THE NEW NATURALIST

A SURVEY OF BRITISH NATURAL HISTORY

WILD FLOWERS OF CHALK & LIMESTONE

The aim of this series is to interest the general reader in the wild life of Britain by recapturing the inquiring spirit of the old naturalists. The Editors believe that the natural pride of the British public in the native fauna and flora, to which must be added concern for their conservation, is best fostered by maintaining a high standard of accuracy combined with clarity of exposition in presenting the results of modern scientific research. The plants and animals are described in relation to their homes and habitats.

The text and line illustrations are here reproduced unaltered, but the process of manufacture used to achieve an economic price does not, unfortunately, do full justice to all the photographs; and those originally in colour appear in black and white.

THE NEW NATURALIST

WILD FLOWERS OF CHALK & LIMESTONE

by

J. E. LOUSLEY

WITH 52 COLOUR PHOTOGRAPHS
BY ROBERT ATKINSON, JOHN MARKHAM,
BRIAN PERKINS AND OTHERS
29 PHOTOGRAPHS IN BLACK AND WHITE
20 MAPS AND 15 DIAGRAMS

Bloomsbury Books
London

First edition 1950
Second edition 1969
Reprinted 1976

This edition published 1990 by
Bloomsbury Books an imprint of
Godfrey Cave Associates Limited
42 Bloomsbury Street, London WC1B 3QJ
under license from William Collins Son's & Co. Ltd.

ISBN 1870630 54 8

To the memory of
my great-great-grandfather
JOB LOUSLEY (1790-1855)
who loved the Berkshire downs, and added
to our knowledge of their flora

CONTENTS

PAGE

EDITORS' PREFACE xv

AUTHOR'S PREFACE xvi

CHAPTER

1 FLOWERS, AND CHALK AND LIMESTONE SOILS 1
Calcicoles and calcifuges—Basic and acid soils—Characteristics of limestones and their soils—Scenery—Geographical distribution of plants—Soils and geology—Geological maps—Superficial deposits—Soil tests—Plants as soil indicators.

2 BOX HILL: THE COMMON FLOWERS OF CHALK 17
Trees—Shrubs—Herbs.

3 BOX HILL: THE ECOLOGY OF THE CHALK 34
Habitat factors—Geology and soil—Clay-with-flints—Topography—Water-supply—Plant communities—Chalk grassland—Chalk scrub—Chalk woodland—Succession—Human interference.

4 THE NORTH DOWNS 49
East Kent—West Kent—Surrey.

5 THE SOUTH DOWNS AND THE ISLE OF WIGHT 67
Sussex—South Hampshire—Isle of Wight.

6 OTHER CHALKLANDS SOUTH OF THE THAMES 78
North Hampshire—Salisbury Plain—Dorset—North Wiltshire—Berkshire—Calcicoles in Thames meadows.

7 CHALKLANDS NORTH OF THE THAMES 88
The Chilterns—Bedfordshire—Cambridgeshire—Breckland—Norfolk and Suffolk—Lincolnshire and Yorkshire.

8 LIMESTONES OF SOUTH-WEST ENGLAND 103
Limestone compared with chalk—Dorset coast—Torquay and Berry Head—Plymouth—Mendips—Avon Gorge.

9 THE JURASSIC LIMESTONES 121
Lias and Oolite—Bath—Cotswolds—Oxfordshire—Northamptonshire—Rutland and Lincolnshire—Yorkshire.

CONTENTS (*continued*)

CHAPTER		PAGE
10	LIMESTONES OF WALES AND THE WELSH BORDER Geological systems represented—Wye Valley—South Wales—Barmouth—North Wales—Basic soils of igneous rocks.	138
11	THE DERBYSHIRE DALES General characteristics—Matlock—Monsal Dale to Buxton—Dovedale—Manifold Valley.	155
12	THE MAGNESIAN LIMESTONE Characteristics of the rock and soils—Special plants—Flora from Nottinghamshire to Durham.	168
13	CRAVEN IN YORKSHIRE An upland flora—Limestone pavement—Wharfedale—Gordale—Malham Cove—Ribblesdale—Ingleborough.	176
14	OTHER LIMESTONE DISTRICTS OF NORTH ENGLAND Hutton Roof Crag—Silverdale—Humphrey Head—Whitbarrow—Scout Scar—North Westmorland—Wensleydale and Swaledale—Upper Teesdale.	192
15	LIMESTONES OF SCOTLAND AND IRELAND Scotland—Firth of Forth—Cambrian limestone. Ireland—Differences between English and Irish floras—Burren—Aran Islands—Ben Bulben—Killarney.	200
16	SUMMARY AND CONCLUSION Relative importance of kinds of limestone and geographical situation—Richness of calcicole flora in rarities—Plant conservation.	211
	DISTRIBUTION MAPS	215
	REFERENCES	226
	BIBLIOGRAPHY	229
	INDEX	236

* As explained on the second page, these plates are here reproduced in black and white.

* PLATES IN COLOUR

FACING PAGE

1 Traveller's Joy, *Clematis vitalba*, in fruit 2
2 Stemless Thistle, *Cirsium acaulon* 3
3 Musk Thistle, *Carduus nutans* 10
4 Clustered Bellflower, *Campanula glomerata* 11
5 Fragrant Orchid, *Gymnadenia conopsea* and Pyramidal Orchid, *Anacamptis pyramidalis* 14
6 Bee Orchid, *Ophrys apifera* 15
7a Autumn Lady's-tresses, *Spiranthes spiralis* 30
7b Fly Orchid, *Ophrys insectifera* 30
8 Dogwood, *Thelycrania sanguinea*, in fruit 31
9a Wayfaring Tree, *Viburnum lantana*, branch in flower 46
9b Wayfaring Tree, *Viburnum lantana*, branch in fruit 46
10 Deadly Nightshade, *Atropa belladonna* 47
11 Beech, *Fagus sylvatica*, branch in flower 62
12 Early Purple Orchid, *Orchis mascula* 63
13 Henbane, *Hyoscyamus niger* 68
14a Lady Orchid, *Orchis purpurea* 69
14b Monkey Orchid, *Orchis simia* 69
15 A disused chalk pit 72
16 Field Eryngo, *Eryngium campestre* 73
17a Cypress Spurge, *Euphorbia cyparissias* 82
17b Ground Pine, *Ajuga chamaepitys* 82
18 Candytuft, *Iberis amara* 83
19 Early Gentian, *Gentianella anglica* 90
20 Large-flowered Chalk-eyebright, *Euphrasia pseudokerneri* 91

		FACING PAGE
21	Common Teasel, *Dipsacus fullonum* with Wild Parsnip, *Pastinaca sativa*	98
22	Orchids of a Hampshire beechwood	99
23	Cuckoo Pint, *Arum maculatum*, in fruit	106
24	Rare Cuckoo Pint, *Arum neglectum*	107
25	Large Autumn Gentian, *Gentianella germanica*	114
26	Military Orchid, *Orchis militaris*	115
27	Lizard Orchid, *Himantoglossum hircinum*	122
28	Gog Magog Hills, Cambridgeshire	123
29	A Cambridgeshire chalk pit	126
30	Field Fleawort, *Senecio integrifolius*	127
31	Early Spider Orchid, *Ophrys sphegodes*	142
32	Cheddar Gorge, Somerset	143
33	Wasp Orchid, *Ophrys trollii*	146
34	Malham Cove, Yorkshire	147
35	Bracken, *Pteridium aquilinum* on limestone	154
36	Limestone pavement, Ingleborough, Yorkshire	155
37	Wooded limestone pavement, Ingleborough, Yorkshire	158
38	Baneberry, *Actaea spicata*, in fruit	159
39	Bloody Cranesbill, *Geranium sanguineum*	174
40	Melancholy Thistle, *Cirsium heterophyllum*	175
41	Dark-flowered Helleborine, *Epipactis atrorubens*	178
42	Rigid Buckler Fern, *Dryopteris villarii*	179
43	Common Pink, *Dianthus plumarius*	186
44	Irish limestone pavement	187
45	Spring Sandwort, *Minuartia verna*	194
46	An Irish Saxifrage, *Saxifraga rosacea*	195
47	Mountain Avens, *Dryas octopetala*	202
48	Maidenhair Fern, *Adiantum capillus-veneris*	203

It should be noted that throughout this book Plate numbers in arabic figures refer to Colour Plates, while roman numerals are used for Black-and-White Plates

PLATES IN BLACK AND WHITE

		FACING PAGE
I	Box Hill, Surrey	18
II	Interior of a Box grove; Box Hill, Surrey	19
IIIa	Flowers of the Box, *Buxus sempervirens*	26
IIIb	Spray of Yew, *Taxus baccata*	26
IVa	Dark Mullein, *Verbascum nigrum*	27
IVb	Yellow-wort, *Blackstonia perfoliata*	27
V	Shakespeare's Cliff, Dover	34
VI	Man Orchid, *Aceras anthropophorum*	35
VII	Late Spider Orchid, *Ophrys fuciflora*	42
VIII	The Beechwood on Selborne Hanger	43
IX	The Seven Sisters, Sussex	50
Xa	Pasque Flower, *Pulsatilla vulgaris*	51
Xb	Pasque Flower, *Pulsatilla vulgaris*	51
XI	Spiked Speedwell, *Veronica spicata*	58
XII	Berry Head, near Brixham	59
XIII	Ivy Broomrape, *Orobanche hederae*	66
XIV	Wall Pennywort, *Umbilicus rupestris*	67
XV	Avon Gorge from Clifton Suspension Bridge	74
XVI	Great Orme's Head	75
XVII	Thistle Broomrape, *Orobanche reticulata*	94
XVIII	Miller's Dale	95
XIX	Woolly-headed Thistle, *Cirsium eriophorum*	110
XX	Nottingham Catchfly, *Silene nutans*	111
XXI	Limestone Polypody, *Thelypteris robertiana*	190
XXII	Scout Scar, Kendal	191

FACING PAGE

XXIIIa Keys of Ash, *Fraxinus excelsior* 206

XXIIIb Mezereon, *Daphne mezereum*, in fruit 206

XXIVa Vernal Squill, *Scilla verna* 207

XXIVb Pyramidal Bugle, *Ajuga pyramidalis* 207

FIGURES IN THE TEXT

		PAGE
1	Maps showing the areas in which the most important Limestones of botanical interest outcrop. a. Chalk b. Jurassic (Oolitic and Liassic) c. Carboniferous Limestone d. Other Limestones	12
2	Geology of Box Hill	36
3	Diagrammatic section through escarpment of North Downs, Box Hill	41
4	The North Downs	55
5	The South Downs	70
6	Other chalklands south of the Thames	80
7	Chalklands north of the Thames	96
8	South-west England	104
9	The Mendips and Avon Gorge	112
10	Jurassic areas of England and Wales	124
11	Wales and the Welsh Border	145
12	The Derbyshire and Staffordshire Dales	163
13	Magnesian Limestone	169
14	The Craven District of Yorkshire	177
15	Carboniferous Limestone areas of northern England	193
16	Ireland	204

Note.—The geological boundaries shown on these sketch-maps are approximate only and are included for the sole purpose of showing the relationship between the various plant habitats described. They have been taken from the proof of a new map of the Distribution of Limestone prepared for the National Planning Series.

DISTRIBUTION MAPS

PAGE

1 Pasque Flower, *Pulsatilla vulgaris* 216

2 Rock Pepperwort, *Hornungia petraea* 216

3a Hoary Rock-rose, *Helianthemum canum*
b White Rock-rose, *Helianthemum apenninum* 217

4a Bitter Milkwort, *Polygala amara*

b Kentish Milkwort, *Polygala austriaca* 217

5a Yorkshire Sandwort, *Arenaria gothica*

b Norwegian Sandwort, *Arenaria norvegica* c Irish Sandwort, *Arenaria ciliata* subsp. *hibernica* 218

6a Perennial Flax, *Linum anglicum*
b Hair-leaved Goldilocks, *Aster linosyris* 218

7a Honewort, *Trinia glauca*
b Mountain Stone-parsley, *Seseli libanotis* c Banberrry, *Actaea spicata* 219

8 Tuberous Thistle, *Cirsium tuberosum* 219

9a Spring Gentian, *Gentianella verna*
b Large Autumn Gentian, *Gentiana germanica* 220

10 Blue Gromwell, *Lithospermum purpurocoeruleum* 220

11a Western Spiked Speedwell, *Veronica hybrida*
b Spiked Speedwell, *Veronica spicata* 221

12 Cut-leaved Germander, *Teucrium botrys* 221

13 Military Orchid, *Orchis militaris* 222

14 Early Spider Orchid, *Ophrys sphegodes* 222

15 Lady's Slipper Orchid, *Cypripendium calceolus* 223

16a Round-headed Rampion, *Phyteuma tenerum*
b Rigid Buckler Fern, *Dryopteris villarii* 223

EDITORS' PREFACE

During the last two hundred years, successive armies of amateur field botanists have, by their exertions, helped to make the wild flora of Britain the best known of any country in the world. Mr. J. E. Lousley is one of the leading present-day representatives of this great amateur tradition. He lives and works in London and has developed a special affection for—and a unique knowledge of—the chalk downs and beech woods so typical of South-eastern England. Knowing this " weakness " of his we decided to ask him to undertake the first of a series of New Naturalist books on the wild flowers of particular habitats—and the present volume on chalk and limestone is the result. Though the south-eastern chalk is a favourite week-end field of operations for Mr. Lousley, it is obvious that he has also visited and studied most of the other important limestone areas in Britain, from the Devonian limestones of Devon to the Oolite of the Cotswolds and the great areas of Carboniferous Limestone in the north. He has revisited most of the areas described while writing his book. During his wanderings he has been fully awake to the ecological background against which any worth-while study of plants must be made, as is well brought out in his book, but it is the flowers themselves—the peculiarities of their distribution, the characters which distinguish them from their allies, and the history of their discovery in Britain—that fill the centre of his vision and provide the inspiration of his book.

Very few types of habitat can boast a larger proportion of rare and beautiful wild flowers than the limestone—nor more lovely scenery in which to search them out—and Mr. Lousley has undoubtedly taken hold of his opportunities with both hands. His book will, we hope, inspire many to follow in his footsteps across the thyme-scented chalk uplands, through the green shades of the Cotswold beechwoods, or across the limestone pavements of the north, and to learn something of the rich flora that makes them so fascinating to explore.

The Editors

AUTHOR'S PREFACE

I HAVE WRITTEN this book as an amateur for amateurs in the belief that first-hand experiences are likely to be of greatest interest to field naturalists. Most of the places described have been revisited since the end of the recent war to confirm or elaborate earlier notes which in some cases proved to be out of date.

Limits of space have dictated the omission of much that I wished to say and the task of selection from the available material has proved difficult. If I appear to have given undue prominence to rarities it is because these so often provide the most suitable examples of plant geography and illustrate differences between the habitats better than subtle variations in the proportions and behaviour of the commoner species.

The title has been regarded as including trees and shrubs, since to botanists these are as much flowers (phanerogams) as are the herbs. It would be invidious to omit the few ferns closely associated with calcareous soils. Some maritime flowers have been included as growing on chalk or limestone sea cliffs but, in general, species found on limy soils or rocks at an altitude of over 1000 feet have been treated as mountain flowers and therefore as coming within the scope of another book in the NEW NATURALIST series.

Every effort has been made to select one of the places where it is most plentiful for the discussion of each species. This selection has been based on my personal experience and it does not follow that visits in other seasons would produce the same displays as those I have described. It must also not be assumed that failure to mention a plant at any particular place implies that it does not grow there: the accounts of many of the habitats would have become mere lists if all the species had been included.

The English names used, with few exceptions, are taken from Rayner's *Standard Catalogue of English Names of our Wild Flowers.* Although some of these names are not particularly well chosen it seems better to follow a list already in use than to adopt a miscellaneous selection which may mislead. Usually the scientific names are taken from J. E. Dandy's invaluable *List of British Vascular Plants* (1958), to which the reader is referred for synonyms and author's names. The use of scientific names has been reduced as much as possible and after the first mention they are usually not repeated for very common trees and flowers to which there is frequent reference. In the case of rarer species they are repeated at intervals for the benefit of readers not familiar with the English names.

Although the public have free access to most of the chalk and limestone habitats described, it must be made clear that no statement or description in this book should be taken as implying that any Right-of-way exists in these places. Permission to trespass is very rarely refused to genuine botanists and should always be requested as a matter of courtesy.

The experiences described in the following chapters are in large measure due to the companionship, help and encouragement of many botanical friends over a number of years. To mention some and leave out others would be invidious, but their assistance is not appreciated less because it must remain anonymous. Parts of the manuscript at various stages have been read by Messrs. J. D. Grose, R. H. Hall, J. E. Prentice, E. C. Wallace and Drs. W. A. Sledge and J. F. Hope-Simpson, and I am most grateful for their help; although it must not be assumed that they are in any way responsible for the text as printed. The first proof has been read by Messrs. R. Graham, D. McClintock, John Raven and E. C. Wallace, who have all assisted with valuable suggestions. I am also greatly indebted to the Editors of the NEW NATURALIST series for much help and encouragement.

PREFACE TO SECOND EDITION

Considerable changes have taken place in some of the habitats, and in many of the names given to plants by botanists, since publication of the first edition of this book in 1950, and the text has been heavily corrected. I am grateful to Mr. David McClintock for reading the proof and making many valuable suggestions.

J. E. L.

CHAPTER I

FLOWERS, AND CHALK AND LIMESTONE SOILS

I MAKE NO apology for being an enthusiast over the flowers of chalk and limestone. As a schoolboy I soon realised that I found a greater variety of plants on the chalk than on other soils, and most of my botanising was done on the North Downs within cycling distance of my home in South London. An annual stay with grandparents near Reading offered opportunities of getting to the Berkshire Downs. Holidays in Somerset and Devon provided an introduction to the joys of the flora of the older limestones. Later on, when choice of places to visit was entirely my own, I found that chalk and limestone areas were automatically selected for a very large proportion of my field work.

Although chalk is a limestone—indeed the white Upper Chalk is one of the purest British limestones—it differs in its softer nature from the other, usually older, British limestones. Hence the sense in which " chalk " and " limestone " are used in this book is in accordance with popular usage.

My preference is by no means unusual. The majority of the thousands of people who flock to Box Hill or Ivinghoe Beacon, the Great Orme or Berry Head, Cheddar or Ingleborough, are not botanists, but many of them find the flowers in these places an additional attraction. Some of them doubtless realise that the plants differ from those of other soils. The botanist is so well aware of it that he may travel right across England to make for one particular bit of chalk or limestone where he knows that certain rare flowers are to be found.

Many of these rarities have never been found in Britain on other soils. The only places where the Monkey Orchid and the Military Orchid, *Orchis simia* (Plate 14b, p. 69) and *O. militaris* (Plate 26, p. 115), have been seen are on chalk. All our localities for the White Rock-rose, *Helianthemum apenninum*, are on limestone. A very long list might be given of scarce and beautiful wild flowers which are similarly restricted; they will be discussed in later chapters.

There are also a great many more widespread plants which are almost limited to chalk and limestone. Good examples are Chalk Milkwort, *Polygala calcarea*, and Round-headed Rampion, *Phyteuma tenerum*, which are locally abundant on much of the southern chalk though never found in the north of England. Conversely the Dark-flowered Helleborine, *Epipactis atrorubens* (Plate 41, p. 178), is widespread on the limestone of the north and west. Horseshoe Vetch, *Hippocrepis comosa*, and Clustered Bellflower, *Campanula glomerata* (Plate 4, p. 11), are plentiful on *both* chalk and limestone. In addition there are many flowers such as Salad Burnet, *Poterium sanguisorba*, and Carline Thistle, *Carlina vulgaris*, which are specially abundant on soils over these rocks but are also sometimes found on others. Finally there are numerous common species which are not exacting in their soil requirements—such as Common Birds-foot Trefoil, *Lotus corniculatus*—abundant there just as they are elsewhere.

Thus the flowers found on chalk downs like Box Hill or limestone crags such as the Great Orme are a mixture. Some could be seen equally well in many other places, but a great many, and this applies particularly to the rarities, grow specially on soils containing a high percentage of lime. These plants are called *calcicoles*—a word made up from the Latin *calx*, "chalk," and *colo*, "I inhabit," i.e. plants dwelling on chalky soils. The derived adjective is *calcicolous*. Botanists generally use these terms in a very much narrower sense than one might suppose from their literal meanings. They only include as calcicoles those plants which show not only the positive characteristic of thriving on calcareous soils but also the negative attribute of avoiding soils deficient in lime. Those which grow equally well elsewhere cannot be regarded as chalk or lime "lovers." They are not calcicoles.

There are certain flowers which avoid the chalk and limestone. One of the best examples is Foxglove, *Digitalis purpurea*, which is

PLATE I

John Markham

TRAVELLER'S JOY, *Clematis vitalba*, in fruit. A useful indicator of calcareous soils in the south of England. Sussex; October

PLATE 2

Brian Parkins

STEMLESS THISTLE, *Cirsium acaulon*; a nuisance to picnickers on chalk downs. Surrey; July common on other soils in most parts of the British Isles. Similarly, Broom, *Sarothamnus scoparius*, is practically absent from calcareous soils. These two plants are such excellent soil indicators that on train journeys it is often easy to tell immediately the line leaves chalk or limestone by their presence on the railway banks. The term applied to plants which avoid lime is *calcifuge*, from the Latin *calx* and *fugio*, "I flee." It is the converse of calcicole.[1]

Every serious gardener is well aware that some plants have these strong soil preferences. Even under the artificially easy conditions of cultivation, which frees flowers from the competition of their neighbours, they may often be a matter of life or death. It is hopeless to try to grow most members of the Heath Family, *Ericaceae*, on chalk, and if Rhododendrons or Ling, *Calluna vulgaris*, are planted in such situations they will probably soon die. On the other hand Buddleia, *Buddleja davidii*, and many other plants thrive on the shallowest of chalk soils; and limestone is commonly used for rockeries. Gardeners select the plants they grow according to the nature of their soil. This they can modify over a limited area by adding lime if it is too acid, or peat if too mild. Thus by taking the appropriate measures they can grow species which are quite unsuited to their natural soil.

Soils found in the country show contrasts similar to those of gardens. On moorlands and heaths they are acid, or, as gardeners would say, sour. Those formed where chalk or limestone are close to the surface are usually basic or mild. These differences are primarily due to the nature of the rocks from which the soils are derived.

Limestones are rocks which contain at least 50 per cent of carbonate of lime, which is known to chemists as calcium carbonate, $CaCO_3$. This is a basic (alkaline) substance which neutralises acids, and farmers spread ground limestones on their fields to prevent the soil from becoming sour. Chalk has been used for this purpose since very early times and many small chalk-pits remain to remind us of the practice. The net result is similar to that attained by the use of lime (oxide of calcium, CaO) though there are important differences in the action.

[1] The best definitions of calcicoles and calcifuges are those given by J. F. Hope Simpson: "Calcicoles are regarded as species affecting the more important types of calcareous soils and rare or absent from acid soils, and calcifuges are the reverse." —*Journal of Ecology*, XXVI, p. 218, 1938.

These terms are used throughout this book but some botanists have employed *calcipete* or *calciphile* for plants showing degrees of preference for lime, and *calciphobe* for the reverse—with corresponding adjectives in each case.

Calcium carbonate effervesces vigorously with cold dilute hydrochloric acid, and this is one of the tests by which limestones can be recognised.

Another characteristic of these rocks is that they are all soft enough to be scratched with a knife. This is true even of the hardest forms (known as marble). The purest of the limestones, such as much of the Upper Chalk which is commonly 95-98 per cent calcium carbonate, are white. Others are greyish, or stained yellow or red.

Flowers which grow on chalk and limestone do so because the conditions suit them better than those elsewhere, but the particular reasons are complicated and not yet fully understood. Some plants seem to be restricted by the *chemical* characteristics of the soil in which they grow. One example is the Privet, *Ligustrum vulgare*, which thrives equally on the driest of chalk downs and in wet East Anglian fens. In spite of the great contrast in other conditions both localities agree in being strongly basic owing to the presence of calcium carbonate. But the more common reasons are probably due to the physical characteristics of the ground. Limestones are dry, well aerated and warm. Plants which grow on them never have their roots waterlogged. They are able to commence growth early in the spring and many of them flower in May and June and remain more or less dormant during the driest summer months which follow. Others send their roots deep down into the well aerated soil to a level where they are assured of a more constant water supply even in times of drought: these include some of the later flowers like Wild Thyme, *Thymus drucei*, Perforate St. John's Wort, *Hypericum perforatum*, and Small Scabious, *Scabiosa columbaria*.

Some of the finest scenery in the British Isles is to be found on chalk and limestone. The broad outlines of the views which attract and delight visitors are directly due to the nature of the rocks. Where these are soft, as in the chalk areas, the hills are rounded and undulating. Even the steepest escarpments, like those of the North Downs and Ivinghoe Beacon, have all their edges smoothed off. Cliffs are never formed naturally except by the sea, and the soft outlines of the chalk make ideal walking country. Here the wild flowers have often been preserved from destruction by the use of the land as sheep walks throughout the centuries. This, in turn, has produced a short dense springy turf with orchids and other characteristic flowers.

On the harder limestones there are cliffs and steeper slopes.

Cheddar and the Avon Gorge (Plate XV, p. 74), parts of the Wye Valley, and the Great Orme (Plate XVI, p. 75), are examples which are particularly well known. In such places the choicer flowers grow on ledges where difficulty of access and immunity from any threat of cultivation has served to protect them.

The details of the scenery are supplied by the trees and flowers, and the vegetation in turn is dictated, like the topography, by the nature of the rocks. Visitors sometimes fail to appreciate how much the beauty of Box Hill owes to its famous Box Trees, *Buxus sempervirens*, or Selborne Hanger (Plate VIII, p. 43) to its Beeches, *Fagus sylvatica*, or Cheddar (Plate 32, p. 143) to its Yews, *Taxus baccata*, and Whitebeams, *Sorbus aria*. The downland turf is made up of plants which only grow together in this way on calcareous soils, and the association of flowers differs from those found on all other soils. With a little practice places where chalk or limestone is near the surface can be recognised immediately; the plants collectively give characteristic detail to the scenery.

In my travels all over the British Isles I have been impressed with the very gradual changes in the flora when the various chalk and limestone districts are compared. They are like a length of cinematograph film. Each frame differs only in detail from its neighbours, just as the chalk flowers of Reigate Hill, Box Hill and Hackhurst Downs are very similar. Pictures farther apart show much greater differences, and if the distance is sufficiently great they may at first sight seem to have little in common when examined as "stills." Thus the chalk flowers of the Dover cliffs and the limestone plants of the Burren in Co. Clare may seem to be quite unconnected. But when the cinematograph film is projected and the pictures are shown on the screen in quick succession they are shown to form a continuous story. The links which form a series between the scattered frames are seen in their proper place. The chapters in this book cover habitats scattered all over the British Isles and each place described has its own characteristics. By bringing them all together in one volume they can be compared as a series gradually changing from east to west, and from south to north. It is the first time this has been attempted for the calcareous soils of any country.

The reasons for these differences between the flowers of various districts can be distinguished under two heads—variation in climate and the incidence of the geographical distribution of species. The second is to a great extent dependent on the first.

Eras	*Divisions of Geological Time* Major Divisions	Sub-divisions
QUATERNARY		Glacial ... ...
KAINOZOIC ...	OLIGOCENE ...	....
MESOZOIC ...	CRETACEOUS ...	Upper Cretaceous ... ...
		Lower Cretaceous ... ...
	JURASSIC ...	Middle and Upper Jurassic
		Lower Lias ... ...
PALEOZOIC ...	PERMIAN ...	... ...
	CARBONIFEROUS	Lower Carboniferous ... ...
	DEVONIAN ...	Middle and Upper Devonian ...
	SILURIAN ...	... ...
	ORDOVICIAN ...	... ...
	CAMBRIAN ...	... ...
EOZOIC	PRE-CAMBRIAN	... ...

(Local limestones of minor botanical

MENTIONED IN TEXT

Outcrops of Botanical Interest	Chapters	Maps on Pages
Chalky Boulder Clay of E. Anglia, etc.	7	—
Isle of Wight limestones	5	—
Lower, Middle and Upper Chalk of:		
North Downs	2, 3, 4	55
South Downs and Isle of Wight	5	70
Salisbury Plain, Dorset Heights, Berkshire Downs ...	6	80
Chilterns, E. Anglian chalk, Lincolnshire and Yorkshire	7	96
Kentish Rag (near Maidstone), Bargate Stone (near Godalming)	4	—
Oolites of:		
Dorset coast (including Portland and Purbeck) ...	8	} 124
Cotswolds, Oxfordshire, Northamptonshire Uplands and Lincoln Edge	9	}
Limestones of lower part:		}
Near Bristol and at intervals across England to Kingston-upon-Hull	9	}
Glamorgan (Dunraven)	10	}
Magnesian Limestone in a south-north belt from Nottingham to the Tyne	12	169
Massive Limestone of:		
Mendips and Avon Gorge	8	112
Wye Valley, S. Wales (Gower and Tenby), N. Wales (Great Orme and Clwydian Hills)	10	145
Derbyshire Dales	11	163
Craven district of Yorkshire	13	177
Parts of Westmorland, Cumberland, N. Yorkshire, Northumberland	14	193
Central lowlands of Scotland, Burren, Sligo and Killarney	15	204
Massive limestone of S. Devon (Plymouth, Torquay, Berry Head)	8	104
Woolhope, Wenlock, and Aymestry Limestones of Shropshire, Herefordshire, Radnorshire and Worcestershire...	10	145
Basic rocks at Breidden Hill (Montgomeryshire)	10	145
Durness Limestone of N.W. Scotland	15	—
Scattered very small outcrops in Wales, Scotland and Ireland	15	—

iterest also occur in other beds.)

Even in a small area like the British Isles the climate varies considerably and the differences are more important to some kinds of flowers than to others. Just as the human species is adaptable and can live under conditions varying from tropical heat to polar cold, so there are some plants which can endure a considerable range of climate. Flowers like Common Birdsfoot Trefoil, Horseshoe Vetch, and Clustered Bellflower, are to be found growing just as well on the limestone of the north of England as they do on the chalk of the south. But many others are much more exacting. For example, the much wetter conditions of Westmorland and west Yorkshire suit Birds-eye Primrose, *Primula farinosa*, and Globe Flower, *Trollius europaeus*, which would never grow on the dry chalk of the South Downs even if they were planted there. Then there are plants like Maidenhair Fern, *Adiantum capillus-veneris* (Plate 48, p. 203), which cannot stand much frost. They thrive on limestones of the west coast of England and Ireland but would be killed under the extreme conditions of the average east coast winter. There are many contrasts of this kind and they will be emphasised in later chapters.

But in addition there are plants which are so local that present climatic conditions can hardly be the only explanation of their rarity. For example, there are three small Sandworts, *Arenaria ciliata*, *A. gothica*, and *A. norvegica*. In Britain the first is found only on a short length of cliff in Ireland (see p. 208), the second occurs only on a few limestone tracks on the side of a Yorkshire mountain (see p. 185), while *A. norvegica* is restricted to small areas in north-west Scotland, the Hebrides, Shetland and Ireland. It seems certain that there must be other places where each of these plants could find the conditions under which it thrives, and the explanation of their present rarity must be looked for in the past history of the species. In this particular case the three Sandworts belong to a group with a circumpolar type of distribution. The scattered localities where they are now found are likely to be relics of a time when they were more widespread. Although we do not know for certain why they have disappeared from the intervening districts, it is highly probable that they were destroyed during periods of glaciation in past ages. Thus to explain the present distribution of plants in Britain it is necessary to plot the places where they occur elsewhere and also to study the geological and climatic history here and overseas.

From a careful study of the areas over which each species is found in Britain and abroad it has become clear that our country has been invaded by plants from more than one direction. For example, some probably came in from the south-east (see Chapter 4). Others found in the west of Ireland also grow in Spain and Portugal and the Mediterranean district (see Chapter 15). In some cases plants have not spread far from the districts where they entered our country; in others they have extended over more or less wide areas. Plants, and especially rare plants, become very much more interesting if we know something of the climatic conditions under which they can live and of how they have come to the places where they grow. Such facts are most conveniently considered if their habitats are arranged geographically.

But a purely geographical arrangement would not suffice. Limestones (including chalk) are rocks which are mainly composed of the base *calcium carbonate*. Such rocks can occur in strata of all ages and, far from being uniform, they vary widely in degrees of impurity and hardness. Limestones are sedimentary[1] and mostly of marine origin, though some were laid down in fresh water, and sand, mud and other impurities as well as calcium carbonate were involved in their formation. The purity of much of the Upper Chalk (often 98 per cent or more) is exceptional; most limestones are far less pure. It is obvious that these differences may be reflected in their floras, and although very little scientific work has so far been done on this subject it is one which deserves attention.

The problem is complicated by the fact that the occurrence of plants is influenced by the characteristics of the soil round their roots rather than by the geology of their habitats. The latter determines such features as steepness of slopes produced under given climatic conditions, and drainage. Geology provides the outline of the picture but other factors are also involved in deciding whether soil conditions are acid or alkaline.

Soil is the superficial unconsolidated layer of the earth's crust and is a highly complicated mass of organic and inorganic material. The latter is itself the weathered products of rocks. It follows that in general limestone rocks are likely to give rise to calcareous soils, but there are many exceptions to this assertion. Examples will be given in later chapters, but perhaps the one which impressed me most was a shallow

[1] With the exception of crystalline marbles which are metamorphic and of no botanical importance.

depression on the top of a block of limestone in Westmorland. This contained peaty soil only 1½ in. deep in which grew calcifuges, in marked contrast to the calcicoles on the adjacent rock. Although the example just given is an extreme one, less sudden soil changes due to various causes are very common, and hence it is only practical to produce reasonably accurate soil-maps of small areas. The distribution of the chief geological formations (which influence the soil in a general way, but not always in detail) is shown on the small-scale maps (Fig. 1, p. 12) and in the Table.

It has already been explained that limestone rocks are largely sedimentary. At certain periods in the ancient past conditions in our part of the globe were particularly favourable to their formation, and for this reason strata of some ages are richer in limestones than others. The geologist marks his maps primarily according to the *times* when the rocks near the surface were made, and this he is able to do by a careful study of the fossils they contain and the sequence in which they occur. For example, there is the well-known Cretaceous system of some eighty million years ago. At the beginning of the period the fine sands and clays of the Wealden Beds were laid down in fresh water in the south of England. Then sea invaded the area and the sands and clays of the Greensands and Gault were deposited. These include only very local and small areas of calcareous rock (e.g. Kentish Rag), but towards the end of the period the sea advanced still farther and an accumulation of calcareous ooze formed the Chalk.

Geological maps show this as outcropping over considerable areas (Fig. 1a, p. 12). In some places it can be seen as the familiar soft white rock of the Upper or White Chalk, which is often almost pure limestone. At others it outcrops as the less pure Middle Chalk, while some exposures of the Lower Chalk (and Chalk Marls) are very muddy and impure. Not only does the Chalk itself vary but also the higher ground is frequently covered with superficial deposits of very different rocks (see below). It will be evident that the indication ot Chalk on small-scale generalised geological maps covers a wide variety of rock conditions. Nevertheless areas so marked indicate where limestone habitats are *likely* to be found and serve to link together in an orderly fashion the places where they occur.

Next in botanical importance to the Cretaceous, the Carboniferous is the period of geological time when limestones were laid down over wide areas of our country. Sands and shales were also deposited and

PLATE 3

Brian Perkins

MUSK THISTLE, *Carduus nutans*; easily recognised by its nodding heads. Surrey; July

PLATE 4

Brian Perkins

CLUSTERED BELLFLOWER, *Campanula glomerata;* a common autumn flower on chalk and limestone. Surrey; July

much of the land-surface shown as Carboniferous has outcrops of these rocks (and very impure limestones) on which acid soils form. But once more the map is a useful guide. Its markings *include* all the places where limestone of this period comes to the surface and is the basis of calcareous soils.

Similar considerations apply to the Permian, which is the period which produced the Magnesian Limestone. They also apply to the Jurassic. There are smaller outcrops of calcareous rock in the Devonian and other systems. The lithological divisions shown on the maps on page 12 include all places where extensive limestones of botanical importance are to be found in the British Isles.

Reference has already been made to superficial deposits which cover large areas of the limestone-bearing divisions of small-scale generalised maps of " solid " geology such as those just mentioned. These are " rocks " (often gravels, sands or clay) which may give rise to neutral or even acid soils. They have been formed in the following ways :

1. *Residual Deposits.* In the formation of these the original limestone rock has been broken up by frost and dissolved away by rain-water (in which it is soluble to the extent of about 1 in 16,000 parts). When the calcium carbonate is removed the impurities are left as sands or clays on which grow plants different from those of calcareous soils.
2. *Drift Deposits derived from extraneous sources.* These consist of material removed from other areas during the Ice Ages and dropped by the glaciers. Sometimes the drift has been carried for very great distances, and is very unlike the limestones over which it is deposited. Other drifts are calcareous.

Superficial deposits of both kinds are to be found on various limestones, but perhaps the Chalk is the best-known example to use as an illustration. This is the softest of all our limestones and weathers most quickly. When all the calcareous material has been removed the residue sometimes consists of fine particles of very sticky clay mixed with angular flints. The latter are similar to those which are often to be seen in chalk-pits or in cultivated fields on the downs. When this residue accumulates to any depth it gives rise to a soil on which calcifuges can grow. In part, it forms the basis of the " Clay-with-Flints " deposits which often extend over considerable areas on the

a. Chalk

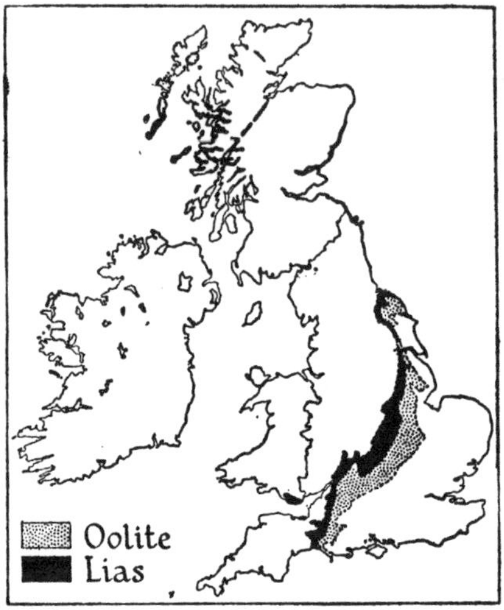

b. Jurassic (Oolitic and Liassic)

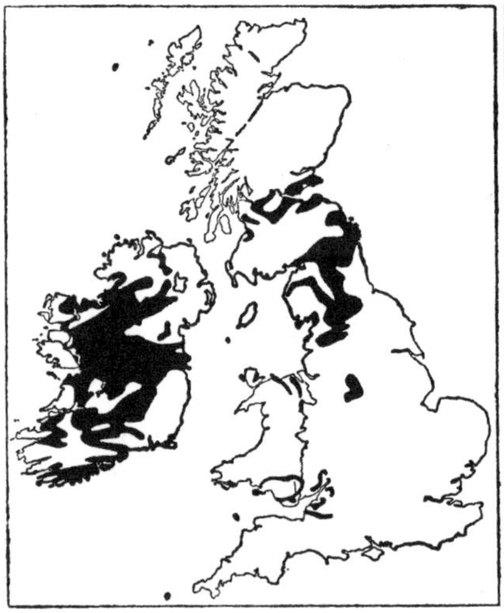

c. Carboniferous Limestone

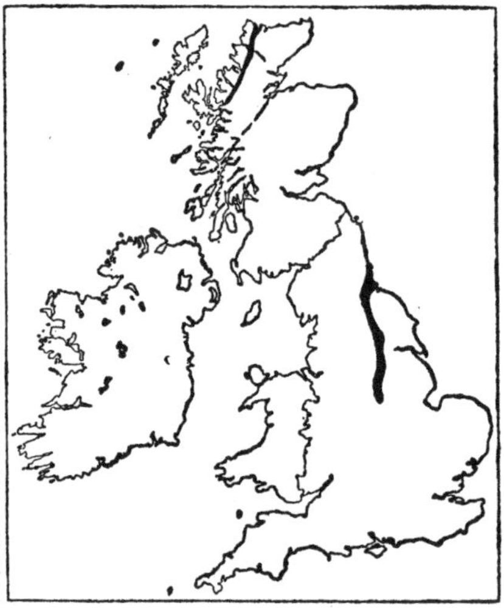

d. Other Limestones

FIG. 1

Maps showing the areas in which the most important limestones of botanical interest outcrop

flattish tops of the downs in south-east England. Some of the Chalk was once covered with more recent beds such as those laid down in Eocene times, and here and there patches of these Tertiary deposits still remain. In places they form pebbly or sandy areas such as those in many places on the chalk of north Kent. In others they seem to have contributed to the beds which the Geological Survey mark as Clay-with-Flints. In most parts of the North Downs their flora provides a very sharp and sudden contrast to that of the adjacent chalk soils because they carry neutral or even acid soils. Good examples which will already be familiar to many readers are to be seen in the Box Hill district. Here Clay-with-Flints carries woodland on the top of the hill and on the higher parts of the spurs (see Chapter 2), and associated sands carry heathland composed of calcifuges at Headley and Walton Heaths.

Superficial and Tertiary deposits characteristically occur on flat or undulating country—in Surrey on the plateau above the 500-ft. contour. On slopes, provided the angle is sufficiently steep, loose material has long been washed away, leaving the chalk at or near the surface. On escarpments and on the sides of valleys this is usually the case.

There are, however, products of a process of *soil* development which are sometimes confused with superficial deposits. The latter are *geological* " rocks," but areas of slightly acid soils (such as " chalk heath ") due to *leaching* are of a different nature. As rain-water percolates through the surface layers of permeable soils it carries off the soluble salts in solution. Calcium carbonate is one of the salts that is removed, and if the process is continued long enough the material left behind gradually becomes less calcareous and may be converted from a strongly basic condition into an acid one. In regions of heavy rainfall in the north and west of Britain such changes take place relatively quickly and leached areas are common : in the south and east the process is slower and of less frequent occurrence. Where they are found it is easy to mistake them for superficial deposits. In fact the formation of Clay-with-Flints is essentially an extension of this leaching process.

North of the Thames there is also the problem of Glacial Drift over the Chalk. Ice sheets came south from Scandinavia and Scotland as far as North London and brought many kinds of rock with them. They also eroded the chalk where they passed over it. As a result most of the Yorkshire, Lincolnshire and Norfolk chalk is now covered with material brought in this way. A great deal of it gives rise to soils which are not calcareous—or only very slightly so—and hence the flora of these areas is far less rich in calcicoles than the chalk south of the Thames (see Chapter 6).

As some sort of compensation the glaciers left behind them a deposit known as Boulder Clay which is calcareous over considerable areas. This is an important source of calcareous soils best known to botanists in parts of East Anglia, where it is the home of some particularly interesting and beautiful wild flowers such as Oxlip, *Primula elatior*, and Crested Cow-wheat, *Melampyrum cristatum* (see p. 99).

Although chalk has been chosen as an example, deposits also occur over other limestones. They are often loosely but conveniently referred to collectively as " Drift," and they are marked on the " drift " editions of the Geological Survey maps. These should always be used by botanists in preference to the " solid " editions, which ignore them. But it must be remembered that the geologists have been unable to show all the very numerous small areas of drift deposits which occur over the limestones. Once again it must be stressed that geological maps should only be regarded as useful indications of where calcareous soils are likely to be found and not as evidence of them.

In order to be sure that a soil is rich in lime more reliable guides are essential. These are to be found in chemical tests of the soils and also in using the plants which grow on them as indicators.

One very simple test is to add a few drops of dilute hydrochloric acid to a soil sample. If an appreciable amount of calcium carbonate is present (say more than 5 per cent) strong effervescence will follow and continue for some time, just as it does when the same test is applied to limestone rock. When this occurs the soil may be accepted as calcareous. With a little practice it is not difficult to judge from the weakness or violence of the reaction whether the soil contains a little limestone or a lot.

Another method is to test the soil water to ascertain whether it is acid or alkaline and to what extent. If it is very alkaline it can be assumed that this is due to the presence of considerable quantities of calcium carbonate, since other bases are relatively scarce in British soils. The easiest way to make the test is to use the B.D.H. Soil Testing Outfit which is employed by farmers and gardeners, and may be obtained through chemists for a few shillings. The outfit

PLATE 5

Robert Atkinson

FRAGRANT ORCHID, *Gymnadenia conopsea* (left) and PYRAMIDAL ORCHID, *Anacamptis pyramidalis* (right). These two common orchids of open downland are easily distinguished by the shape of the spikes and flowers. From Oxfordshire and Buckinghamshire; June.

Robert Atkinson

BEE ORCHID, *Ophrys apifera;* common on calcareous soils and showing a remarkable resemblance to a bee visiting a flower. From West Kent; July

includes a bottle of special liquid which is carefully made up to change colour according to the acidity or alkalinity of the soil water being tested. If this is very acid it turns red; if neutral, green; if basic, blue or bluish-green. For a few additional pence a colour chart may be obtained, and if the outfit is used according to the instructions and the resulting colours carefully compared with the chart, the estimates of soil reaction will be sufficiently accurate for our purpose.[1] If the liquid turns a deep bluish-green the soil may be regarded as calcareous.

The plants themselves act as most useful indicators as to whether soils are calcareous or not, but unfortunately a great deal of experience is necessary before they can be relied on. The trained field botanist can tell at a glance in most cases when he passes from other soils to limestone. Often he knows to within a yard or two where the change takes place, but his deductions are based on the association of different kinds of plants which he sees rather than on the presence or absence of individual species. Attempts to use these as indicators are usually successful only in the case of the rarer flowers whose requirements are most exacting; efforts to show that widespread plants grow only on calcareous soils generally fail as wider experience reveals numerous exceptions.

It is, however, comparatively easy to state a negative case. If strong plants are found of the best marked calcifuges such as Ling, *Calluna vulgaris*, Fine-leaved Heath, *Erica cinerea*, Whortleberry, *Vaccinium myrtillus*, Foxglove, *Digitalis purpurea*, Sheep's Sorrel, *Rumex acetosella*, or Heath Bedstraw, *Galium saxatile*, it is almost certain that the soil is not calcareous.

As positive indicators the most reliable guides are certain mosses and also grasses such as Upright Brome, *Bromus erectus*, and Tor Grass, *Brachypodium pinnatum*. Of the more conspicuous plants my own experience would suggest Traveller's Joy, *Clematis vitalba* (Plate 1,

[1] For scientific work the soil reaction is usually expressed by a figure known as the "Hydrogen Ion Concentration" or "*pH* value." The standard of neutrality is approximately 7: if the soil is acid the figure is lower, if basic it is higher. The usual reactions encountered on calcareous soils range from *pH* 7 to *pH* 8. These figures are shown on the B.D.H. colour chart, and correspond to the bluish-green colours of the Indicator liquid. More accurate results are obtainable by using indicators which react over a narrower range of values and for this purpose the B.D.H. Capillator Outfit is usually employed. Test papers impregnated with indicators are also available for use instead of liquids. In the laboratory it is possible to measure *pH* values directly and more accurately by electrometric instruments.

p. 2), and Dark Mullein, *Verbascum nigrum* (Plate IVa, p. 27), but these do not occur in the north. The shrubs Wayfaring Tree, *Viburnum lantana* (Plate 9, p. 46), Dogwood, *Thelycrania sanguinea* (Plate 8, p. 31), and Whitebeam, *Sorbus aria*, are seldom found off calcareous soils, but these again are mainly southern. More widespread indicators include:

Common Rock-rose, *Helianthemum chamaecistus*.
Hairy Violet, *Viola hirta*.
Mountain St. John's Wort, *Hypericum montanum*,
Bloody Cranesbill, *Geranium sanguineum* (Plate 39, p. 174).
Kidney Vetch, *Anthyllis vulneraria*.
Dropwort, *Filipendula vulgaris*.
Mountain Bedstraw, *Galium pumilum*.
Small Scabious, *Scabiosa columbaria*.
Clustered Bellflower, *Campanula glomerata* (Plate 4, p. 11).
Yellow-wort, *Blackstonia perfoliata* (Plate IVb, p. 27).
Hoary Plantain, *Plantago media*.

If several of these are found together it is highly probable that there is a great deal of calcium carbonate in the soil. Such conditions can also occur off the limestone as, for example, in dunes where comminuted sea-shells provide calcareous material, but in such places the soil may be chemically very similar to that of the downs.

It follows from the statements made in the last few pages that the really characteristic plants of the limestone and chalk areas are to be found only where the soil is calcareous. These calcicoles include many of our rarest British wild flowers, and also some of the most common and beautiful ones. Their variety and interest are probably unequalled by those of any other habitat, and time employed in their search is spent in some of the most delightful country in Britain. There is certainly no need to apologise for being an enthusiast over flowers of the limestone and chalk.

CHAPTER 2

BOX HILL: THE COMMON FLOWERS OF CHALK

THE BEST known and the finest place to begin a survey of limestone flowers is Box Hill in Surrey. Thousands of people toil up its steep chalky slopes every summer week-end and most of them pause to admire its plants. To almost every Londoner it has provided a pleasant introduction to the downland flora. Its riches and beauty are also known to visitors from all parts of the country. Fortunately for botanists the multitude are conservative in their habits, and few of them wander far from the spur which leads from the railway station to the tea-places and view-points. Solitude and a profusion of flowers can be found in the less frequented valleys even on the busiest Bank Holiday. In spite of the toll taken by visitors, Box Hill remains as good a place for plant-hunting as it was when I first knew it over 40 years ago.

The National Trust owns the hill and some of the adjacent country, and under their management it should remain in its unspoilt state. The Juniper Hall Field Centre of the Field Studies Council provides facilities for studying the natural history of the district. Students are accommodated right at the foot of Box Hill in an ideal situation, and people from all parts of England attend courses at all seasons of the year and see one of our best examples of a chalk flora.

For these reasons Box Hill has been chosen for rather more detailed treatment than it is possible to give to the other places described in this book. In this chapter the reader will be introduced to flowers which will in most cases be referred to in connection with other parts of the British Isles. In the next there will be an account of simple ecological observations of general application.

The most prominent features of the flora of the hill are the trees and shrubs which provide a patchwork of soft and charming colours throughout the year. The Box, *Buxus sempervirens*, with its tough dark evergreen leaves, is conspicuous in all seasons. It covers the almost precipitous slope above the Mole with a dense grove under which very few herbs can grow (Plate IIIa, p. 26). It has given its name to the hill which must be one of the best-known in England. In a lease dated 25 August, 1602[1] the tenant covenanted to "use his best endeavours for preserving the Yew, Box, and all other trees . . ." and to account half-yearly for what had been sold. Six years later the receipt for Box-trees cut down upon the Sheep Walk on the Hill amounted to £50. In 1712 it was stated that the value of those felled within the preceding few years was as much as £3,000. As a native in Britain the tree is extremely local and restricted to very calcareous soils (see also pp. 55, 94 and 128). At Box Hill it is at its best.

But in spring and summer, apart from the slope just mentioned which the thick, snaky stems of the Box dominate, other trees are more conspicuous. Of these, the finest contrast is between the very dark green (almost black from a distance) of the Yew, *Taxus baccata*, and the silvery foliage of the Whitebeam, *Sorbus aria*. The first is a conifer which shows no apparent morphological variation although it grows in practically all the chalk and limestone areas in Britain. Cattle are often poisoned by the foliage and the seeds also contain the dangerous alkaloid taxine, but the scarlet fleshy cups known as arils which envelop them are freely and eagerly eaten by birds. Very often the shoots end in a little cone-shaped tuft of leaves united together which encloses a gall with the larvae of a dipterous insect (*Taxomyia taxi*).

The Whitebeam is a much more variable tree and a whole range of different leaf-shapes may be found within a short distance. In the north and west of England, in Wales, Scotland and in Ireland, it is mostly replaced by allied species which will be discussed later. The white appearance so conspicuous at a distance is due to a snowy felt on the under-surface of the leaves. It is a handsome tree throughout the warmer months. From early May onwards the silvery appearance of the young leaves is very beautiful. Later in that month, in favourable seasons, it is covered with heads of sickly-smelling white flowers and these are succeeded by bright-red fruits in autumn. Finally the leaves

[1] Manning & Bray (1804): *History of Surrey*, I, p. 560.

By courtesy of Raphael Tuck & Sons Ltd.

Box Hill, Surrey

PLATE II

J. E. Lousley

Interior of a Box Grove; Box Hill, Surrey

drop off to form a white carpet on the ground. The word " beam " is an Anglo-Saxon term for tree akin to the German *Baum*, so " Whitebeam tree " is a pleonasm.

Although it is not confined to calcareous soils most of our native Beech, *Fagus sylvatica*, is to be found on the chalk of south-eastern England. Its essential requirement is good drainage and it often forms " hangers " on the shallow soils of the escarpments. Nevertheless the finest woods are often—as at Box Hill and on the Chilterns—to be seen on the deeper earth of the Clay-with-Flints. Gilbert White referred to the Beech as " The most lovely of all forest trees," and I think he was right. When walking through one of these woods I always have a feeling that I am in a cathedral. The smooth fluted trunks branching out in curved vaulting, with the subdued light and coolness on hot summer days due to the close canopy overhead, all contribute to this impression. It is obvious to the eye that relatively little light penetrates the foliage, and this is probably the main reason why so few flowers grow on the thick layers of reddish-brown old leaves which accumulate on the ground.

The next two very characteristic trees of calcareous soils are less abundant at Box Hill than they are in the north and west. The Ash, *Fraxinus excelsior*, is recognised in summer by the divided (compound) leaves which have about four pairs of leaflets with an odd one at the end. Just as the Beech is easily known in the winter by its long tapering light-brown buds, so the Ash is recognised by short, stout, sooty buds on olive-green twigs which are flattened in a characteristic manner. The stalk of the leaves has a curious furrow which collects rain-water and this may sometimes be absorbed. Flowers appear before the foliage as dense purplish clusters. They are followed by the fruits, known as " keys " (Plate XXIIIa, p. 206), which remain on the trees throughout the winter and then spin away in the wind to fall some distance away. It has been shown by a German botanist[1] that the Ash trees of dry calcareous soils, the " lime-ashes," belong to a different physiological race from those of marshes. The descendants of the former are satisfied with less moisture and flourish under drier conditions, so each race is adapted to its own type of habitat. Apparently their external appearance is exactly the same.

Wych Elm, *Ulmus glabra*, seldom grows to its full height of 60

[1] Büsgen, M. (1929) : *The Structure and Life of Forest Trees*. Third, revised edition by Dr. E. Münch, English translation by T. Thomson, p. 411.

feet or so on the chalk downs. The leaves are large (3-5 in. long), rough, and very unequal at the base, so that the larger side extends farther down the stalk. In early May in some years (1948 was a good one) the bunches of bright green fruits are produced abundantly and the tree then looks as though it is covered with delightfully pale foliage.

White Birch, *Betula pendula*, occurs occasionally on the chalk, though it is much more plentiful on the Clay-with-Flints. The closely allied Downy or Common Birch, *B. pubescens*, is not always easy to distinguish in the south of England although the characters given in the floras seem straightforward enough on paper. The difficulty is partly (perhaps mainly) due to hybridisation. In Yorkshire it is found on limestone but I do not remember it on chalk in the south. Scots Pine, *Pinus sylvestris*, is to be seen at intervals along the steep face of the North Downs on the shallowest of chalk soils. Although originally planted it has a tendency to extend its ground from seed. It shows to advantage against the skyline (cf. Plate 28, p. 123). Small trees of the Common Oak, *Quercus robur*, are to be seen here and there on Box Hill, but its deep roots have no opportunity of full development on shallow chalk soils—it is more characteristic of the damper clay soils such as those of the Weald. Sycamore, *Acer pseudo-platanus*, is fairly plentiful in places. It is not a native tree but spreads rapidly by means of its winged fruits and grows freely from seed on calcareous soils. The indigenous Field Maple, *Acer campestre*, with foliage which turns a lovely golden yellow in the autumn, is plentiful all over the downs but especially in hedgerows.

Three shrubs, Dogwood, *Thelycrania sanguinea*, Privet, *Ligustrum vulgare*, and Wayfaring Tree, *Viburnum lantana*, often grow together. If all are present, and in quantity, as is frequently the case on the North Downs, it is almost certain that the soil is highly calcareous. Dogwood (Plate 8, p. 31) is always easy to recognise by the reddish colour of the twigs, to which the second part of the scientific name refers. In the winter, after the leaves have fallen, this is often so noticeable that a whole thicket of the shrub will show up red from a distance. In autumn the foliage turns purple-red. Privet is half-evergreen—the leaves are renewed each spring but some of them remain on the shrub throughout the winter.

The Wayfaring Tree (Plate 9a and b, p. 46) has always been a favourite with me. To call it a tree is something of a misnomer, for although it can grow to a height of about 15 feet it is commonly very much shorter. It is the only British shrub with naked buds; i.e., the flower and leaf buds have no hard protective scales but are merely covered with a pair of folded leaves clothed with felt, which is sufficient to preserve them from damage during the winter. Flower buds form during the summer and may be seen well advanced long before the foliage drops. As the white blossoms are collected into heads at the ends of the shoots, the display during the short flowering season at the end of April and beginning of May is very fine. On Box Hill I have seen flowers produced on young plants only about two feet tall, giving the impression that the bloom is out of all proportion to the size. The fruits are at first red, turning black later, so that in early autumn many of the clusters are made up of a mixture of both colours. The leaves of the Wayfaring Tree are broad and wrinkled, and grow in pairs opposite to one another on the stem. They are covered with a felt of dense star-like hairs which unfortunately collect the dust when it grows on roadsides (as by the "Zig-zag" up Box Hill) where, as a result, the bush sometimes looks greyish-white in midsummer.

Another very common shrub on the chalk downs is the Hawthorn, *Crataegus monogyna*, which grows there just as freely as it does on most other soils. On Box Hill it is the host of a small race of Mistletoe, *Viscum album*, which is less than half the size of the same species parasitic on Apple and Poplar elsewhere. Juniper, *Juniperus communis*, is a much more characteristic shrub of calcareous soils though local on these hills. It is a conifer well able to resist wind, and on the exposed escarpment it often provides shelter for young plants of other species of shrub and tree. The "berries" take several seasons to mature and may often be seen in several stages—green, pale and dark blue, and finally black—on the same bush. On the slopes of Box Hill towards the east (and elsewhere) large numbers of Juniper may be seen in a dead and dying condition, but the reason for this is not yet fully understood. Young seedlings are rare, and it is possible that intense grazing by rabbits prevents regeneration of this long-lived shrub and that the old ones are simply dying of old age without a fresh supply of younger ones to take their place.

Roses are abundant on calcareous soils and the Box Hill district is an excellent area in which to commence their study. In addition to the well-known Dog Rose, *Rosa canina*, in many forms, Field Rose,

Rosa arvensis, and other species equally or more common on other soils, there are two which are specially associated with the chalk. The best known of these is Sweetbriar, *R. rubiginosa*, a low-growing erect shrub with small blunt roundish leaflets covered thickly with scented glands underneath. The sepals remain on the top of the fruit until it reddens and often stand bolt upright to form an attractive crown. In addition there is the False Sweetbriar, *Rosa micrantha*, which in most downland areas is more common. This is a larger, more sprawling bush with usually narrower leaflets with fewer glands and with a less pronounced scent.

Spindle Tree, *Euonymus europaeus*, is one of the most sought-after chalk shrubs by those who gather autumn fruits for decoration. At all times of the year it may be recognised by the smooth, green, four-angled twigs. The small green flowers are inconspicuous, but the plant attracts attention in the fall from all country ramblers. The leaves turn a brilliant reddish hue, and the pink fruits split open into four lobes to expose the bright orange covering to the white seeds buried within—one of the most striking colour contrasts to be seen in nature.

At the same season Traveller's Joy, *Clematis vitalba* (Plate 1, p. 2), is an important element in the Box Hill colour scheme. It is one of the best indicators of calcareous soils in the south of England, and I have often amused myself on train journeys by noticing how accurately its presence or absence marked changes in the geology. Its rope-like stems, resembling those of tropical lianas, festoon hedgerows and sprawl over trees on the edges of woods. Their bark splits away in long narrow shreds. The abundance of white flowers produced is attractive enough, but it is the mass of silvery fruits with their persistent styles, lasting well on into the winter, which are best known. These give the plant its alternative name of Old Man's Beard.

The plants discussed so far have been trees and shrubs—the conspicuous features which individually make substantial contributions to the scenery. But the smaller flowers growing in the short, dense turf of the slopes are more characteristic of downland and collectively are responsible for much of the joy and beauty of Box Hill. In March I have seen large areas of the grassland so coloured with the blooms of the Hairy Violet, *Viola hirta*, that the whole hillside looked blue from a distance. These showy early blossoms appear before the leaves have fully expanded and set very little seed. A couple of months later, hidden away near the base of the long-stalked summer leaves, flowers of another kind are to be found setting seed in abundance. These are like little swollen fleshy buds with tiny malformed and often pink petals; they never open and are self-fertilised. The fruits rest on or near the surface of the ground, and thanks to the attraction of an oily body attached to each of the whitish seeds, ants carry the latter away from the parent plant and thus help it to colonize fresh ground.

On Box Hill the flowers of the Hairy Violet vary very greatly in size and colour but it is easily recognised as a tufted plant with hairy, rather pointed leaves with spreading hairs on their stalks. But these characters will not serve to differentiate it from the closely allied Chalk Violet, *Viola calcarea*, which is a rarity found here and in a few other widely scattered places on the chalk and limestone. This is smaller with narrower petals, of which the four uppermost are arranged in the form of a St. Andrew's Cross, and with such a tiny conical spur that it is sometimes almost imperceptible. In their extreme forms the two plants are very distinct but they are connected by many intermediates. Some botanists (including myself) incline to the view that the Chalk Violet is really only a late-flowering (semi-cleistogamous) state of the Hairy Violet. This is supported by the fact that it does not flower until May, varies a great deal in numbers in different seasons, and that the flowers are a sort of half-way stage between the large spring flowers of the commoner species and its summer flowers described above.

The Sweet-scented Violet, *Viola odorata*, is a precocious flowerer, with fragrant blossoms, long runners, and rounder leaves which are shining and almost without hairs in the spring. In the Box Hill district it is usually white- instead of blue-flowered, and it has been shown by S. M. Walters that of this there are two white varieties, one with bearded and the other with beardless lateral petals. Hybrids with the Hairy Violet are common.

In May the slopes where the Violets grow are bright with the flowers of Milkworts. Of these, two are plentiful on the chalk. On the North Downs the Chalk Milkwort, *Polygala calcarea*, is locally abundant and may be known from allied species by the rosettes of broad leaves at the bases of the flowering stems. These rosettes in turn are produced on wiry stems which lead back to a central root.

The arrangement is not always easy to follow when the plants are growing in thick turf, but if you can find one on chalk rubble with very little surrounding vegetation there is no difficulty. The colour of the flowers of the Chalk Milkwort is usually a delightful bright blue, but they are occasionally white and in 1946 I found a whole colony at Buckland, a little farther along the hills, with uniform pale magenta blooms. This species is practically restricted to the chalk and a few places on the limestone, but the Common Milkwort, *P. vulgaris*, which lacks the leaf rosettes, is very catholic in its soil requirements. It varies a great deal in the colour of its flowers, and sometimes pale and dark blue, and red, may be found growing together.

Salad Burnet, *Poterium sanguisorba*, is another early-flowering plant which is as common on Box Hill as on most calcareous soils in England and Wales. The young leaves smell and taste like cucumber and at one time they were used as an addition to salads. Sheep feed on it eagerly, no doubt finding the unusual flavour an attractive relish to the downland turf. The flowers are collected into roundish heads about half an inch across at the top of a wiry stem a foot or so high.

In May the typical downland orchids start to appear, and for these Box Hill has long been famous. In spite of the depredations of visitors, who pick them selfishly in large numbers because they regard them as quaint and rare, they are still plentiful in the district. I am convinced that if people realised how interesting these plants are they would treat them with greater care and they would be still more plentiful. Perhaps the most fascinating of them all is the Man Orchid, *Aceras anthropophorum* (Plate VI, p. 35), which is usually about nine inches tall with many flowers in a dense spike. The lip is usually yellow and shaped like the body of a man with divisions to represent the arms and legs. The sepals are green, edged with brown or red, and curved in the form of a hood. But there is an alternative resemblance to the human race which amuses people with imagination. The hood may be regarded as portraying the head of a dwarf with the lip for his flowing beard. Surrey and Kent are the counties where Man Orchid is to be found in the largest numbers—the farther one gets away from the south-east the less plentiful it is, and it is not found at all in the west of England, Wales, Scotland or Ireland.

The Fragrant Orchid, *Gymnadenia conopsea*, and the Pyramidal Orchid, *Anacamptis pyramidalis*, flower a little later. As they are often confused by beginners they are shown side by side on the same colour plate (Plate 5, p. 14) so that the differences can be clearly seen. In addition to those obvious in the picture it should be noted that the Fragrant has a most delightful scent rather like a carnation (though some people find it over-strong), and the Pyramidal has erect guiding plates at the base of the lip which are found in no other British orchid. Some years ago my friend W. H. Spreadbury found a most remarkable specimen on Box Hill in which all the individual flowers *appeared* to be upside down. Actually they were the right way up, for in the Pyramidal, and most other British orchids, there is normally a twist in the ovary and this had not been made. This aberration has never appeared in the same spot again.

The Bee Orchid, *Ophrys apifera*, is one of our best-known wild flowers (Plate 6, p. 15) and is all too frequently picked. The resemblance to a Bee visiting a flower is so close that children are often afraid to touch it, and it would seem likely that bees themselves are aware of the likeness. Darwin showed that the orchid was commonly self-pollinated, but almost certainly cross-fertilisation also occurs and certain bees may be the agents.

The Musk Orchid, *Herminium monorchis*, like the Bee, varies greatly in numbers from year to year, but I have never failed to find a few plants in certain places on and near Box Hill. It is a small slender plant, usually about six inches in height, and extremely inconspicuous. A very strong and pleasing smell of honey is given off by the rather tubular yellowish flowers, which are less than a quarter inch long. It has a long flowering season but July is the best month to search for it. Autumn Lady's-tresses, *Spiranthes spiralis* (Plate 7a, p. 30), is about the same height but a rather stouter plant, flowering in August and September—the last of our native orchids to blossom. The small white flowers are very sweet-scented and are arranged in an extremely elegant spiral round the stem, twisting sometimes from right to left and sometimes in the opposite direction. As a result there is a certain resemblance to old-fashioned ways in which ladies once twisted their hair. Unlike most of our orchids, Autumn Lady's-tresses has no rosette of leaves at the base of the flowering stem, these having withered earlier in the summer. Instead there is a new rosette about an inch away which lives through the winter and decays before the flowers appear the following August. This may be compared with the Bee Orchid, of which I have found leaves under light snow on Box Hill in February soon after they appeared above ground. These are still to be seen at the base of the flowering stems in summer and only wither as the blooms turn to seed. Lady's-tresses is most abundant on the parts of the hill most frequented by trippers and they often picnic in their hundreds quite unaware that an orchid is growing all round them. There are other orchids still to be found on the grasslands and in the woods of Box Hill.

Having followed one group of plants through the summer, it is now time to return to the June flowers. At this season yellow blossoms predominate, and one of the most common and conspicuous is Common Rock-rose, *Helianthemum chamaecistus*. This is a low shrubby plant with flowers about an inch across. The delicately thin fugitive petals drop almost immediately they are picked. Generally they are of a uniform buttercup yellow, but rarely there are orange spots at their base, and sometimes they may be sulphur or even white. These variations are constant on the same plants from year to year, and once located they can generally be seen again in other seasons in the same place.

The next three plants are all members of the Leguminosae (Pea Family). Kidney Vetch, *Anthyllis vulneraria*, owes the second part of its scientific name to its supposed vulnerary (wound-healing) qualities. The flowers are usually pale yellow, and in fruit the calyx becomes white and inflated. Sheep are very fond of it and on the Continent the plant is cultivated on a considerable scale, but it is rarely grown over here. Common Birdsfoot Trefoil, *Lotus corniculatus*, has bright yellow flowers with the standard striped with red at the base. As they go over, the colour deepens and becomes more or less orange, and when dried for herbarium specimens there is sometimes yet another change to green. The plant gets its popular name from the brown cylindrical pods spread out finger-wise, thus recalling the foot of a bird. These pods twist suddenly as they split on maturity and the movement throws out the seeds a little distance from the parent. Horse-shoe Vetch, *Hippocrepis comosa*, has more graceful flowers of a paler yellow with delicate brown lines marked on them. There should be no difficulty in distinguishing it from the Birdsfoot Trefoil by the leaves, which have about 7 to 11 elliptical leaflets minutely pointed at their ends, and also by the pods. These are brownish, about an inch long, curved into a semi-circle or ring, and made up of a series of joints, each of which is swollen over a single seed—a second seed in

John Markham

a. Flowers of the Box, *Buxus sempervirens*

John Markham

b. Yew, *Taxus baccata*. Underside of spray with male flowers

PLATE IV

Brian Perkins

a. Dark Mullein, *Verbascum nigrum*. On the North Downs, Leatherhead, Surrey

A. E. Hick

b. Yellow-wort, *Blackstonia perfoliata*; Fleam Dyke, Cambridgeshire

each joint being usually abortive. One might expect the pods to split open across the narrow joints, but in fact the breaks take place through the widest parts. Horse-shoe Vetch is hardly ever found off calcareous soils, on which it is very widespread.

Fairy Flax, *Linum catharticum*, is a slender wiry little plant with small glaucous green stem-leaves in pairs, and numerous white flowers about a quarter of an inch across with a yellow eye. In some of the books it is called Purging Flax, with allusion to its purgative qualities. A seventeenth-century recipe recommended bruising the plant and then placing it whole in a pipkin of white wine left on the embers of a fire to infuse all night.[1] The writer referred to it under the pleasant name of " Mil-mountaine " and warned his readers that the effect was somewhat drastic.

I have always had a soft spot for Squinancywort, *Asperula cynanchica*. Its pink flowers are an ornament to most of our chalk downs in June, and on the limestone it goes as far north as Westmorland—its northern limit in Europe. But it is the quaintness of the name, which rolls so easily off the tongue, which pleases me. As Pryor puts it, this was earned on account of " its supposed efficacy in curing the disease so-called in old authors, viz. the quinsy." The French and medieval Latin names are very similar, and there is no doubt that the English name has come right down to us from the days when the study of plants was in the hands of simplers and old wives.

Downland flowers often bloom over such a long period that it is particularly difficult to arrange them in the sequence at which they are at their best. Thus Yellow-wort, *Blackstonia perfoliata* (Plate IVb, p. 27) may be in blossom as early as the end of May—yet I have seen it out as late as October on Box Hill. The flowers are the brightest of yellows and make a pleasing contrast to the characteristic undivided glaucous leaves which are arranged in pairs joined round the stem (connate). It is a true calcicole of wide distribution in our islands though less common towards the north. The flowers close up at night. The small genus to which it belongs was named by Hudson in honour of John Blackstone, an English botanist and apothecary who died in 1753.

Hoary Plantain, *Plantago media*, is abundant on chalk hills and easily recognised at all times of the year by the oval, hoary leaves.

[1] Thomas Johnson in Gerard's *Herbal* ed. 2 (1636), p. 560 ; on the authority of John Goodyer and a Dr. Lake of Winchester.

The flower-stems are even more woolly, and when the heads show the purple stalks of the yellowish-white anthers they are quite attractive. Like its relatives which can withstand so much trampling in garden lawns, the Hoary Plantain is a most difficult plant to destroy and hence it is to be found even on the most frequented parts of the downs. Much the same can be said for the Stemless Thistle, *Cirsium acaulon* (Plate 2, p. 3), which is able to put up with any amount of bad treatment. The name would often seem to be a misnomer, for not infrequently the stems are of sufficient length to be noticeable, but nevertheless more ramblers can claim acquaintance with its spiny leaves than with its flowers. As it increases very rapidly vegetatively, it forms large patches—often a yard or two yards across—from which other vegetation is more or less excluded. To select one of these inadvertently as a resting-place is an uncomfortable experience for which the handsome purplish-red heads of flowers nestling amongst the leaves are small compensation.

Two Umbellifers are very common on chalk. Some of the quieter parts of Box Hill have masses of Wild Parsnip, *Pastinaca sativa*, a coarse plant with bright yellow flowers. Various subspecies are recognised on the Continent but, although the leaf-shape of our downland material varies a good deal, no attempt has been made to "split" the Parsnip in Britain. Wild Carrot, *Daucus carota*, should also be recognised very easily by any gardener who has ever allowed his crop to go to seed, though in this case also the cultivated and wild plants are not identical. Recent research has shown that the Carrot of the vegetable garden is probably derived from a Mediterranean subspecies and not from our wild British plant. The heads of flowers arranged on stalks set out like the ribs of an umbrella are worth careful examination. Those on the outside are irregular with the petal directed outwards enlarged to make the head more prominent. The inner flowers have all the petals more or less the same size, and careful examination with a lens will show that some are male and others female. The central flower is often a deep purple colour.

By August most of the chalk down flowers are those which will go on until well into the autumn. Whereas the predominant colour earlier is yellow, blues, reds and purples now become general. Two Scabiouses are particularly characteristic. One, the Small Scabious, *Scabiosa columbaria*, is widespread on chalk and limestone in Britain.

Each flower-head consists of some 70 to 80 separate bluish-lilac flowers collected together in the same way as the daisies (Compositae). Those round the edge are rayed, making the whole head more conspicuous, and in these the anthers are pushed out and expanded well before the stigmas mature. The fruits are hard and spiny, with another covering (the involucel) outside the calyx. They are crowned with five dark purple spines with teeth all along their edges, and these catch in the hair of animals or the clothing of humans and thus assist in the dispersal of the seeds.

The Small Scabious has the parts of its flowers in 5's, but in Field Scabious, *Knautia arvensis*, they are in 4's. This has much larger and more purplish blooms, and although common on chalk and limestone it also occurs on other soils. Usually in all the flowers of the heads the anthers open first, shed their pollen, and wither before the stigmas are protruded. In this way self-pollination is rendered very unlikely. But Darwin also showed that some plants occur with only female flowers and these are said to be more numerous early in the season. It seems that their numbers as compared with the hermaphrodite blossoms vary in different parts of the country.

Thistles are usually regarded as pests rather than flowers of beauty, but although downland farmers have good reason to destroy it, the Musk Thistle, *Carduus nutans*, is a handsome plant, as the illustration (Plate 3, p. 10) shows. The blooms smell of musk and are protected by a series of rather broad bracts ; there is only one head at the end of each downy stalk, which is leafless towards the top. Carline Thistle, *Carlina vulgaris*, also shows a strongly marked preference for calcareous soils. Its pale-yellow " everlasting " flowers expand fully in sunshine in dry weather and close up again when it is wet. On this account country people sometimes collect them for use as barometers, or rather as hygrometers—for it is the humidity of the atmosphere and not the air-pressure which they indicate. On the downs they last well into the winter until the wind and rain destroy them.

Dark Mullein, *Verbascum nigrum* (Plate IVa, p. 27), is another very characteristic plant of calcareous soils in the south, although it is absent from the northern limestones. It is easily distinguished from the other Mulleins by the numerous and usually unbranched stems, which come up from the rosette of leaves with heart-shaped bases, and by the beautiful tufts of purplish hairs on the stamens. It is said to be absolutely sterile to its own pollen, so cross-fertilisation is essential to the production of seed. The books usually give the Dark Mullein as a biennial but this is certainly not always true. I have known Surrey plants which have lived for years, increasing annually in size so that eventually they became more like a small colony than a single individual.

Great Mullein, *V. thapsus*, sometimes called High Taper, has long dense spikes of stalkless, rather pale yellow flowers and woolly leaves with bases which run down the stem (decurrent). Almost the whole plant is covered with matted white hairs which, when examined under the microscope, are seen to be intricately branched. This wool, stripped from the leaves, was formerly used as tinder owing to the ease with which it ignited when dry. The Great Mullein, like most of its allies, is a biennial, and in the first year it produces only the rosettes of woolly leaves which are such familiar sights in spring and autumn. On Box Hill I have found hybrids with the Dark Mullein showing a perfect mixture of the characters of the two parents.

I always associate August on the chalk downs with the delightful scents of leaves of Labiates—Wild Thyme, *Thymus drucei*, Marjoram, *Origanum vulgare*, Wild Basil, *Clinopodium vulgare*, and other less common plants. The first two are closely related to foreign species grown in herb gardens for use as flavourings, but the native Thyme and Marjoram will serve as coarser substitutes. In addition to the " complete " blossoms, which contain fully-formed stamens and pistils, there are female flowers in which the stamens are aborted. These appear a little earlier and are smaller, so that a careful search is necessary to find them.

The Eyebrights, *Euphrasia spp.*, are extremely interesting from several points of view. They are partially parasitic in that they normally obtain part of their food materials from other plants by means of attachments from their roots on to those of their hosts. For this purpose they attack Grasses, Sedges and probably other plants, and the dense mass of roots present in the downland turf provides them with excellent opportunities.

Recent researches have shown that the British Eyebrights, all formerly included under the aggregate name of *Euphrasia officinalis*, can be divided into about 25 species. Some of these are very distinct and very little study will suffice to distinguish them. The most handsome of the kinds found on calcareous soils is Large-flowered Chalk

Robert Atkinson

a. AUTUMN LADY'S-TRESSES, *Spiranthes spiralis;* a frequent, but often overlooked, little orchid.
Bedfordshire; September

Robert Atkinson

b. FLY ORCHID, *Ophrys muscifera;* frequent on the edges of calcareous woods.
Oxfordshire; June

John Markham

DOGWOOD, *Thelycrania sanguinea*, in fruit. The red twigs make identification easy even in the winter. Hertfordshire; September

Eyebright, *E. pseudokerneri* (Plate 20, p. 91), for which the type locality is Box Hill. Pugsley described this as "a beautiful plant of dwarf, robust and bushy habit, with small, dark foliage and large, bright flowers." It is one of the autumn gems of the downs, coming into flower in August and being at its best in September. Well grown plants are a mass of bloom, and the individual blossoms seem enormous in comparison with the size of the plants. It is fairly common on the South and North Downs, and also found in East Anglia, but it is one of the few British species which, so far as our present knowledge goes, are endemic—i.e., not found outside this country.

The other species which is common on Box Hill is the Common Eyebright, *E. nemorosa*. This has much smaller flowers which are less prettily marked and it is more straggling. For those who are interested in such fine points, it should be mentioned that, as found here, it is usually the variety *calcarea*, which is dwarfer and coarser than the usual state of the species.

Clustered Bellflower, *Campanula glomerata*, is common on calcareous soils in all parts of England and extends into Wales and Scotland. It is not surprising that over such a wide range it varies very greatly in size. The Box Hill specimens (Plate 4, p. 11) may be taken as about the average, and many people think they have found something different when, on the wet limestone cliffs of the north, they find strong, robust plants some two feet high with much more numerous flowers and less hairy leaves. The other extreme is seen on very dry coastal cliffs in Sussex and the Isle of Wight, where it may be found a mere inch or two tall, with only one or two flowers, and extremely hairy. It was such plants that led the painstaking Dr. William Withering into a first-class botanical howler a little over a century ago. On two diminutive specimens of the Clustered Bellflower he described a species new to science, and went so far astray that he classified them as Gentians—under the name *Gentiana collina*!

The only true Gentian to be found on Box Hill is far less beautiful than the rarer species described in later chapters. Autumn Gentian, *Gentianella amarella*, has reddish-purple flowers which open and close with surprising speed, according to changes in the temperature. Since it is warmer when the sun is shining, the opening is generally observed as clouds roll away, and the time taken for the change may sometimes be as little as 20 seconds. The bitter taste of the stem and leaves is said to offer protection against grazing, but this is certainly of little value in the face of attacks from the hungry rabbits of the downs. When they nibble the young shoots down to ground level the plants branch out from the base and grow into very floriferous bushy little tufts on which the flowers are sometimes divided into 4's instead of 5's. It was from Box Hill that Pugsley described a new variety of the Autumn Gentian with greenish-white tetramerous (divided into 4's) flowers as variety *pallida*.

Finally there are two plants which belong to bushy places and wood borders rather than to the chalk grassland. Ploughman's Spikenard, *Inula conyza*, has small yellowish flowers collected into numerous heads about half an inch long and is usually about a couple of feet in height. The leaves are rather like those of the Foxglove, and more than once I have thought that I had found this calcifuge on chalk until I quickly realised my mistake. In a similar difficulty, rub a leaf, and if it has an aromatic smell it is certainly not Foxglove. It was the " sweet and aromaticall flavour which his roots containeth and yieldeth " which led the Elizabethan Gerard to confuse this plant with a foreign herb with roots which provided an ointment, and hence to the application of the name "Plowmans-Spikenard."

Deadly Nightshade, *Atropa belladonna* (Plate 10, p. 47), is common on Box Hill—perhaps too common in view of the large number of children brought there for picnics. All parts of the plant are poisonous as they contain the deadly alkaloids atropine and hyoscyamine in various proportions, but drugs are generally prepared from the leaves and roots. It is the fruits, which are about the size of cherries and of very attractive appearance, which are responsible for most cases of accidental poisoning. Somewhat strangely it seems that many animals are immune from serious effects following their feeding on Belladonna. Birds eat the berries. Rabbits gnaw the leaves and stems and, as shown in the illustration, the foliage is often eaten by caterpillars. On limestones Deadly Nightshade is sometimes locally abundant, but elsewhere it is generally found only round abbeys and similar places where it was probably originally planted for medical use.

The plants discussed in this chapter are all to be found on Box Hill and many of them are widespread on calcareous soils. Readers from all parts of the country will be able to find some of them in their own districts ; others are restricted to the south of England. They do not exhaust the treasures of the hill ; on the contrary it must be stressed that the visitor will find many other fascinating plants for himself. The selection of characteristic chalk plants which has been given will serve, by comparison with other districts, to illustrate the common factor which runs through all the floras of calcareous soils in the British Isles. Distance brings into effect the influence of the limits of geographical distribution of species. For this reason it will be found, as a general rule, that the farther we get away from Box Hill in the following chapters, the greater the differences in the kinds of wild flowers observed.

CHAPTER 3

BOX HILL: THE ECOLOGY OF THE CHALK

PLANT ECOLOGY is a modern development of field botany. It is the study of plants in relation to their environment and of their association together in what are called "plant communities." By investigating the conditions under which they live (habitat factors), the ecologist is able to define the requirements of species and to show why some of them are commonly found growing together, while others are rarely or never associated. His work provides an essential approach for the proper understanding of plants in their homes.

An excellent account of the habitat factors of British plants has been provided by Dr. W. B. Turrill in his book on *British Plant Life* in the NEW NATURALIST series. There he adopts the following classification :

A. *Inorganic.*
- 1. Climatic.
- 2. Edaphic (soil).

B. *Organic.*
- 3. Biotic (animals and plants).

In addition some writers have included another inorganic group to cover topographic and physiographic factors, but Dr. Turrill shows that these are not basically distinct. They act indirectly through the other factors. Because of this it is convenient to consider them first in the case of Box Hill.

Box Hill rises to a little over 650 feet on the east side of the gap formed by the River Mole where it breaks through the North Downs. Above the Mole it forms a magnificent river-cliff which drops some 300 feet at a slope of about 3 in 4, facing west. A long south-facing escarpment drops about the same height at an average slope of

PLATE V

Robert Atkinson

Shakespeare's Cliff, Dover, with Sea Cabbage, *Brassica oleracea*, on the chalk cliff

Robert Atkinson

Man Orchid, *Aceras anthropophorum*; Oxfordshire

1 in 3, overlooked from the well-known viewpoint at the Salomon's Memorial—a stone semi-circle on which directions and distances are marked. The high ground on the top of the hill runs out in tongues northwards, with intervening steep-sided valleys.

The geology is fairly simple (Fig. 2, p. 36), the divisions present being as follows:

A. *Clay-with-Flints.* This covers most of the ground above 500 feet (thus running out in tongues along the northern spurs).

B. *Upper Chalk.* Outcropping in a narrow belt at the crest of the southern escarpment (including the Salomon's Memorial), above the river cliff, and in a broader belt including most of the Zig-zag and Juniper Bottom to the north.

C. *Middle Chalk.* At the surface over most of the southern escarpment and the river cliff, and by Headley Lane.

D. *Lower Chalk.* Outcrops below the hedge at the bottom of the southern escarpment and along the end of the river cliff nearest to Dorking.

The Clay-with-Flints gives rise to a deep soil of red-brown loam, often with layers of slowly decaying leaves and other rotting vegetation at the surface. Upper and Middle Chalk have shallow calcareous soils of the *rendzina* type. In these the humus layer at the top passes gradually into the lower whiter layers of rock fragments merging into the parent chalk beneath. There is no second ("B") horizon of redeposited material as in soil profiles of a more mature type. The whole mass is permeated with free calcium carbonate which corrects any tendency to acidity. Deep layers of undecayed vegetable matter do not collect. The Lower Chalk is made up of marls and greyish-white soft rock and bears grey loamy soil. Most of it slopes gradually and is easily cultivated. The change from the steep uncultivated Middle Chalk to the meadows and arable fields of the Lower Chalk is abrupt and coincides with the hedge running along the base of the escarpment.

A very easy way to appreciate the influence of geology on the vegetation is to look south from the Salomon's Memorial. In the far distance the South Downs can just be seen, and on a clear day it is possible to pick out their higher hills such as Mount Harry (near Lewes), the Devil's Dyke (near Brighton), and Chanctonbury Ring (near Worthing). The South Downs, like the North Downs, are a chalk range with flowers characteristic of calcareous soils (see Chapter

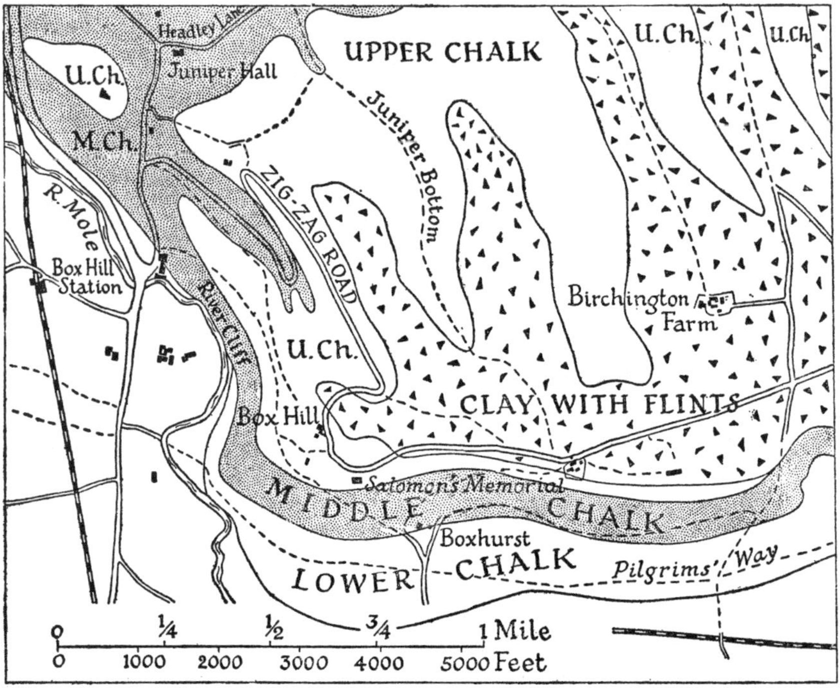

FIG. 2
Sketch map of geology of Box Hill

5). In the middle distance are the clays and sands of the Weald and the Greensand of the Surrey Hills. Leith Hill (conspicuous on account of its height and characteristic tower), at a distance of about six miles, is one example which will be familiar to many readers. There one finds calcifuges such as Ling, *Calluna vulgaris*, Whortleberry, *Vaccinium myrtillus*, and abundant Bracken, *Pteridium aquilinum*, instead of the short dense turf of the chalk hills.

Throughout the large area of country between the South and North Downs calcareous soils are practically absent. It is not until the observer from the Memorial allows his eye to follow the escarpment on which he is standing that he will again be looking at a chalk flora. This escarpment runs from the east past Buckland, Colley and Reigate Hills, and west by Denbies, White Downs, Hackhurst and Albury Downs to the Hog's Back. Most of the way it is excellent chalk grassland varied by occasional brushwood and hangers of Beech, Yew or Box.

Turning now to the north, a short walk from the Salomon's Memorial leads to the plateau on the top of Box Hill which is covered with Clay-with-Flints. Here the vegetation is obviously different from that of the Chalk. Some of the trees are the same—such as Beech, which is dominant over most of the woodland. But here it commonly grows to a height of over 100 feet with tall trunks with few lower branches, so that their leafy canopy is high. Yew and Box occur towards the edge of the Clay-with-Flints and are often larger than on the chalk. The tree which gives the best indication of the change in the geology is the Common Oak, *Quercus robur*. On shallow soils over chalk this is scarce and stunted. On Clay-with-Flints it is common and fairly well grown.

Beech and Oak are the characteristic trees of these woods with an equally characteristic low shrub layer of Brambles, *Rubus spp*. Here and there are patches of Bracken. The ground flora includes Bluebell, *Endymion non-scriptus*, Wood Sorrel, *Oxalis acetosella*, and Dog's Mercury, *Mercurialis perennis*. The surface of the soil is covered with deep layers of fallen leaves and is sticky and wet in winter. Under such conditions it tends to become acid, owing to the accumulation of humus, and beyond the limits of Box Hill the Clay-with-Flints sometimes carries extensive calcifuge vegetation.

The nature of the chalk soils is greatly influenced by topography. Where the slope is very steep the rate of erosion is such that it prevents soil from forming at all, and then the bare rock with lumps of chalk and powdery débris is exposed. This is accentuated by trampling, since the feet of walkers tend to send loose material rolling down the slope. A good example is to be seen on the track leading up Box Hill from the Burford Bridge Hotel. Here erosion takes place so fast that the National Trust have been obliged to place wooden stakes in the ground to retard the process. Between the trees on the river cliff there are several open areas where soil—and hence turf—has failed to form owing to the steepness of the slope.

The gradient at which turf can form has not been investigated on Box Hill, but it is probably not very different from that on the Hampshire chalk, for which two examples can be given. Adamson (1922) found that a slope with an average gradient of 30·6° had a continuous ground flora, while one with a gradient of 36·5° was either bare or had a very sparse vegetation. The investigations of Tansley and Adamson (1925) showed that 37-38° was the greatest angle at which closely grazed chalk grassland could maintain itself.

Such steep gradients are rare on Box Hill, but even the more usual 20-30° has an important influence on depth of soil, temperature, amount of light available, water-content, and the extent to which leaching has taken place. Material washes down slopes, so that it is usual to find that the soil on slopes is shallow on the escarpments and sides of the valleys but deeper at the bottom of the valleys. Similarly water in the form of rainfall is lost to the steeper slopes more rapidly than when the gradient is low. Leached material is carried off quicker when the angle is high, and thus the soil remains more calcareous than at the bottom of the valleys. On the north-facing slopes the sun's rays are spread out more than they are on those facing south. Therefore they receive less warmth and less light.

Maintenance of adequate water supply is one of the most serious problems facing plants on the chalky slopes. To reduce to a minimum the loss by transpiration, many of them are low growing. Their aerial parts thus carry on their life entirely in the relatively humid zone just above ground level, protected from the full force of drying winds. Some, like Fairy Flax, *Linum catharticum*, have small leaves, so that the area from which water can be lost is less. Others have thick cuticles like Autumn Gentian, *Gentianella amarella*, and many of the orchids. A few protect their foliage from undue water loss with shaggy hairs as in the case of the Hairy Violet, *Viola hirta*. Some species, like the Man Orchid, *Aceras anthropophorum*, and Bee Orchid, *Ophrys apifera*, die down after flowering and so avoid the driest, hottest summer months. The majority of the chalk flowers are perennials with wiry stems and deep roots adapted to withstand considerable drought.

The depth to which the roots of some chalk plants penetrate is far more than one would expect from the size of their aerial parts. Salad Burnet, *Poterium sanguisorba*, penetrates two feet or more below ground level. Wild Thyme, *Thymus drucei*, and Perforate St. John's Wort, *Hypericum perforatum*, go down more than 15 inches. Other examples of common small grassland flowers with deep roots include Common Rock-rose, *Helianthemum chamaecistus*, Horseshoe Vetch, *Hippocrepis comosa*, and Common Birdsfoot Trefoil, *Lotus corniculatus*.

The efficiency of this method of avoiding the effects of the summer drought on chalk downs has been clearly demonstrated by Anderson

(1928). She showed that, in addition to a considerable loss by evaporation, some 42 per cent of the total rainfall percolates through the porous chalk to below the region tapped by plant roots. Some of this last moisture, however, rises again by capillary action to become available to plants. At ground level there is great seasonal variation in the water-content of the soil. In wet weather this may be as much as 98 per cent, but she found that in a drought it fell to 8·5 per cent, only a part of which could be taken in by roots.

This seasonal variation decreases as one goes deeper into the soil. At a depth of 6 inches the variation is only half that of the top 3 inches of soil. Below 9 inches the fluctuation decreases less rapidly, so that at 27 to 30 inches the variation is only 5 per cent less than that at 6 inches. Since aeration is less good deeper in the soil, Anderson concluded that the optimum level for the roots of herbs on the chalk was between 6 and 9 inches from the surface. This is in fact the level at which most of them are found. The plants that go deeper avoid all risk of damage during the severest of summer droughts. Locket (1946) has shown that this problem of surviving periods of water shortage must be even more serious than was formerly supposed. By experiment he showed that little or no water was lost to solid chalk at a pressure up to one atmosphere. It follows that much of the moisture present in soils of high chalk content is not available to plants.

A covering of continuous turf has the effect of conserving the water in the soil. It also reduces leaching, which occurs much more rapidly in cultivated fields where the natural grass has been broken up.

On the chalk soils of Box Hill the following plant communities may be recognised :

A. Chalk Grassland (S. escarpment, about the Zig-zag ; Juniper Bottom).
B. Chalk Scrub (Bushwood or Brushwood). (Juniper Bottom ; E. end of S. escarpment. Poorly developed about Zig-zag.)
C. Woodland.
   (a) Beechwood—Escarpment Type. (S.W. corner below the Fort.)
   (b) Yew-wood (S. end of river cliff ; E. of Juniper Bottom).
   (c) Boxwood (River cliff).

The places given in brackets indicate where good examples may be seen.

CHALK GRASSLAND is the community which leaps to the mind when downs are mentioned. It is characterised by short, dense, well-drained, springy turf which is ideal for walking or riding. Its popularity with ramblers is well known. The use of chalk grassland for race-courses (as for example Epsom, Lewes, Brighton, Goodwood, Salisbury and Newmarket) is explained by the same qualities. It is the plant community most favoured by the crowds at Box Hill, for here they find the right conditions for picnics and games. No doubt they exercise a considerable influence on its flora in the parts which are most popular.

The chalk grassland on the escarpment is mostly on Middle Chalk with a southern aspect. That about the Zig-zag, Juniper Hill, and a much-scrambled-over stretch on the shoulder along which the main track runs down to the Burford Bridge Hotel, is on Upper Chalk and faces towards the north, or to east or west on the sides of the valleys. The difference between the flowering plants of the escarpment and that of the other places is slight and may be disregarded here.

By the side of the road just above the second bend of the Zig-zag there are two small pits. One of these shows excellent sections through the turf and soil and the rock underneath. There is a depth of about a foot of pale brown soil, darker on top where the interlacing roots of the grasses ramify, and paler with more flints where it joins the white lumpy mass of chalk. These sections are excellent illustrations of the reason downland turf is well drained. Chalk is a very porous rock. A cubic foot can hold two gallons of water ; it can hold over a gallon without appearing to be wet. Hence the water which drains down through the shallow soil soon reaches a rock which can take it in without becoming waterlogged. These sections also demonstrate why chalk turf is springy. For six inches or so below ground level there is a mass of roots which hold the soil together and make it elastic. Most of them come from grasses which form a level sward in contrast with many of the grasses of other habitats which often grow in tussocks.

In this turf competition for space and moisture is keen. The whole of the ground tends to be permanently occupied and seedlings can only establish themselves with difficulty. They have to compete with the vegetative increase of mature plants—especially grasses—already there. Thus the majority of the flowers and grasses are perennials, so that they can continue from year to year without being dependent on the hazards of reproduction from seed. Grasses are the most

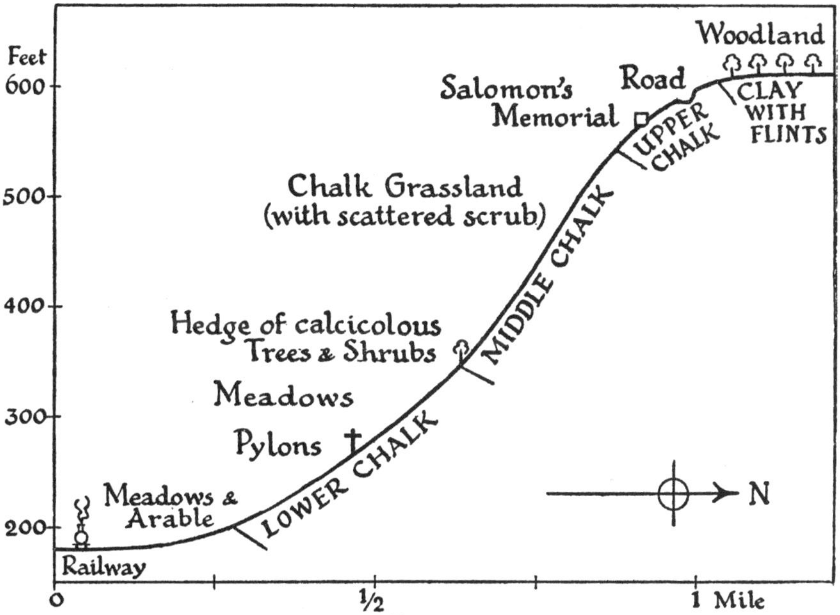

FIG. 3
Diagrammatic section through escarpment of North Downs, Box Hill

characteristic plants of this community, but these are being described in another book in the series.

It is perhaps not surprising that many of the most constant species of chalk grassland are plants common also in other communities. Tansley (1939) compared 62 typical areas spread over five counties and (grasses excluded) he found the following in over 80 per cent of them:

Fairy Flax, *Linum catharticum.*
Common Birdsfoot Trefoil, *Lotus corniculatus.*
Lesser Burnet-saxifrage, *Pimpinella saxifraga.*
Ribwort Plantain, *Plantago lanceolata.*
Wild Thyme, *Thymus drucei.*
Glaucous Sedge, *Carex flacca.*
Stemless Thistle, *Cirsium acaulon.*
Common Hawkbit, *Leontodon hispidus.*
Salad Burnet, *Poterium sanguisorba.*
Small Scabious, *Scabiosa columbaria.*

All these are common on Box Hill, but from experience over a wider area it seems that the first five are not specially associated with calcareous soils. In Tansley's lists of the species found in more than 40 per cent and less than 80 per cent of the areas he examined, about three-quarters of the flowering plants given are to be found frequently on other soils.

Thus the majority of the flowers which are *constant* in chalk grassland are not *confined*, or nearly confined, to this community. Those which are tend to be local and each locality has its own selection. It is this feature which makes the chalk grassland so interesting, for the flora often changes in the space of a few yards. Even within the limited area of Box Hill there is very little repetition.

The number of species showing a high degree of exclusiveness for this community is large. In other words there are many flowers seldom seen elsewhere. These are the plants with which this book is specially concerned, and some of the more attractive kinds to be found on Box Hill have already been described in Chapter 2.

CHALK SCRUB is intermediate between grassland and wood. It merges into both. In some parts of Box Hill there are scattered bushes with grassland in between. In others, scrub fringes the edges of the woods. It is best developed in the less frequented parts of the hill and even better along the escarpment to the east.

The characteristic shrubs of the chalk are Dogwood, Privet, the Wayfaring Tree and Spindle Tree. On Box Hill the latter is rather scarce (probably because people tear off the boughs in autumn on account of the decorative berries), but the first three are plentiful and sometimes form locally pure scrub over small areas. Hawthorn is also abundant. Juniper was probably formerly more common than it is now. Common Buckthorn, *Rhamnus catharticus*, and various Roses, with thorns and prickles respectively, sometimes make progress through the bushes difficult. Traveller's Joy often climbs over them, and its white flowers are conspicuous in late summer as are its silvery plumed fruits in autumn. Scattered among the shrubs there are usually a few young trees of Beech, Yew and Whitebeam, and occasionally Ash. White Birch, *Betula pendula*, is locally more common than it is on most chalk soils.

The flowers to be found amongst the scrub include many of those of the chalk grassland. Hairy Violet, Common Rock-rose, and the Milkworts, commonly grow where the bushes are not too close. Man

PLATE VII

J. E. Lousley

Late Spider Orchid, *Ophrys fuciflora*; South-east Kent

PLATE VIII

Robert Atkinson

Beechwood on Selborne Hanger

Orchid thrives in such places. Where the shrubs are closer or larger so that they cast considerable shade, some of the flowers of wood borders are to be found. Ploughman's Spikenard, Common Bugle, *Ajuga reptans*, and Wild Strawberry, *Fragaria vesca*, are examples. Fly Orchid is sometimes seen, and Deadly Nightshade in places where rabbits are active. Where there is even more shade, Dog's Mercury, *Mercurialis perennis*, is sometimes seen in the scrub.

The three main types of CHALK WOODLAND are named after their dominant trees. Box, Yew and Beech all form woods locally in which the leafy canopy is almost exclusively composed of a single species. All three cut off so much of the light that when they are mature few shrubs and herbs grow beneath them. They differ in that Box and Yew have a dense canopy throughout the year, whereas Beech is deciduous.

The famous Box woods of Box Hill have never been fully investigated by an ecologist. The tree is most numerous on the steep river cliff where it is dominant over considerable areas. Its roots seem to be well adapted to life on a slope so steep that those of most other trees would soon be exposed owing to erosion of the surrounding soil. It grows equally well on gentler gradients over much of the Hill. Inside the Box woods (Plate II, p. 19) light is dim even in summer, and the ground is devoid of herbaceous vegetation.

Yew is a taller tree, but its flat, plate-like boughs of dark evergreen leaves cast an almost equally dense shade. Very locally, on the southern end of the river cliff and on Juniper Hill, it forms almost pure wood. The ground is generally covered by fallen leaves and shrubs and herbs are unable to tolerate the shade. Even finer examples of Yew-wood are to be seen on Buckland Hill, in Norbury Park and below Ranmore Church.

The most interesting woods of the chalk in south-east England are those in which the Beech is dominant. Characteristically they form the well-known " hangers " familiar to all readers of Gilbert White (Plate VIII, p. 43). Tall fluted trunks carry the close canopy, and the ground is littered with deep layers of fallen and slowly decaying leaves. Lack of light almost restricts the plants underneath to those which have their main period of growth early in the year before the foliage of the Beech expands and to those which grow by tracks and on the edges of the wood. In addition there are a few species which are adapted to life in the shade.

This *escarpment type of Beechwood* (as the ecologists call it) should be compared with the *plateau type* to be seen on Clay-with-Flints on the top of Box Hill (see p. 37). The former occurs over a small area on the crest of the slope below the Fort and also near the head of Juniper Bottom. Much better examples are to be found on White Hill, bordering Headley Lane, on the north side of Box Hill.

Frequently the dominant herb is Dog's Mercury, *Mercurialis perennis.* Cuckoo-pint, *Arum maculatum* (Plate 23, p. 106), Yellow Archangel, *Galeobdolon luteum*, and Wood Spurge, *Euphorbia amygdaloides*, are other early flowering species. In June an orchid, the Large White Helleborine, *Cephalanthera damasonium*, is common in these beechwoods. The Narrow-leaved Helleborine, *C. longifolia*, which grows with it in Hampshire (Plate 22, p. 99), is very rarely to be found in Surrey. All these plants complete their vegetative growth before the Beech is in leaf and die down after flowering. Spurge Laurel, *Daphne laureola*, a shrub some 2 to 3 feet tall with evergreen leaves, blooms from January to March.

Birds-nest Orchid, *Neottia nidus-avis*, is a saprophyte, that is to say it lives on the accumulation of decaying leaves and humus. It produces no green leaves and sends a foot-tall spike of yellowish-brown flowers above ground in May. In a good year I have seen it in thousands in the Box Hill district—stretching away up a slope as far as the eye could follow. Yellow Birds-nest, *Monotropa hypopitys*, lives similarly. It may be distinguished from its orchid counterpart by the nodding top of the flowering stem (hence it is sometimes called "Dutchman's Pipe").

In August the flowers of another orchid are to be found round the edges of the beechwoods. Broad-leaved Helleborine, *Epipactis helleborine*, is common in such places. The flowering stems are usually solitary, whereas those of the Purple Helleborine, *E. purpurata*, usually grow in clusters. The latter I have found in the plateau beechwoods, but it may grow in those on the chalk also.

Plant populations are never static. Just as villages turn into towns and cities and spread over the adjacent countryside, so woods grow larger and take in areas which were formerly grassland. In both cases the process is usually slow and may pass almost unobserved during the short span of a human lifetime, but occasionally (as with the growth of London during the present century) it may be accelerated locally so that the change is obvious even in the absence of special measures taken to record it. Both in human and plant populations the tendency is progressive. But it is subject to regression which may be local (as in the case of towns destroyed or abandoned) or widespread (as with a decline in the population of a nation.) The human climax is presumably the covering of the whole country with bricks and mortar. Ecologists agree that in England the climax to the process of plant succession is deciduous summer forest made up of trees appropriate to various soils. On the chalk of south-east England the appropriate general climax forest is Beechwood.

Grassland and scrub are regarded as stages in a succession leading to woodland. The basic theoretical sequence is as follows:

Bare chalk ⟶ Pioneer plants ⟶ Chalk Grassland ⟶ Chalk Scrub ⟶ Woodland

Although this is the general tendency, the actual development as recorded in nature may be very much more complicated. For example, there are fields in the Chipstead Valley (6 miles N.E. of Box Hill) which were cultivated during the 1914-1918 war, and then allowed to go wild. They were immediately invaded by shrubs, and by 1939 their whole area was occupied by bushes which were in some places close enough together to form thickets, and in others fairly widely spaced Even in the open parts there was no continuous turf—the Chalk Grassland stage had been left out. If the shrubs had not been grubbed up when the fields were again cultivated in 1942, trees which had started to grow between the bushes might have formed woodland in years to come.

Details of the succession are extremely complex and often do not conform to the generalised sequence set out in the text-books. Nevertheless, short stages in the tendency can easily be observed on Box Hill. Thus the shrubs often invade grassland. This may be seen on the escarpment east of the Salomon's Memorial and on a small scale about the Zig-zag. There are two fields in a valley above Warren Farm which used to be heavily grazed by farm animals and were at that time covered with short, rather fine grass. Grazing ceased about 30 years ago and the turf became coarser and tussocky. Now there are scattered bushes invading the fields, which are rapidly changing in a way which would have been impossible while they were used for their old purpose.

Left unchecked by the action of man and animals, Beech-wood

would develop over much of the southern chalk. As evidence that woods of this tree now cover areas once cultivated, there is the presence of lynchets (terraces formed by ancient ploughing) within such woods on the South Downs. On Salisbury Plain, near Stonehenge, there is a beech-wood containing barrows which must have been constructed before the trees were there. On Box Hill ancient man has left no similar signs as clear demonstrations of the change that has taken place through the centuries. Nevertheless, in spite of the general correspondence of the scenery to that shown in old views, there is no doubt that over a lengthy period there have been changes.

The position of Yew- and Box-woods in the scheme is somewhat anomalous. Under their dense shade it is impossible for other trees to develop. Therefore they cannot be a direct stage in the succession leading to Beechwood. It is probable that each of them can be a climax over small areas—perhaps those where the slope is too steep even for the Beech.

That the whole of Box Hill is not covered with wood is due to powerful ecological factors which retard the development of the succession or even set it back to earlier stages. The most important of these is man. His influence is included in the biotic group of factors, of the scheme on page 34.

The most obvious way in which human interference retards plant succession on chalk hills is by cutting down shrubs and trees. In some districts, and especially in time of war, this can cause great changes in the vegetation. Historical records show that in past centuries a great deal of timber was removed from Box Hill, and many trees have been felled in the beechwoods on White Hill (just across Headley Lane) within the last twenty years. Another very obvious human influence is that of trampling. On the steeper tracks this may result in the exposure of bare chalk (see p. 37). On gentler slopes the turf remains, but its composition changes with the increase of such plants as Hoary Plaintain, which can withstand trampling. Wherever foot traffic is heavy there are few new bushes and the flora becomes restricted.

On most chalk downs grazing is a far more important factor than those already mentioned. Whether it arises from farm animals such as horses, cows or sheep, or from wild creatures like the rabbit, which was imported to this country, probably in the twelfth century, grazing

John Markham

a. In flower. Somerset; May

John Markham

b. In fruit. Bedfordshire; September

WAYFARING TREE, *Viburnum lantana*
A characteristic shrub of chalk and limestone

PLATE 10

Brian Perkins

DEADLY NIGHTSHADE, *Atropa belladonna*; very poisonous to humans but eaten with impunity by some animals. This picture shows

is almost entirely within the control of man. Farm animals are no longer pastured on Box Hill. In other areas a great increase in Tor-grass, *Brachypodium pinnatum*, has followed their withdrawal. This is now abundant and spreading about the Zig-zag and elsewhere, forming large yellow-coloured patches in the grassland which are conspicuous from a distance. Rabbits are fairly plentiful and doubtless have an appreciable effect on the vegetation near their burrows. By eating the seedlings and removing bark from shrubs and young trees, they prevent woody plants from establishing themselves. Fortunately there are some plants which rabbits are known to avoid; these include Common Rock-rose, Clustered Bellflower, and Common Hounds-tongue, *Cynoglossum officinale*. They are often plentiful near the warrens.

Another way in which man influences the vegetation is by the introduction of alien species. On Box Hill this has seldom occurred except in the case of a few trees. Larch and other conifers have been planted, and Sycamore, *Acer pseudo-platanus*, which was introduced to this country from Central Europe, has spread naturally to many parts of the Hill. Doubtless the fruits of native plants are carried about by visitors on their clothing, and mapping of Burdock, *Arctium spp.*, Houndstongue, and other species with hooked or adhesive fruits, would probably show that they are distributed along tracks in this manner. But the most astonishing example of what must have been the deliberate introduction of seeds of foreign plants is to be seen in a bomb crater in the chalk just off the main National Trust property.

I first heard rumours of a curious Foxglove being found in 1947 and in the following May accidentally discovered the bomb crater myself. Instead of one foreign Foxglove there were four (*Digitalis ambigua*, *D. lutea*, *D. lanata*, and *D. ferruginea*), and they had spread from the crater into the surrounding wood. In addition I found other strange plants such as Sweet Cicely, *Myrrhis odorata*, Elecampane, *Inula helenium*, Motherwort, *Leonurus cardiaca*, Woad, *Isatis tinctoria*, *Cochlearia glastifolia*, and *Lepidium graminifolium*. Altogether there were about 20 foreign species and an assortment which could be provided by very few botanical gardens. How they came to this wild spot has yet to be explained.

This chapter must end on a note of warning. It is impossible to make generalised ecological statements which are more than approximations. Most facts of plant ecology are strictly true only of the very limited areas from which the observations on which they are based have been drawn. This account of the ecology of Box Hill has been deliberately simplified in an effort to make the main facts as clear as possible, and this would not be compatible with a precise scientific statement. The conclusions drawn apply in varying degree to other limestone areas. They indicate the way in which ecological factors are likely to act elsewhere, but it must be remembered that differences, and even apparent contradictions, will be found.

CHAPTER 4

THE NORTH DOWNS

CHALK IS the most important of all the formations which give rise to calcareous soils in the British Isles. On the geological map its outline resembles a great lop-sided "£" sign sprawling right across England, with its northern tip near Flamborough Head. It is the limestone best known to Londoners, and although it comes second to the Carboniferous Limestone in area occupied, it is superior to that formation in the production of continuous stretches over which calcareous soils predominate.

The cross-bar of the "£" sign represents the North Downs, which extend for nearly a hundred miles from east to west. From the "White Cliffs of Dover" they form a ridge right across Kent and Surrey, broken only by narrow gaps such as those of the Medway and Mole. For half the distance the North Downs form a bold, south-facing escarpment on which chalk in one of its purest forms is often near the surface and calcicoles are abundant. This escarpment includes some of the finest scenery in the south of England, and its wild flowers, including many species rare or absent elsewhere, provide a mass of bloom from spring until autumn.

East Kent

It is appropriate that a survey of the limestone flora of Britain should begin at Dover. Travellers approaching our shore by the short sea-route have a magnificent view of some of our richest chalk-lands; and because early botanists sometimes travelled to and from the Continent by this route, it is not surprising that the flora was recorded at a very early date. William Turner (about 1508 to 1568), the "Father of English Botany," listed three plants which are still features of the chalky Dover cliffs. They are included in his book, *The Names of Herbes*, published in 1548, and usually regarded as the starting point of our knowledge of British plant localities. He probably noticed them during a walk taken to pass the time while waiting for a boat.

In May the yellow flowers of Sea Cabbage, *Brassica oleracea*, are abundant on cliffs on each side of Dover and even in the town itself. The leaves are large and fleshy (recalling those of garden cabbages), and as it is still regarded as rather a rarity it is not surprising that Turner states that he had seen it nowhere else.

Samphire, *Crithmum maritimum*, he regarded as plentiful on these cliffs. It is an Umbellifer with yellow flowers, and the fleshy leaves are used for a vinegar pickle. Shakespeare, writing about 58 years after Turner, immortalised it in *King Lear* (Act IV, Scene VI), in the famous lines:

Half-way down
Hangs one that gathers samphire, dreadful trade!

It is believed that he had in mind the great cliff to the west of Dover now known as Shakespeare's Cliff (Plate V, p. 34) but the plant abounds in less forbiding places.

Turner's third Dover plant, the Yellow Sea-Poppy, *Glaucium flavum*, he had also found "in many other places by the sea syde." Like Samphire, it is widespread round the British coast and also grows on shingle and rocks which are not limestone. But when it occurs away from the sea it is apparently always on chalk. During Hitler's war a deep defence ditch was cut along the hills behind Folkestone, and in 1948 it still formed a great white snaky gash, exposing the bare chalk for miles. On this Yellow Sea-Poppy and Sea Cabbage were abundant. In Sussex it strays several miles inland in chalk-pits in the Adur and Ouse valleys, and has been found 15 miles from the sea on imported chalk on the railway near Mayfield. In the Isle of Wight it occurs in a chalk-pit four miles from the coast.

That all three plants mentioned by Turner should persist on Dover cliffs is an interesting example of the permanence of vegetation when conditions remain unchanged.

PLATE IX

Seven Sisters near Seaford; a habitat for dwarf forms of chalk flowers

Judges Ltd.

Brian Perkins

a. Pasque Flower, *Pulsatilla vulgaris*; Cambridgeshire, April

Harry Meyer

b. Pasque Flower, *Pulsatilla vulgaris*; Bedfordshire, May

Chalk extends along the coast from Folkestone to Walmer and Deal, forming a broad belt running west (and slightly north) to the Medway valley and Rochester. In parts it is covered by superficial deposits ; but this country includes considerable areas with highly calcareous soils. This is especially the case on the hills behind Folkestone and Dover, east of Wye, and above the Medway valley. It is the home of some of our rarest wild orchids.

The most handsome of these is the Lady Orchid, *Orchis purpurea* (Plate 14a, p. 69). In some woods on chalk and chalky clay, and occasionally on the open downs, its flowers are to be seen in fairly large numbers. But when they grow near villages or roads they are liable to be picked before they are fully open. The lip (labellum) of the flower forms an outline recalling the sketches which Victorian children used to draw of crinolined ladies, and the deep brown hood may be likened to their bonnets. Yet this outline is variable, and in a sufficiently large colony individuals can sometimes be found with very narrow lobes, while others are exceptionally broad. The former have been confused with the Military Orchid, *O. militaris*, and even recorded as such, but the dark colour of the hood makes such confusion inexcusable.

The Lady Orchid is specially a Kentish plant. Outside the county it has been found only in Surrey and Sussex, and there extremely rarely. Yet in Kent I have seen it at many localities extending from near Dover almost to the outskirts of London. In one place to which Mr. Francis Rose directed me in 1946 it was growing in a station placed on record in the year of the Great Fire of London—another example of the permanence of some plants when they are not unduly raided.

The Late Spider Orchid, *Ophrys fuciflora* (Plate VII, p. 42), has probably never been found outside Kent, though there is an old record from Surrey and a very doubtful one from Gloucestershire. Within the county it occurs in small scattered colonies over a ten-mile stretch of chalkland. In 1946 I spent a day with some friends searching as many of the recorded places as we could, and we were fortunate in finding the orchid in five of them, not including another spot where I have known it for over twenty years. The total number of plants seen was small and although, like many of our orchids, the Late Spider is more plentiful in some years than in others, it must be regarded as one of our scarcest wild flowers. The pattern and colouring of the lip varies greatly and it has sometimes been confused with the Bee Orchid, *O. apifera* (Plate 6, p. 15), a relatively common flower. The easiest way of distinguishing the two plants is by the two upper petals, which are green in the Bee and pink in the Late Spider.

The Early Spider Orchid, *O. sphegodes* (Plate 31, p. 142), is locally plentiful on some coastal cliffs and also on downland in one inland district in Kent. It is also found in quite large colonies in Sussex and Dorset, and has been observed in other counties, though in most of them increased cultivation of the downs has led to its extinction (Distribution Map, p. 222). Flowering begins as early as March and continues until May, being normally over before the two last-mentioned species are out. The name is not inapt for there is a fanciful resemblance between the labellum and the body of a bloated brown spider.

For many years the Lizard Orchid, *Himantoglossum hircinum* (Plate 27, p. 122), was regarded as appearing more regularly in Kent than in any other part of England. Then for a time it seemed to be lost, and other counties acquired a reputation as the home of this strange species. Most orchids are erratic in their appearance, but the Lizard is the most capricious of them all with the exception of the Spur-lipped Coralroot, *Epipogium aphyllum* (see p. 89). The first news of the Lizard's appearance in a new locality often comes from school-teachers, clergymen or journalists rather than from botanists. It is found as solitary individuals or in colonies by roads or tracks, on railway banks, or chalk downs (or on sand-dunes), and then generally disappears quite suddenly after a very few years. Its record persistence in recent years seems to have been one for 26 consecutive summers at one place in east Kent; but the usual period is very much shorter.

Kent acquired a reputation for the Lizard Orchid very early in botanical history. It was first recorded from Britain in 1641 from near Dartford and persisted in the district for over two centuries. During the eighteenth and nineteenth centuries there were also sporadic records from four other counties; but most of the records were still from various parts of Kent. Since 1900, the Lizard Orchid has shown a remarkable increase elsewhere, both in range and frequency, but right up to the recent war it was on the chalk of the extreme south-east of England that it was found most often. Professor Good, in a valuable paper summarising the history of its distribution and features of its biology, has come to the conclusion that the most probable explanation of the distributional changes and increases in numbers is connected with changes in our climate.

It is not surprising that such an erratic and bizarre plant has held an irresistible fascination for at least one Man of Kent. My friend John Jacob of Dover made the quest for "Lizzies" his life work from the time he saw his first in 1885. For 25 consecutive years of those that followed he never missed a season without seeing the plant somewhere or other. The list of localities he wrote out for me before his death is a long one. There can be little doubt that he held the record for having seen the greatest number of "Lizzies" in England.

John Jacob's flair for tracking down odd plants of the Lizard Orchid led to an interesting journey which we shared in 1925. Earlier that year two elderly ladies had found what they took to be a wild Aspidistra; they dug it up and kept it in a pot at their home. Towards the end of June it came into flower, and they then realised that they had found something very much out of the ordinary and tried to get the plant named. Their inquiries came to Jacob's notice and he called on the ladies and collected the plant with the object of placing it on show in Dover Museum.

We took the plant on the train together and during the journey gained practical experience of a feature of the Lizard Orchid which was new even to Jacob. In the ordinary way in the open air in day-time the most unpleasant smell given off by the flowers is not noticeable. On this occasion it proved to be exceedingly objectionable, and the reminiscence of the he-goat implied by the scientific name *hircinum* was shown to be well founded. Our journey took us through lengthy tunnels in which the carriage windows were closed in accordance with custom, and on this warm summer day the smell was over-powering. If the ladies who dug up this rare orchid in ignorance had kept it in their house they would have met with a just reward!

Orchids are more numerous in Kent—and especially east Kent—than in any other part of England. In addition to the very rare species already mentioned, some of the more widely distributed kinds are more abundant than elsewhere. This is particularly the case with the Man Orchid, *Aceras anthropophorum* (Plate VI, p. 35). In Kent it reaches its maximum frequency and grows, not only on chalk downs, its usual haunt, but also in woods. Surrey and Sussex are its next best counties, in others it is very local and rare. Fly Orchid, *Ophrys insectifera* (Plate 7b, p. 30), Autumn Lady's-tresses, *Spiranthes spiralis* (Plate 7a, p. 30), and the Fragrant and Pyramidal Orchids, *Gymnadenia conopsea* and *Anacamptis pyramidalis* (Plate 5, p. 14), are amongst others which the reader is likely to find in Kent.

Broomrapes, like orchids, need protection. They also produce large numbers of very small seeds and are faced with heavy odds against their seeds finding the right conditions for germination and growth to maturity. Like orchids, they include species which are intensely rare, and two of these are to be found in Kent.

The Clove-scented Broomrape, *Orobanche caryophyllacea*, is a fine plant, over a foot in height, parasitic on the roots of Hedge Bedstraw, *Galium mollugo*. It was first discovered by G. E. Smith, and I was delighted to see it in 1948 on two of the chalky banks where he observed it before the end of the eighteenth century. Here it is very local and probably erratic in appearance, as both spots had been searched on several previous occasions without success. As Smith observed, the flowers "when newly expanded, distil a fragrant scent of cloves." Oxtongue Broomrape, *O. picridis*, is even rarer—a few individuals leading a precarious existence threatened by falls of cliff. Fortunately there are times (as in 1939) when they are quite inaccessible, and these give them a breathing space to recover from periods when it can be reached and picked.

Chalk and Common Milkworts, *Polygala calcarea* and *P. vulgaris* (see pp. 23, 24), are handsome species common on many of the Kentish downs, but the special rarity allied to them is inconspicuous and only to be found by the most careful search. Kentish Milkwort, *P. austriaca*, is the tiniest and daintiest of its genus, and found only within the county now that its Surrey station has been destroyed by building. It was first found near Wye in 1871, and I have recently seen it in several places in that district. In 1945 Mr. Francis Rose discovered it about twelve miles to the north-west, providing an interesting link between the district where it was first found in Britain and a spot on the downs a few miles from Sevenoaks, the only other place where it is now known (Distribution Map, p. 217).

The belt of chalkland has a less varied flora in the stretch west of Wye, and it is not until the Medway valley is in sight that the scenery and the flowers improve. The Medway between Rochester and Maidstone is flanked on both sides by magnificent chalk hills with steep escarpments rising above the river. Those on the west side will be considered later.

Rochester and Chatham are on chalk east of the Medway. On an elevated open space known as " The Lines " in the latter town the very prickly Purple Star-thistle, *Centaurea calcitrapa*, is abundant. Here it thrives in spite of the crowds who knock it about and, no doubt, measures taken by the authorities to reduce it. The outer parts of the flowers (phyllaries) terminate in stiff yellow spines which spread out in all directions and render them very difficult to handle. These resemble caltrops in arrangement (the spiked iron balls used in ancient warfare to hamper the advance of enemy cavalry and infantrymen) and to these the scientific name refers.

FIG. 4
The North Downs

A little to the south, and on the same side of the river, there is a most scenic range of hills starting from near Wouldham and running through Burham Downs to Boxley Hill and Detling. They provide some excellent country for the botanist. There are fine hangers of Beech, good woods of Yew, and very locally the rare Box. The last has given its name to the village of Boxley, whence the tree was brought to the notice of the botanical world by John Aubrey (1626–1697). This is one of the few places where it is usually accepted as a genuine native tree in Britain (see also pp. 18, 94 and 128).

Some of the woods are almost pure Yew, dark and cool on the hottest summer day, and with very little ground vegetation. In one of these there is a fine colony of Caper Spurge, *Euphorbia lathyrus*, growing far from the nearest house and regarded as part of the natural flora though sometimes grown to provide capers for true caper-sauce. It was first recorded from here in 1862 and the discoverer remarked that it was capricious in appearance. From observations in my own garden it is clear that the seeds have the power of remaining dormant in the soil for very long periods until the appropriate conditions stimulate germination. In woods, this stimulus is probably provided by the increase of light and warmth following felling of the trees. This may well explain why the plant, which has narrow, leathery leaves arranged in four rows cross-wise on the stem, is to be found in some seasons but not in others.

On the edges of the woods and in scrub Stinking Hellebore, *Helleborus foetidus*, attains an unusual luxuriance. In one spot there is a large patch of Meadow Clary (sometimes called Meadow Sage), *Salvia pratensis* (see also p. 58), which my friends have known here for several years, but never found in flower. When I visited it the shoots which would have produced blooms had all been bitten off by rabbits and this probably happens annually.

In this district, as in most parts of Kent and Surrey, the slopes of the hills are highly calcareous, while the tops are often covered with superficial deposits (cf. p. 11). On one bushy slope there is a colony of Field Fleawort, *Senecio integrifolius* (Plate 30, p. 127), which was first recorded over a century ago, but in recent years knowledge of the precise spot had been lost. The locality is the only one where the plant has been found in Kent, and local botanists spent many unsuccessful hours in attempting its rediscovery. Then in 1947, when away in Caernarvonshire collecting material for this book I received a small tin containing a fragment of Field Fleawort with a jubilant note from Mr. Francis Rose announcing that he had found it at last. The following year I was able to see it for myself.

Apart from the hill slopes, chalk is exposed in the old cement workings along the lower part of the valley. In one old working there is a sight to be seen which is probably unique in the whole of Britain —hundreds of plants of the hybrid between Canadian Fleabane, *Conyza canadensis*, and Field Fleabane, *E. acer*. The former is a North American weed, with small silvery flowers, which was first noticed in England in the seventeenth century. It is now abundant on the London bombed sites and elsewhere. The latter is a blue-flowered composite of well-drained soils especially plentiful on chalk. In spite of the fact that the hybrid between them has been known for a good many years, it has only been found a very few times. There is no difficulty in recognising it, as it is usually a slender plant like *canadensis* but with blue flowers and more spreading branches like *acer*. At Burham the hybrid has been found in quantity for several years growing with masses of the parents.

The Isle of Thanet

The Thanet chalk is separated by a gap of over six miles from the main mass of the chalk of Kent. The holiday towns of Margate, Broadstairs, and Ramsgate, have spread out over much of it. Cultivation and the construction of aerodromes has ruined the natural flora of the remainder. Nevertheless Thanet has at least three flowers of special interest.

In 1809 invalid troops from the ill-fated Walcheren Expedition were landed at Ramsgate and their bedding straw was distributed. It is supposed that it contained seeds of the Hoary Cress, *Cardaria draba*, which was found here by botanists some twenty years later. At that time the plant was very local but it spread rapidly, and some forty years after its discovery it had become a serious pest in many parts of Kent. Now it is to be found in many districts of England, Wales and even Ireland, and is still increasing its range.

Another plant specially associated with Thanet is Longleaf, *Falcaria vulgaris*, which is abundant in chalky districts across the Channel in France. The colony near Broadstairs, where I first knew it, had been ploughed up, but there is another 200 yards away, and in 1948 I saw a lot of it near the North Foreland. There are also records from Birchington, and from Wingham on the other side of the Stour valley. Longleaf is a perennial Umbellifer, with thick, deep roots which form extensive patches in the fields where it grows. With us it ripens relatively few fruits, and this led to some difficulty when it was first found in 1858. The finder sent a specimen to the famous Dr. Lindley, who replied curtly that he refused "to name an umbelliferous plant without perfect fruit-seed." In spite of this, there should not be the slightest trouble in recognising Longleaf by the curious narrow leaves with sharp teeth along their edges. The species is now firmly established in several scattered inland counties, where it may have been introduced with clover seed. Thanet is so near to the Continent that I cannot help feeling that there is a possibility that it may be native there.

The third flower is certainly an alien of recent introduction. Hoary Mustard, *Hirschfeldia incana*, has a rosette of hairy leaves from which arise wiry stems bearing small yellow flowers. I noticed it in a couple of places on chalky roadsides in Thanet, to which district it has probably spread from the railway sidings at Richborough. Having regard to its rapid increase in that neighbourhood in recent years, it may soon become plentiful on the chalk.

West Kent

Near Maidstone there are outcrops of calcareous sandstone in the Hythe Beds of the Lower Cretaceous. This " Kentish Rag " may contain as much as 90 per cent of calcium carbonate, and it is possible that its influence on the flora may be important locally. So far as my own observations go, the associated calcicoles, with the possible exception of Wild Liquorice, *Astragalus glycyphyllos*, are all species which affect limestones on account of their physical rather than their chemical qualities, but the subject requires further study. In any case, the Kentish Rag is of insignificant importance as a home of limestone plants in comparison with the North Downs. The reason for this is no doubt its association with sandy beds, and hence high porosity and marked leaching so that calcareous material is soon lost.

The chalk ridge is five miles wide where it is broken by the Medway valley. On the west side of the river the scenery and flowers are just as fascinating as those already described on the east.

In one place the rare little Hairy Mallow, *Althaea hirsuta*, has led a somewhat chequered existence for at least a century and a half. It grows in chalky cultivated fields and, like many other annuals, is much more plentiful in some seasons than in others. Sometimes the crops are unsuitable, and this is probably the general explanation of why it has from time to time been reported as extinct. But adverse weather conditions at the time the seedlings should appear may also play a part. With the Hairy Mallow grow Ground Pine, *Ajuga chamaepitys* (Plate 17b, p. 82), and Broad-leaved Cudweed, *Filago spathulata*. Not far away is our oldest locality for Meadow Clary, *Salvia pratensis*, a handsome sage with lovely blue flowers an inch in

PLATE XI

A. W. Graveson

Spiked Speedwell, *Veronica spicata*; Norfolk

PLATE XII

Judges Ltd.

Berry Head near Brixham (Devonian Limestone)

length. Specimens gathered in the seventeenth century from this spot are still in existence. In recent years it has been found in several new places in the county (I have seen it in four others myself), and elsewhere in England. In most of these new localities it has probably been introduced with grass-seed, but here above the Medway, and in Oxfordshire, it has been with us so long that its claims as a native plant cannot reasonably be disputed. Yet another rarity from the same district is Cut-leaved Germander, *Teucrium botrys*, which grows on broken chalky ground on an uncultivated down.

The Pilgrim's Way runs westward from near here along the foot of the south-facing escarpment of the chalk. For much of its length to the Darenth gap and beyond—indeed right across Surrey—it is now represented by convenient tracks or quiet roads giving easy access to the fine chalkland flora of these hills. Field Eryngo, *Eryngium campestre* (Plate 16, p. 73), is an interesting example of the uncommon plants which have been found near it. This flower was found in 1930, and the photograph from which the illustration was made was taken after I had known the patch for about fifteen years. During this time it had neither increased nor decreased, and this suggests that the Field Eryngo had been there for a long time. New arrivals usually increase or decrease rapidly until they attain equilibrium with the other vegetation with which they have to compete. Unfortunately this colony has now been destroyed.

The northern edge of the chalk country runs above the Thames between Gravesend and Dartford, and was the scene of many excursions made by early botanists. In the days before the construction of good roads it was easier (and no doubt cheaper) to travel by water. For this reason Gerard, Johnson and other London herbalists found it convenient to make the districts near the Thames their favourite hunting grounds. Hence many British flowers growing on chalk were found for the first time in north Kent.

Since Elizabethan times the demand for chalk for cement and other purposes has led to the quarrying of a vast network of pits between Gravesend and Dartford. The older ones are now overgrown with shrubs (Plate 15, p. 72) and their sides are gay with Red Valerian, *Centranthus ruber*, with flowers in several shades of red or sometimes white. Snapdragon, *Antirrhinum majus*, also grows in some of the pits and on railway cuttings in such abundance that it is difficult to realise that the two plants are not native. The floors of the old quarries are often damp owing to the water-level being just below the surface. This explains why in one of them Marsh Helleborine, *Epipactis palustris*, and a Marsh Orchid, *Dactylorhiza praetermissa*, grow side by side with the usual chalk plants which thrive on well-drained soils.

In this district the Italian Catchfly, *Silene italica*, grows on at least one series of chalky banks. It resembles the Nottingham Catchfly, *Silene nutans* (Plate XX, p. 111), from which it may most easily be known by the long peduncles which carry the clusters of flowers well away from the stem. The last is a widely distributed species which is plentiful on the chalk cliffs of east Kent and is mentioned several times in later chapters. The Italian Catchfly, on the other hand, seems to be restricted in Britain to north Kent. It is usually seen by botanists with the flowers closed—its dingy appearance being enhanced by the collection of road dust on the sticky hairs with which it is covered. The blossoms open at dusk, giving off a sweet scent attractive to night-flying insects. I once saw the Italian Catchfly in perfect condition when I took a friend to see it late one evening, and the extent of the transformation was a great surprise. The flowering dates given in most of the books are much too late—the plant is at its best in late May.

North Kent is the headquarters of White Mullein, *Verbascum lychnitis* var. *album*. From the Medway to the Surrey border it is frequent on chalky banks and roadsides, and on one of my visits to Charles Darwin's famous "Orchid Bank" I found it there. This spot has probably changed very little since the famous naturalist used it for much of the work published in his *Fertilisation of Orchids*, and it is still a delightful strip of chalk grassland flanked to the west by a wood of Beech and Yew. Hairy Violet, Squinancywort, Yellow-wort, Viper's Bugloss, *Echium vulgare*, and Marjoram make the place bright with colour throughout the summer. Of the orchids which grow there, the Musk, Pyramidal and Sweet-scented have been exceptionally fine. Fortunately the "Bank" is strictly private; and steps have been taken to preserve it as an additional memorial to Darwin's work.

Kent has the richest calcicole flora of any county in the British Isles. In other words, the number of different species to be found on its calcareous soils is greater than elsewhere. This statement remains true even after allowance is made for maritime species like Yellow Sea-Poppy, Sea Cabbage and Samphire, which are not to be found in inland counties. For an explanation it is necessary to study the distribution of British plants abroad as well as within our islands.

Professor Matthews, in his paper on "The Geographical Relationships of the British Flora," has divided our flowering plants into fifteen groups (which he calls *elements*) according to their world distribution. From these it is possible to deduce the probable directions from which they entered Britain. One of these groups contains species found chiefly in central and southern Europe, which become less common towards the north of their range. Most of them extend into north Africa and south-west Asia. This group Matthews calls the "Continental Southern Element," and it includes 127 of our British plants. Over a hundred of these have been found in Kent and the majority grow on limy soils. Of the flowers already referred to in this chapter he lists the following as belonging to the Continental Southern Element:

Man Orchid, *Aceras anthropophorum*
Ground Pine, *Ajuga chamaepitys*
Hairy Mallow, *Althaea hirsuta*
Pyramidal Orchid, *Anacamptis pyramidalis*
Yellow-wort, *Blackstonia perfoliata*
Box, *Buxus sempervirens*
Purple Star-thistle, *Centaurea calcitrapa*
Field Eryngo, *Eryngium campestre*
Yellow Sea-Poppy, *Glaucium flavum*
Lizard Orchid, *Himantoglossum hircinum*
Bee Orchid, *Ophrys apifera*
Late Spider Orchid, *O. fuciflora*
Early Spider Orchid, *O. sphegodes*
Lady Orchid, *Orchis purpurea*
Clove-scented Broomrape, *Orobanche caryophyllacea*
Oxtongue Broomrape, *O. picridis*
Meadow Clary, *Salvia pratensis*
Autumn Lady's-tresses, *Spiranthes spiralis*

The list also includes many of the commoner chalk plants. The concentration of this group in Kent is remarkable and significant.

It is deduced that they entered Britain from the south—as indeed also did members of some of Matthews' other groups. In Kent they found dry and calcareous soils for which they show a preference. Some species such as the Bee Orchid and Autumn Lady's-tresses have spread widely while others like the Late Spider Orchid and Clove-scented

Broomrape have failed to extend their range. From this and other causes the county has a high proportion of rare or uncommon plants of calcareous soils in addition to the common ones.

SURREY

Where the chalk enters Surrey from the east it is about six miles in width from north to south. As it crosses the county it gradually narrows until, near the western boundary, it becomes restricted to the steep-sided narrow ridge of the Hog's Back. Except for part of this last ten miles, the northern (dip) slope is very gradual, with much of the surface covered with Clay-with-Flints and other superficial deposits. Here the chalk flora is seen chiefly in steep-sided, dry valleys which have been cut in the dip-slope by former streams. The south-facing escarpment, on the contrary, is steep, with chalk near the surface nearly all the way. Eroded into embayments, it provides magnificent scenery and such excellent hunting grounds for flowers as South Hawke near Woldingham, Reigate, Colley, Buckland, Betchworth and Box Hills, White Downs and Hackhurst Downs, and Pewley Hill, near Guildford.

The North Downs of Surrey must not be regarded as a mere continuation of those of Kent. There is, of course, a close resemblance in the general features of the flora, but the detail differs. Some of the Kentish wild flowers have hardly been found in Surrey—examples are Lady Orchid, Early Spider Orchid and Meadow Clary. A few, like Clove-scented Broomrape, have never been found in the neighbouring county. Others, such as Man Orchid, are much more local there. By way of compensation, Round-headed Rampion, *Phyteuma tenerum*, which is extremely rare in Kent, is plentiful on some of the Surrey Downs (Distribution Map, p. 223). Early Gentian, *Gentianella anglica*, which was unknown in Kent until three plants were discovered in 1946, is to be seen in several places in Surrey.

One species which botanists associate especially with Surrey is the Cut-leaved Germander, *Teucrium botrys*. It was found for the first time in Britain in 1844 by T. Ingall and W. Bennett " in a wild, stony locality " in the Box Hill district. Fortunately, the spot still remains little changed in spite of the passage of a century. Shortly afterwards it was found in another place in the chalk-hills south of Croydon, and

PLATE II

John Markham

BEECH, *Fagus sylvatica;* the flowers and beautiful young fringed leaves of this characteristic tree of the south-eastern chalk. Hertfordshire; May

Robert Atkinson

Early Purple Orchid, *Orchis mascula;* a common orchid of woods. Oxfordshire; May

later still near Chipstead. I have seen the Cut-leaved Germander at all three localities in recent years, but two other Surrey stations have been lost. As already mentioned, the plant also grows in Kent, and it seems to be permanent now in Hampshire and Gloucestershire and is on record for Wiltshire (Distribution Map 12, p. 221).

Ground Pine, *Ajuga chamaepitys* (Plate 17b, p. 82), is much more widespread than Cut-leaved Germander, with which it is associated at least in one place. In appearance it resembles a little conifer, and indeed the leaves smell like one, but the bright yellow blooms immediately reveal that it is a flowering plant. It demands an extremely chalky soil, but apart from this its requirements are not very exacting, for it grows equally well in cultivated fields, gardens, and even clearings in woods.

Epsom and Walton Downs merge into one another to form a fine stretch of chalk grassland familiar to all visitors to the famous races. Rising to 500 feet, their gentle slopes provide conditions for plant life rather different from those of the steeper hill slopes. Left to nature, the grasses here would be taller and coarser, but generations of trampling and horse-racing have left their influence.

Cypress Spurge, *Euphorbia cyparissias* (Plate 17a, p. 82), is probably one relic of the use to which the downs have been put. This is a handsome plant throughout the summer. When the flower heads appear in April and May they are bright golden yellow, which is shown up to perfection by the contrast of the dull-green, slender leaves. Later they turn a flaming red. This Spurge grows round the edges of scrub and it is tempting to suppose that it is as native here as it is in similar places in France. I have seen it also on chalk at Dover and in a second place not far from there, which supports this theory. As contrary evidence there are the facts that Cypress Spurge has increased greatly during the twenty years I have known it at Epsom, and that most of its wildest-looking British localities are places associated with horses—and especially with horse-racing. On balance, I think it is probable that its seeds have been brought in with fodder from abroad. On Epsom Downs its behaviour may be compared with that of the Twiggy Spurge, *Euphorbia uralensis*. This undisputed foreigner from central Europe occurs in half a dozen large patches ranged round the course just where one would expect alien seeds from fodder to fall. It is interesting to notice that in each patch the leaf-shape is uniform but differs in outline and width from those of plants in the other patches.

Before the Derby was run at Epsom the race took place on downs a few miles away. Here the Early Gentian, *Gentianella anglica* (Plate 19, p. 90), is abundant in most seasons. It flowers in May and June—and this alone is sufficient to distinguish it from other British Gentians which bloom later. The purplish-blue blossoms are conspicuous enough on a bright sunny day, but it is most difficult to find them in cold cloudy weather when they remain closed. On the same downs Curtis's Mouse-ear Chickweed, *Cerastium pumilum*, and Fine-leaved Sandwort, *Minuartia hybrida*, are also to be found. Both are extremely rare in south-east England.

The flora of Box Hill has already been described. Parts of it are typical of the chalk escarpment along nearly all of which most of the flowers described are to be found. Special mention must, however, be made of two woodland plants which grow off the escarpment on the chalk to the north of Box Hill.

One of these, Green-leaved Houndstongue, *Cynoglossum germanicum*, is still to be found in a place first recorded in 1666. In addition I have seen it in three other spots in the district in small colonies which are probably temporary, like several others found by various observers. These are more in keeping with its behaviour in other counties, for it is now a very scarce plant no longer to be found in the majority of the places from which it has been recorded. No reason is known for this apparent decrease in the Green-leaved Houndstongue during the last two centuries. The flowers are at their best towards the end of May, and it usually grows on slopes under beech trees.

Martagon Lily, *Lilium martagon*, is a handsome purple-flowered plant well-known in old-fashioned gardens. In Surrey it grows in three chalky copses, in two of which it was discovered just before 1830.

Between Box Hill and Guildford the escarpment of the chalk remains almost equally steep. There is still the same sharp contrast between the flora of the limy slopes and that of the Clay-with-Flints and other superficial deposits on the flattish top—for example, at Ranmore Common and Netley Heath. Grazing, which is now uncommon on the Surrey chalk grassland, takes place on the Denbies estate below Ranmore, and its effect can be seen in the finer and shorter grasses. Here a row of Yews have a lop-sided outline—an excellent example of the result of exposure to the prevailing wind.

White, Hackhurst and Albury Downs follow in succession along the hills, which terminate in steep Pewley Hill above the town of Guildford. All are good places for chalk flowers.

Some four miles to the south of the chalk escarpment at Guildford there is an interesting flora of calcicoles to be seen about Godalming. The coarse sands and fine pebble beds of the Bargate Beds of the Greensand are more or less calcareous, and are sometimes cemented into Bargate Stone, which is used locally for building. On these Beds Shining Cranesbill, *Geranium lucidum*, is locally plentiful, Wild Liquorice, *Astragalus glycyphyllos*, persists on at least one dusty roadside, Narrow-leaved Bitter-cress, *Cardamine impatiens*, occurs sporadically in the woods, and a very rare sedge, *Carex depauperata*, is still to be found. In comparison with the chalk the calcicole flora is of trifling importance and may be compared with that of the Kentish Rag near Maidstone.

The chalk at Guildford is broken by the narrow valley of the Wey. On the west side it continues as a narrow ridge, the Hog's Back, sloping steeply to the north as well as to the south. The old quarries along its sides have an interesting flora. But most readers will know the Hog's Back best from the main road which runs along the top. Here dark-leaved Yews contrast with the snowy-white under-surface of the leaves of Whitebeam. For the rest, the hedges are mainly composed of Wayfaring Tree and Privet festooned with Traveller's Joy. One little patch of downland is a favourite picnic ground for motorists. A few years ago this was still gay with various wild orchids, Hairy Violet, Squinancywort, Kidney Vetch, Round-headed Rampion and Autumn Gentian. Now trampling and flower-gathering have ruined the place. A strip of grassland a little farther on was formerly the only Surrey locality for Field Fleawort. Road widening and traffic destroyed it.

Hampshire

Two miles before reaching Farnham the chalk plants come to an end, and it is not until well beyond that town that calcareous soils again occur. Then the chalk broadens out into a wide mass in Hampshire. This country, at the junction of the North and South Downs, was immortalised by Gilbert White in his *Natural History of Selborne*. As Gunther has remarked, " it is perhaps better known to, though less visited by the English reader, than any other inland area in England."

Rising above the village of Selborne is a steep hill of chalk with its " long hanging wood, called The Hanger." White continues (Letter I) : " The covert of this eminence is altogether beech, the most lovely of all forest trees, whether we consider its smooth rind or bark, its glossy foliage, or graceful pendulous boughs." The Beech there now is just as lovely as it was in 1767 (Plate VIII, p. 43). Unfortunately very little space in the famous *Letters* is devoted to flowers —White was primarily an ornithologist.

But of the chalk plants he found room to mention Stinking Hellebore, Yellow Bird's-nest, Autumn Gentian, Bird's-nest Orchid, Broad-leaved Helleborine, Spurge Laurel and Mezereon. Most of these still grow at Selborne with others listed by Gilbert White. It would be interesting if someone living near could compile a good localised list of the plants now growing in the parish to compare with Gilbert White's incomplete records. Canon Vaughan's account of 1877 needs bringing up to date.

PLATE XIII

W. H. Spreadbury

Ivy Broomrape, *Orobanche hederae*; Torquay. (Devonian Limestone)

R. H. Hall

Wall Pennywort, *Umbilicus rupestris*; North Wales

CHAPTER 5

THE SOUTH DOWNS AND THE ISLE OF WIGHT

THE SOUTH DOWNS form the bottom of the " £ " sign which represents chalk on the geological maps of England. They extend some sixty miles west from the sea at Beachy Head until, a little across the Hampshire border, they lose their identity in the great mass of central chalk into which they merge. There is scarcely a mile of this long stretch without fascinating plant communities, and some of the wildest and finest scenery in the south of England is included. Those who know the Sussex Downs will appreciate Gilbert White's words[1] : ". . . I still investigate that chain of majestic mountains with fresh admiration year by year ; and I think I see new beauties every time I traverse it." Those beauties are made up as much of the wild flowers, shrubs and trees as of the rounded curves of the hills.

SUSSEX

The South Downs, like the North Downs, start by rising straight up out of the sea. Beachy Head, over 500 feet in height, is still sufficiently under the influence of salt winds to offer a strange mixture of downland and maritime plants. Some of the seaside flowers, like Samphire, *Crithmum maritimum*, grow on the almost vertical cliffs, but only occasionally reach the top. Others like Sea Beet, *Beta maritima*, reach the top but do not extend beyond the edge of the cliff. Yet others such as Slender-headed Thistle, *Carduus tenuiflorus*, grow abundantly both on the edge and some distance inland.

[1] *The Natural History of Selborne*, Letter XVII dated 9 Dec., 1773.

Along the seaward edge of the downs is a narrow strip of ground where the grasses are browned and seared and there is much bare soil. The cause of this is probably in part the result of exposure to salt winds, but it is perhaps equally due to the drying effect of loss of moisture from the cliff-face.

A few yards inland from the cliff is a belt of short downland turf which is a favourite promenade of visitors to Eastbourne. Characteristic chalk flowers abound. In places exposed to the full force of the sea-winds they are dwarfed to a size which renders them hardly recognisable as being the same as those of more sheltered spots. Thus in August, 1946, I listed the following species as occurring *less than two inches in total height.* The measurements given in brackets are the usual height of the plants elsewhere.

Dwarf Spurge, *Euphorbia exigua* (6 in.)
Lesser Burnet-saxifrage, *Pimpinella saxifraga* (12 to 18 in.)
Slender-headed Thistle, *Carduus tenuiflorus* (18 in. to 3 ft.)
Black Knapweed, *Centaurea nemoralis* (18 in. to 2 ft.)
Small Scabious, *Scabiosa columbaria* (12 to 18 in.)
Wood Betony, *Betonica officinalis* (18 in.)
Dwarf Centaury, *Centaurium capitatum* (1½ in.—as here)
Round-headed Rampion, *Phyteuma tenerum* (12 to 18 in.)
Autumn Gentian, *Gentianella amarella* (6 to 9 in.)

The reduction to a common low level of height of such a varied collection of flowers is remarkably interesting. The Beachy Head breezes, which Richard Jefferies appreciated so highly, reduce the stature of the plants and the size of their leaves, but the flowers remain almost as large as usual. Sometimes these characters may perhaps be inherited. The result is a fascinating set of miniatures which only those who are prepared to look closely can find and appreciate.

Although Beachy Head and the coastal downs along the top of the Seven Sisters and Seaford Head—a stretch of some eight miles—have an exciting chalk-flora, they are not uniformly typical limestone areas. On top of the great mass of the chalk are patches of reddish sands (Lenham Beds) which bear a contrasting vegetation. These patches are often marked by thickets of Gorse, *Ulex europaeus,* and Brambles, *Rubus spp.,* and contain species which are no part of the subject of this book. They afford cover for rabbits which severely graze the surrounding downland and by their nibbling often distort

Robert Atkinson

HENBANE, *Hyoscyamus niger*; an uncommon plant on chalk downs and usually associated with rabbit burrows. Kent; July

Robert Atkinson

a. LADY ORCHID, *Orchis purpurea;* a very local plant almost restricted to Kent. Kent; May

Robert Atkinson

b. MONKEY ORCHID, *Orchis simia;* one of our rarest orchids, only found in recent years in Kent and Oxfordshire on the chalk. From Oxfordshire; June.

such plants as Eyebright and Autumn Gentian into little bushy structures very unlike their normal growth.

In this district the very rare little Small Hare's-ear, *Bupleurum baldense*, has occasionally been found. On the mainland it only grows elsewhere on the limestone of south Devonshire; in both localities it is rare and difficult to find. I have seen it twice in Sussex, and on both occasions it was growing in rather bare places with exceptionally small plants of the Dwarf Spurge and Field Madder, *Sherardia arvensis*. Both of these have been mistaken for Small Hare's-ear at times. Another rare plant of these seaside downs is Dwarf Centaury, which is here fairly plentiful in the short turf.

Between Seaford and Eastbourne there are a number of colonies of Mountain Stone-parsley, *Seseli libanotis*, which is to be found elsewhere in Britain only in a limited area on the chalk of Cambridgeshire, Hertfordshire and Bedfordshire (Distribution Map 7, p. 219). The leaves are very like those of the Wild Carrot, *Daucus carota*, of which it might be taken for a stout and stocky example. But the bracts under the heads of flowers are undivided, whereas those of the Carrot are divided into narrow segments. The absence of spines on the fruits is another easy point of distinction. The flowers are in compact heads (umbels) and absolutely white, which is noteworthy as a great many flowers so described in the books are actually tinged with other colours. On the last occasion I went to look for Mountain Stone-parsley this was demonstrated in a very striking way. We had been out botanizing all day and daylight had failed long before we passed the place where the plant grew. Then one member of the party happened to mention that he had never seen it, and in a fit of rather light-hearted adventure we stopped the car, scrambled up a bank and stumbled across the down. It was pitch dark and none of us really expected to find the flower. Actually our task proved to be a very easy one for the whiteness of the flowers of the Mountain Stone-parsley showed up in the darkness, and at once distinguished it from the other members of the Carrot Family (*Umbelliferae*) with which it grew. It is likely that they serve as a beacon to night-flying insects. Another interesting feature is the way in which the stalks of leaves which have decayed away form a protective fringe round the base of the stem.

Early Spider Orchid, *Ophrys sphegodes* (Plate 31, p. 142) and Field Fleawort, *Senecio integrifolius* (Plate 30, p. 127), occur locally on these downs and farther west. It has been claimed that the last species actually attains its greatest frequency in Sussex, but it ranges in small scattered colonies very widely over the English chalk. In most of the places where it grows the plant varies greatly in quantity from year to year, for reasons which are not yet understood. The Round-headed Rampion is another plant which is more plentiful on the Sussex downs than elsewhere. There is plenty of it in Surrey and a good deal in parts of Wiltshire, Dorset and Hampshire, but it is strangely absent from the Isle of Wight.

There are many places on the chalk of this part of Sussex where

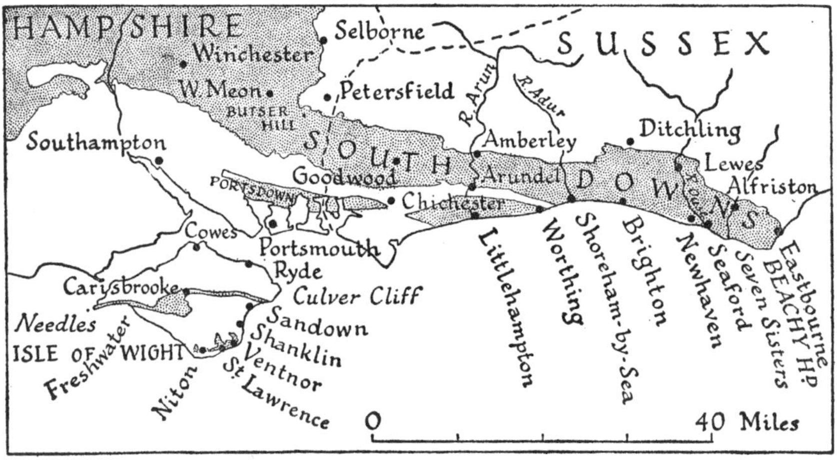

FIG. 5
The South Downs

the Purple Star-thistle, *Centaurea calcitrapa*, is to be found. It usually grows by tracks along the flanks of the downs, though in one place I have seen it plentifully on the cliffs.

Across the Cuckmere valley there is another fine stretch of coastal chalk culminating in Seaford Head, and after a gap of about three miles the chalk starts again at Newhaven and forms a cliff right along to Brighton. Along the last stretch there are again extensive patches of superficial deposits. In a few places the Hoary Stock, *Matthiola incana*, grows on the face of the chalk cliffs, where it is usually quite safe from the attentions of unscrupulous collectors. It is one of our most handsome flowers, and nearly all the places where it grows in England are on chalk sea-cliffs. The Sea Cabbage, *Brassica oleracea*, is very rare on this coast in contrast to its abundance near Dover. At Cuckmere Haven it grows on shingle, where it has increased greatly during the recent war—it is hoped that it will spread back on to the chalk cliffs where it has been very rare in recent years.

Inland there is a fine chalk flora about Lewes with some unusual features. Lewes Race-course, Mount Caburn and Mount Harry are among the best places. On the lower slopes of Mount Caburn the Scarce Sweetbriar, *Rosa agrestis*, is more abundant than in any other place in Britain. For about a mile it is about the most common rose, and it is difficult to suggest any reason why it should thrive here and yet be so scarce elsewhere. Not far away is a chalk-pit where Hoary Mustard, *Hirschfeldia incana* (see p. 58), an alien from the Mediterranean, is thoroughly naturalised. It is believed that its seeds came in with oil-cake at least forty-five years ago. In the district I have seen a single plant of the Mezereon, *Daphne mezereum*, in a copse on a steep chalky slope, and I once just missed seeing the Lizard Orchid, *Himantoglossum hircinum*, which disappeared the year before my visit. There is no harm in recording them now for, unfortunately, both have gone, though they may one day be refound.

Westward from Lewes the chalk forms a fine escarpment facing north, as travellers by rail to Brighton and Eastbourne will remember. Ditchling Beacon, Wolstonbury Hill, Newtimber Hill and the Devil's Dyke are all places on these hills well known for their wild flowers. There are plenty of orchids, and these include Man Orchid, *Aceras anthropophorum*, though this is much less plentiful than on the Surrey and Kent North Downs. It becomes ever rarer as one goes west. In a few places the Meadow Clary, *Salvia pratensis*, has been found.

The South Downs are interrupted by the broad flat-floored valleys of successive streams such as the Adur and the Arun, which cut through them on their way to the English Channel. Thus beyond the Adur another series of chalk downs extends for over ten miles behind Worthing and Littlehampton. The best-known hill is Chanctonbury, surmounted by a fine earthwork. The beeches here forming Chanctonbury Rings are said to have been planted in 1760 by Mr. Charles Goring, a local landowner. But from the botanist's point of view, by far the best stretch is that from Rackham Hill to the end of the range at Amberley Mount. It is along here that the Fly Honeysuckle, *Lonicera xylosteum*, grows in its best British locality. At Amberley it has been known for almost a century and a half, growing plentifully in copses and hedges on the slope of the wild downs. Unlike the well-known climbing Common Honeysuckle, *L. periclymenum*, it is a shrub, and the corolla tube is relatively short, so that the honey can be reached by insects which have not got a long proboscis. Another interesting plant which seems to be permanent in the same district is the Yellow Vetchling, *Lathyrus aphaca*. Its leaves are reduced to slender tendrils, while their ordinary functions are taken over by the large heart-shaped stipules which grow in pairs.

The Arun valley not only forms a gap in the chalk hills but it also separates the relatively treeless eastern part of the South Downs from the well-wooded areas to the west. To the east, superficial deposits are also less extensive. For a natural boundary the division is exceptionally sharp. Along the whole stretch of the hills we have been considering from Beachy Head to Amberley there are no extensive woods and the downs have few copses. West of the Arun there are the great wooded areas of Arundel and Goodwood Parks, Charlton Forest and Westdean Woods, and many others. There are extensive Beechwoods, the finest Yew-woods in Britain, and considerable areas of Ash. The general pattern of the vegetation is different, and while there are good open downland stretches (particularly on the northern escarpment), wooded country is the general rule. The difference is probably in part due to the increased rainfall, but I think even more to preservation of the trees from destruction in large estates.

In the Arun valley the White Mullein, *Verbascum lychnitis* var. *album*, is to be found. Its other main areas are north Kent and Surrey and as far away as North Wales. By contrast, Madder, *Rubia peregrina*, which one associates with the wetter, western limestone parts of Britain, is found in several places on chalk near the Arun. This is one of the few districts where it grows away from the sea. Germander Whitlow-grass, *Draba muralis*, which is usually a limestone plant but very rare indeed in chalk districts, also grows near here.

Most of the specially interesting flowers of the hills between Arundel and Amberley are woodland species. Stinking Hellebore, *Helleborus foetidus*, is found in several places, though in Arundel Park it is said to have been planted. It has been there for at least seventy years and the evidence for the planting seems to be extremely vague. Gladdon, *Iris foetidissima*, is common. Rare Cuckoo-pint, *Arum neglectum* (Plate

PLATE 15

Brian Perkins

A Disused Chalk Pit at Greenhithe, Kent, showing recolonisation by shrubs and trees after working has been abandoned. June

Brian Perkins

FIELD ERYNGO, *Eryngium campestre;* a rare spiny Umbellifer found in a few places on chalk and limestone. Kent; August

24, p. 107), is found at several places on the chalk here and is larger and much handsomer in leaves, flowers and fruit than the common species, *A. maculatum*. In a number of woods north of Arundel, Caper Spurge, *Euphorbia lathyrus*, is most probably truly native.

West of Arundel the chalk is less well known to botanists. Goodwood is the third Sussex race-course on chalk (the other two are Brighton and Lewes), but the spectators who sit on the Trundle are more interested in the races than in the wild flowers around them. Four miles to the west is Kingley Vale, with the finest woods of Yew in England—and indeed perhaps in the whole of Europe. In March and April the slopes below these woods are blue with masses of Hairy Violet, which here occurs as several varieties. The locality has been carefully studied by ecologists, as have also an interesting group of woods and downs on the Sussex-Hampshire border. Here, grouped on each side of the railway's main line from London to Portsmouth, are Ditcham Woods, Butser Hill, War Down, and Chalton Down, which have been described in detail in ecological papers. The main road to Portsmouth actually runs in a deep cutting between the steep slopes of War Down and Butser Hill.

Hampshire and the Isle of Wight

Beyond the county boundary the chalk soon broadens out into the great central mass which stretches right through Hampshire to Salisbury Plain. This will be considered in the next chapter.

South of the South Downs there is a smaller chalk area which extends over the Hampshire border to form the steep slopes of Portsdown behind Portsmouth. From here Nottingham Catchfly, *Silene nutans*, is recorded. But a much more important habitat for calcicoles is the narrow ridge of chalk which stretches for some twenty miles right across the Isle of Wight. In the east it rises straight out of the sea at Culver Cliff, near Sandown. In the west it forms the high downs at Freshwater cliffs, which run out into the Needles. In addition to being well known to holiday-makers, these localities are exceedingly interesting to the botanist. The intervening inland parts of the ridge deserve to be better known than they are.

At Culver Cliff there is an excellent opportunity of contrasting the flora of the chalk with that of the sand and clay. The walk from

Sandown is at first along the top of reddish cliffs with long, coarse grasses. Then there is an abrupt change to the short, dense, characteristic downland turf at the point where the white cliffs begin. All the common chalk plants such as Yellow-wort, Squinancywort, Salad Burnet, Common Rock-rose, Horse-shoe Vetch, Small Scabious and Marjoram are there. Wayfaring Tree, Privet and Traveller's Joy in the hedges also mark the change in soils.

A few maritime species such as Portland Spurge, *Euphorbia portlandica*, and Yellow Sea-Poppy, *Glaucium flavum*, reach to the top of the cliff at Culver. One unusual feature is the presence of the usually sand-loving Field Bugloss, *Lycopsis arvensis*, on the chalk. It also grows on the bare white rock near the Needles. When I was last on Culver Cliff in July, 1947, I noticed an interesting example of the way war-time activities can sometimes protect a plant. Within a stout iron fence erected round some guns there was a wonderful display of Pyramidal Orchid, *Anacamptis pyramidalis*, in very large numbers. Outside, on the downland to which the public had free access, only a few scattered plants could be found.

At Freshwater Downs at the far western end of the ridge there is a very similar abrupt change to the chalk. This is again due to the almost vertical inclination of the strata. Thus, on the south side of Alum Bay, it is easy to mark almost to a yard the point at which the yellow sandy cliffs change to the white chalk, with a consequent contrast in floras.

From my own experience I should have said that the best part of Freshwater Downs was near the Tennyson Monument on High Down. Local botanists, however, contend that more species are to be found on Afton and Compton Downs, east of Freshwater Gate, than on the west side. The flowers show a strong general resemblance to those of Beachy Head described earlier in this chapter. Maritime species ascend to the top of the precipitous cliffs, where the common chalk flowers are windswept and dwarfed.

Perhaps Hairy Rock Cress, *Arabis hirsuta*, is the most remarkable of all the plants which are here dwarfed by the wind and dry conditions. It is usually over twelve inches in height, but on Freshwater Downs I found it less than two inches tall. In this condensed state many people would have found great difficulty in naming it. Other plants dwarfed to one to two inches included Wood Betony, Small Scabious, Wild Carrot, Black Knapweed and Yellow-wort. The list should

PLATE XV

Robert Atkinson

Avon Gorge from Clifton Suspension Bridge (Carboniferous Limestone). Clifton and Durdham Downs on right, Leigh Woods on the left

PLATE XVI

Judges Ltd.

Great Orme's Head (Carboniferous Limestone). The toll road round the Head can be seen on the right

be compared with the one from Beachy Head on page 68. The dwarf forms of Freshwater Downs have attracted the attention of many botanists, but none of them have gone to such lengths as T. Wulff, an enthusiastic young Swede who visited this country in 1894. On his return to Sweden he wrote a scientific paper on the subject which was published in a Swedish journal. He also issued a pamphlet which he distributed to his friends. Wulff's excitement was such that to a number of these forms he gave special names, and the dwarf Carline Thistle he referred to as a " most distinguished variety." It is hardly necessary to mention that British botanists have ignored his names, as it is not considered desirable to describe forms of plants which seem to be only the result of local climatic conditions. This does not apply to Dwarf Centaury, *Centaurium capitatum*, a species described as new to science from here, with differences in the flower as well as stature.

One interesting plant which is abundant here, and indeed throughout most of the Isle of Wight chalk, is the Bastard Toadflax, *Thesium humifusum*. It is easily detected by the pale yellow colour of its foliage. The maritime plants which grow on the top of the Freshwater cliffs include Thrift, *Armeria maritima*, and the rare Hoary Stock, *Matthiola incana*. The latter is mentioned because the places where it grows are nearly all completely inaccessible, and although the plant is easily seen from the top of the cliff there is no danger of it being collected to excess. With the Hoary Stock grows Sweet Alyssum, *Lobularia maritima*, a garden plant which is thoroughly naturalised.

The two extremes of the east-to-west ridge are familiar to all visitors to the Isle of Wight. With the exception of the immediate vicinity of Carisbrooke Castle, the intervening chalk downs are less well known although they include a lot of very interesting country. As usual, the flowers which are most representative of the chalk are to be found best on the slopes of the hills; the tops are often covered with patches of other deposits.

Along wood borders and in clearings in one of the valleys running up into these hills Greater Calamint, *Calamintha sylvatica*, is found in its only British locality. Years ago it grew also on limestone at Torquay, but there it has not been confirmed since its discovery in 1864; the locality may have been built over. It has also been recorded from two shrubberies on the mainland of Hampshire, but in these places it may have been deliberately planted, and in any case it has not been seen recently. In the Isle of Wight it is undoubtedly native. When I first saw it there the plant was in great quantity though it had always been restricted to a strip of wooded down about half a mile long. In 1947 I could find very little, but the shrubs had grown up and there is reason to believe that the Greater Calamint does not thrive under such conditions.

In addition to the main ridge, the Isle of Wight contains an isolated chalk area around Ventnor to the south. The flora here differs considerably from that of the country already described, and although it seems to have fewer kinds of chalk flowers, the lack of quantity is more than made up by quality. The differences may in part be due to impurity of the rock, but the more important factor is undoubtedly the climate. The chalk flowers round Ventnor are as much sheltered from the winds as those of Freshwater Downs are exposed to them, and the district enjoys an exceptionally mild winter. This is almost certainly the reason why the Rare Cuckoo-pint, *Arum neglectum*, which is a plant of southern distribution, is so plentiful. Unlike the common species, *A. maculatum*, its leaves appear above ground during the winter and would suffer considerable damage if subjected to frost and snow. The difference in size is difficult to appreciate from descriptions in books—the Rare Cuckoo-pint is a magnificent plant in all its parts.

Near Ventnor the handsome Purple Cow-wheat, *Melampyrum arvense*, is more permanent than anywhere else in Britain. The English name refers to the beautiful purplish-rose colour of the bracts rather than to the flowers in which yellow is more conspicuous. It has been about here for a century and a quarter, and at one time it was so abundant on two farms that the seeds ground up with the wheat discoloured the flour and rendered it unmarketable. Hence it became known locally as Poverty Weed. One countrywoman described bread made from this flour as " tasting sharp in the mouth," and the farmers pulled up the weed and burnt it. Improved cultivation has had its effect, for in the old Isle of Wight locality I have never succeeded in finding Purple Cow-wheat in an arable field but it still grows in profusion on one chalky bank.

The chalk cliffs by the sea near Ventnor have a number of maritime species. Here there is Sea Beet, *Beta maritima*, Sea Radish, *Raphanus maritimus*, Samphire, *Crithmum maritimum*, Thrift, *Armeria maritima* (this also occurs on the inner cliffs), Alexanders, *Smyrnium olusatrum*, and Hoary Stock. A feature of the Undercliff is the profusion of Ivy Broomrape, *Orobanche hederae*, growing, as its name implies, as a parasite on Ivy, *Hedera helix*. The Kidney Vetch, *Anthyllis vulneraria*, is mostly of an unusual kind with pale lemon flowers. Madder, *Rubia peregrina*, scrambles up amongst the more woody plants.

The two areas of chalk described are the only extensive limestone soils in the Isle of Wight, but the reader may be puzzled at finding chalk-loving plants in other parts of the island. The reason for this is that the geological formation (Oligocene) which covers most of the north has thin beds of limestone built up of fossil shells. For example, on Headon Hill, near Totland Bay, most of the soil is ferruginous sand and it is about the last place where one would expect chalk flowers. Yet here I noticed Privet, Hoary Plantain, Squinancy-wort, Stemless Thistle, Carline Thistle and Vervain, *Verbena officinalis*. Similarly the hedges near Binstead Church are full of Ash, Dogwood, Privet, Field Maple, Traveller's Joy and Wayfaring Tree, while in one place I even saw the chalk-loving Musk Thistle. It is on the same formation (Oligocene) that a curious variety of the Traveller's Joy, with long, narrow lance-shaped leaflets (*Clematis vitalba* var. *timbali*) is found near Thorley.

So many interesting chalk flowers are found in the Isle of Wight that it may surprise people to learn that some which are not rare on the South Downs and Hampshire chalk are apparently absent or extremely rare. These include Chalk Milkwort, *Polygala calcarea*, Field Mouse-ear Chickweed, *Cerastium arvense*, Fine-leaved Sandwort, *Minuartia hybrida*, Round-headed Rampion, *Phyteuma tenerum*, Ground Pine, *Ajuga chamaepitys*, Musk Orchid, *Herminium monorchis*, and Tor Grass, *Brachypodium pinnatum*. Dropwort, *Filipendula vulgaris*, is surprisingly uncommon.

CHAPTER 6

OTHER CHALKLANDS SOUTH OF THE THAMES

THE LARGEST stretch of real chalk downland in Britain is the central area which includes Salisbury Plain. It forms the left-hand bottom loop of the " £ " symbol which represents chalk on the geological map, and extends continuously for a distance of as much as fifty-five miles from east to west. In addition to Salisbury Plain it includes a great part of Hampshire, the North Wiltshire and Berkshire Downs, and much of Dorset. There are outliers in Devon. Unfortunately the chalk flora is, on the whole, less interesting than that of the North and South Downs and Isle of Wight discussed in the last two chapters. From the botanist's point of view, a great deal of the country is too uniform to be exciting.

The characteristic feature of this part of England is the use of the downs ever since prehistoric times as pasture for sheep. The modern flocks are almost trivial compared with those maintained in the past, whose influence has moulded the vegetation as we know it to-day. Sheep are very close-grazing animals, " living lawn-mowers " as H. J. Massingham has called them, and only a limited number of grasses and flowers are able to exist under their constant nibbling. Those that do are the species characteristic of short, dense turf of the kind which still covers countless acres of Wiltshire, Hampshire, Berkshire and Dorset downland. Long treeless miles of uniform flora are characteristic of such country with only occasional areas where the wild flowers are more varied.

North Hampshire

The eastern part of Hampshire has many well-wooded areas. The flowers of Selborne Hanger (p. 66) are representative of many beechwoods in the district. In some woods and copses the Narrow-leaved Helleborine, *Cephalanthera longifolia* (Plate 22, p. 99), is locally plentiful. Round Winchester there is more varied country. For example, on one hill there is an abundance of orchids, including the Spotted, *Dactylorhiza maculata*, Sweet-scented, *Gymnadenia conopsea*, Pyramidal, *Anacamptis pyramidalis*, Bee, *Ophrys apifera*, Marsh, *Dactylorhiza praetermissa*, Frog, *Coeloglossum viride*, Lesser Butterfly, *Platanthera bifolia*, and very locally the Man, *Aceras anthropophorum*. The Marsh Orchids which grow here are short, dumpy forms very different from those of wet marshes. North of Winchester, Field Eryngo, *Eryngium campestre* (Plate 16, p. 73), is to be found. The main locality was ploughed up during the war but the species still persists nearby. In another place Cut-leaved Germander, *Teucrium botrys*, occurs in great quantity on spoil-heaps by the railway. Both these plants are under suspicion of having been introduced to these places by human activities. There is one chalky arable field where Pheasant's Eye, *Adonis annua*, and the curious Round-leaved Hare's-ear, *Bupleurum rotundifolium*, are always to be found when the condition of the crop permits. This district includes the most easterly station known to me for Yellow Star-of-Bethlehem, *Gagea lutea*, but although there are thousands of plants in the copse, only a very few of them produce flowers.

Salisbury Plain

Towards the western side of Hampshire the country is less wooded. Immediately across the Wiltshire boundary is the great, open, undulating sheep-moulded Salisbury Plain. Except in the valleys, the scenery is varied only by occasional earthworks and a few clumps of planted trees. Apart from these, it is mostly continuous close pasture with a very uniform flora. Large areas have been taken over by the military, whose activities restrict, or even prohibit, public access, but generally serve to protect, rather than destroy, the wild flowers. Some of the best plants grow on War Office land. For example, Purple Milk-vetch, *Astragalus danicus*, and Cut-leaved Self-heal, *Prunella laciniata*, grow on downs where access is only possible at certain times. The activities of the Army have had an interesting influence on the plant-life of this region. They have led to the introduction of alien

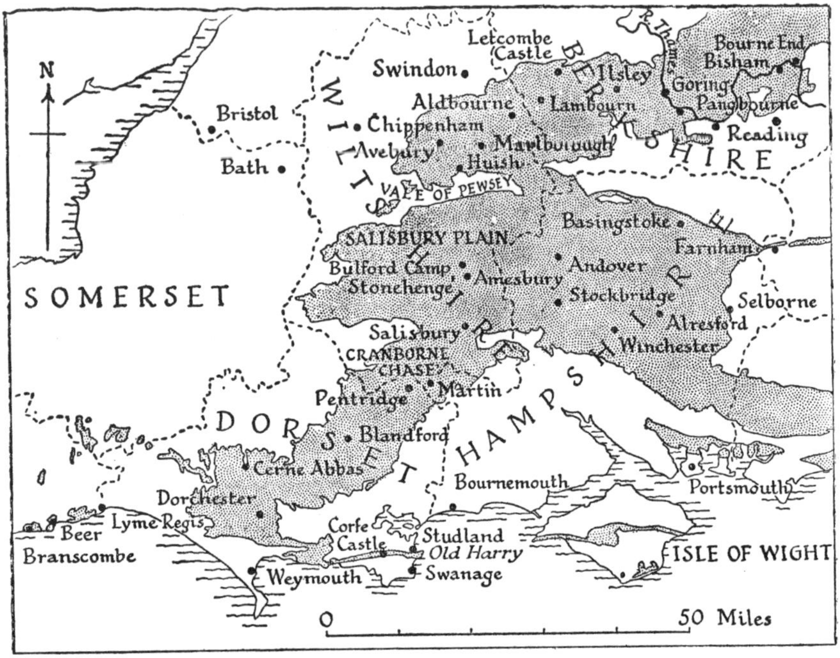

FIG. 6
Other chalklands south of the Thames

species round the great camps, to the breaking up of downland turf by the tracks of the tanks, and sometimes to the increase of flowers, owing to the exclusion of the public and grazing animals. The construction of a new road at Bulford Camp in 1939 brought up the buried seeds of Pheasant's Eye and the scarlet flowers appeared in thousands on the chalk rubble at the side. Now the ground has become grassed over and I believe they have disappeared.

The two botanical features of Salisbury Plain of greatest interest are the abundance of both Tall Broomrape, *Orobanche elatior*, and Dwarf Sedge, *Carex humilis*. The former is a parasite on Greater Knapweed, *Centaurea scabiosa*, and is found in greater plenty here than in any other part of Britain. In July and August the brown, dried spikes of the plant in fruit line many of the roads across the plain like two-feet high sentries. They are conspicuous enough from a fast-moving car, but the Dwarf Sedge is usually only seen after a hands-and-knees search. Actually the practised eye can pick it out from a little distance by the rather pale yellow hue of its wiry foliage, but this requires experience. It covers quite a lot of ground on the Plain and is found particularly on well-drained hilltops and earthworks. The flowers appear in March and April, and are followed by small fruiting spikes hidden amongst the leaves. I have seen these as late as August, but usually they have dropped by then.

One day in 1947 included the achievement of a botanical ambition which I had long cherished. With the help of my Wiltshire friend, Mr. J. D. Grose, I saw the Tuberous Thistle, *Cirsium tuberosum*, in the place where it was first found in Britain. The story is a remarkable one. It was in 1812 that A. B. Lambert, one of the first Vice-Presidents of the Linnean Society, made the discovery. A few years later he showed the plant to his friends, Sir J. E. Smith and the Dean of Carlisle (later Bishop Goodenough), but, unlike most rarities, the knowledge of its exact locality was not passed on to future generations of botanists. It seems that the Tuberous Thistle was collected here again in 1830, 1849, 1881 and 1888, but these finds were not generally known. In fact, the locality found by Professor Buckman in 1857, 25 miles to the north-east, remained the place where later botanists always went to see the plant. Many people must have searched in the hope of refinding Lambert's spot, but they were misled by the idea that it was a woodland species. On the labels of his dried specimens Lambert had given the name of the locality as a wood, and later searchers had taken his statement literally. Mr. Grose knew Tuberous Thistle in various other places, and in his experience he found it a plant of open spaces. Like other searchers, he first looked in Lambert's wood. Then, thinking the wood unsuitable, he carefully explored its borders. Finally he examined the adjacent chalk downs, and here, in 1942, his search was rewarded by refinding a fine colony of the Thistle. There is, of course, no absolute proof that this is the exact spot where Lambert saw it in 1812, but the probability is extremely strong. The downs here are very inaccessible and vast, with few landmarks, and I had no hesitation in following the original discoverer's example and using the name of the nearest wood as the locality on my labels. Unfortunately part of this colony of Tuberous Thistle was ploughed up in 1949.

Dorset and devon

Stretching south-west from Salisbury is a long broad tongue of chalk running right down past Blandford and Dorchester. The main road through these towns runs through the middle of some good country. Round the Bokerly Ditch, Martin Down and the Pentridge Hills, the country is open and undulating, and here there is quite a good chalk flora, which is at its best in May. I have noticed Dwarf Sedge, *Carex humilis*, in great abundance on earthworks in this district, and in one place I found Early Gentian, *Gentianella anglica* (Plate 19, p. 90). West of the main road is wooded Cranborne Chase, which is known to have an interesting flora but has been little explored in recent years.

Around Dorchester the chalk is certainly not at its best from the botanical point of view. The archaeological interest of such well-known spots as Maiden Castle and the Cerne Giant is not reflected in the flora, and west of these places the chalk shown on the map is not rich in characteristic plants so far as Dorset is concerned. There are, however, some small but interesting outliers in Devon. The best of these is a strip of coast between Branscombe and Beer. Here the chalk forms fine sea-cliffs and an undercliff with a magnificent flora. There are the usual shrubs—Privet, Dogwood and Wayfaring Tree, over which scramble Traveller's Joy and Madder, *Rubia peregrina*. Most of the common downland herbs are present. In addition there is Blue Gromwell, *Lithospermum purpurocaeruleum*, which in 1938 I saw here in full flower as early as 17 April. It is usually a limestone plant, and this is the only locality where I know it on chalk, though it was formerly to be found on this rock near Greenhithe in Kent. But perhaps the most exciting feature of Beer Head is the addition of maritime plants. Rock Sea-lavender, *Limonium binervosum*, and Rock Spurry, *Spergularia rupicola*, both with mauvish flowers, grow in chinks of the vertical chalk cliff. Samphire, *Crithmum maritimum*, and Portland Spurge, *Euphorbia portlandica*, are also here. In one place I have seen Hoary Stock, *Matthiola incana*, on the sea-cliff, but perhaps this is only an escape from gardens. As usual by the sea, the Slender-headed Thistle, *Carduus tenuiflorus*, is common. Other interesting plants of the district include Nottingham Catchfly, *Silene nutans*, which is less plentiful than on the Dover cliffs, and Gladdon, *Iris foetidissima*. A useful account of this chalk flora has been written by Mrs. Clare Harvey, who has drawn

PLATE 17

Brian Perkins

a. Cypress Spurge, *Euphorbia cyparissias;* an increasing species on the south-eastern chalk. Surrey; July

Brian Perkins

b. Ground Pine, *Ajuga chamaepitys;* an uncommon Labiate restricted to the chalk of south-east England. Surrey; July

Brian Perkins

CANDYTUFT, *Iberis amara;* locally common on the chalk of the Chilterns and in a few other places. Surrey; July

attention to the rapid transition on the top of the cliff from chalk to the quite acid soil of the clay which covers it inland. The narrow strip of downland turf, close-nibbled by rabbits, and including such plants as Common Rock-rose, Salad Burnet and Squinancywort, merges into the flora of the clay characterised by patches of Bracken and clumps of Gorse, *Ulex europaeus*. With the exception of a small area of metamorphosed chalk in Co. Antrim, which is so untypical that it will not be further considered in this book, and a tiny area in Morvern in the West Highlands, the Branscombe chalk is the most westerly in Britain. It is interesting to notice from Mrs. Harvey's fuller lists how closely the characteristic species present agree with those of our most easterly chalk in Kent. The common plants are almost identical—it is the rarities which differ.

From Dorchester a strip of chalk extends eastwards, forming much of the country behind Lulworth Cove, the Purbeck Hills, and eventually ending at The Foreland by Old Harry Rocks, near Studland. Probably the best known spot on this fine ridge is the mound on which Corfe Castle stands. Around the ruins of the Castle are several plants which may well be relics of cultivation by inhabitants of long ago. Thus there is Borage, *Borago officinalis*, which is one of our oldest garden herbs. In addition to medicinal uses of the plant, the leaves were added to favourite drinks, and the flowers, which abound in honey, attract bees. In fact, Borage is still grown by bee-keepers, and the seeds were included in a mixture sold for their use which I purchased in 1947. Alexanders, *Smyrnium olusatrum*, is another plant which may persist here as a relic of ancient cultivation. It was used as a pot-herb. The Shining Cranesbill, *Geranium lucidum*, which grows on the ruins, is under no suspicion—it is undoubtedly native.

Other plants which have been found on the Purbeck chalk ridge include the Tall and Ivy Broomrapes, *Orobanche elatoir* and *O. hederae*, and Mountain St. John's Wort, *Hypericum montanum*. On the downs near Old Harry there is Henbane, *Hyoscyamus niger*, and a puzzling series of Carrots which seem to be intermediates between the Wild Carrot, *Daucus carota*, and the Sea Carrot, *D. gummifer*. Yellow-wort is far less common on the chalk here than it is on the Jurassic limestones south of Swanage only a few miles away. At Corfe the Fiddle Dock, *Rumex pulcher*, is exceedingly plentiful. It is easily recognised by the curious warty tubercles on each of the three segments (tepals) which envelop the fruits, by the manner in which the stiff branches spread out in all directions, and also by the fiddle-shaped outline of the leaves.

The wild flower for which this area of chalk is most famous is a very local Calamint, *Calamintha baetica*, which is not known from anywhere else on the mainland of Britain. It was first found by H. W. Pugsley in September, 1900, when he was impressed by the large size of the lilac-pink flowers; but although he collected further material in 1912, it was not until December, 1922, that he decided to publish it as an addition to the British flora. The plant is well known in Spain (as the name implies) and Portugal, Morocco and Algeria, but seems to skip the intervening French limestones to reappear in Dorset. Calamints are difficult plants to name and many people have difficulty in distinguishing *C. baetica* from Common Calamint, *C. ascendens*. When growing, the rare Purbeck species may be known by the more numerous stems, which at first grow along the ground and then ascend, thus forming a " knee," by the very hairy leaves, and the larger flowers. But the Common Calamint grows near by and it must be admitted that the differences between the two plants are slender. As Pugsley has pointed out, it is interesting that *C. baetica* should grow on the same chalk ridge, now broken by the sea, as the large-flowered Greater Calamint, *C. sylvatica*, which is found only in the Isle of Wight (see p. 75).

North Wiltshire

Having followed the Dorset chalk into the sea at Old Harry, we must now return to Wiltshire. The Marlborough Downs are immediately north of Salisbury Plain and almost cut off from it by the Vale of Pewsey, exposing Greensand and Gault. Some of the chalk in the immediate vicinity of Marlborough has superficial deposits which bear a calcifuge flora, and, as the mosses show, the Sarsen Stones or Grey Wethers on many of the downs are not calcareous. Probably the finest chalk flora here is that of the escarpment which runs along from Martinsell, Huish Hill, Knap Hill and Milk Hill to Rybury Camp. In one chalky cornfield not far from Marlborough I once saw a fine quantity of Purple Cow-wheat, *Melampyrum arvense*. This was discovered in 1942, after a gap of 47 years since it was last seen in the county. It also turned up in a clover field near

Aldbourne, and it is thought that the seeds may have remained dormant in the soil until war-time ploughing disturbed them.

The main London-to-Bath road runs through a district west of Marlborough where the Tuberous Thistle has been found in a number of places. For most of these we are indebted to the industry of J. D. Grose. The feature of the district which impressed me most on an early visit was the great abundance of the handsome blue-flowered Meadow Cranesbill, *Geranium pratense*, on the dry roadsides. I first knew this plant as a boy in the water-meadows of the Thames Valley, and to see it in such plenty about the downs, away from rivers, came as a surprise. It compelled complete revision of my early ideas of its habitat requirements. Since then I have seen it elsewhere in equally dry chalky places, but I shall never forget my first visit to Avebury. The lesson is, of course, that only long experience can show to what extent a species is adaptable to different habitat conditions.

In this district the most interesting plants are often to be found on earthworks. Silbury Hill will be a familiar example to all motorists who have driven along the Bath road. A great conical artificial mound, 135 feet tall and nearly a third of a mile in circumference at the base, it has a good flora, including Round-headed Rampion, *Phyteuma tenerum*. This plant has been known from near here for nearly three centuries. Earthworks both in Wiltshire and elsewhere frequently have better flowers than the intervening downs. Freedom from interference by ploughing, and provision of well-drained slopes which so many chalk rarities favour, are probably the most important reasons.

Berkshire

Much the same type of country stretches north-west to the Berkshire border and continues in that county. First the Lambourn Downs, then Letcombe Castle and the Ridgeway country leading to Ilsley Downs and to the Thames at Streatley. Along this range there are considerable areas where the chalk is covered by other deposits, and in places there are patches of Ling, *Calluna vulgaris*, on the downs. The general impression one receives of the chalk flora has been well described by Dr. G. C. Druce[1] in the words, " softly swelling downs which are studded with Juniper bushes and redolent of Thyme, and

[1] Druce, G. C., *Flora of Berkshire* (1897), lxviii.

brilliant with the orange flowers of *Hippocrepis*, the Horse-shoe Vetch, and the blue of the Chalk Milkwort." He adds that "though the number of species composing the down-flora is not large, yet the individuals are in countless numbers and are of a very interesting character."

This is true enough, but another feature of downland floras is exceptionally well shown here. In addition to the species which are abundant and widespread, there are others which, for no apparent reason, are restricted to very small areas. Thus the handsome flowers of the Pasque Flower, *Pulsatilla vulgaris* (Plate X, p. 51), are only to be found very locally in scattered patches. Although there are miles and miles of seemingly suitable country, and although the plant has fruits well adapted for dispersal, and fertile seed is set freely, yet it fails to spread. One of the localities where I have seen it was discovered over a century ago by my great-great-grandfather, Job Lousley (1790-1855).

Another very local plant is the Large Autumn Gentian, *Gentianella germanica* (Plate 25, p. 114). It is probably restricted in Berkshire to one earthwork, where it grows with Autumn Gentian, *Gentianella amarella*. The latter flowers a little earlier than the rarer species, and this is quite a useful character additional to those given in the books. It was from this locality that the hybrid between the two Gentians was first described. As an example of a more widespread plant, which is nevertheless restricted to small areas, Field Fleawort, *Senecio integrifolius* (Plate 30, p. 127), may be instanced. This is found at intervals all along the range, but in each place it grows only for a few hundred yards.

From the steep slopes of Streatley Hill (which has long been a famous botanical hunting-ground) the chalk extends on the Berkshire side of the Thames to Reading. About Pangbourne especially there is a good deal of Pale Toadflax, *Linaria repens*, which shows a decided preference for the chalk. Near Sulham and Tilehurst good chalk plants have been found. Beyond Reading much of the chalk shown on the map is obscured, but there is a nice little bit of downland south of the Thames opposite Bourne End. Here, on Winter Hill, there is an especially fine display of a rather local and large-flowered Eyebright, *Euphrasia pseudokerneri*. This is only found on calcareous soils and has already been described in connection with Box Hill. Mention must also be made of the interesting flora of the beechwoods of Quarry Wood, Bisham. Just over a century ago the Military Orchid, *Orchis militaris*, was found here.

This chapter concludes the account of the chalk south of the Thames and seems an appropriate place to refer to the occurrence of calcicoles in the water-meadows. During the course of its long journey the river passes through a great deal of limestone and chalk country, and the streams which discharge into it contain calcareous matter in solution and even in suspension. As far down as the outer suburbs of London the amount of this is surprisingly great. Thus Dr. North states that Thames water near Ditton was found to contain 16·84 parts of calcium carbonate per 100,000, and he quotes the Royal Commission on Water Supply appointed in 1867 as reporting "that the average quantity of dissolved material carried down by the Thames past Kingston was 548,230 tons per annum, of which about two thirds was calcium carbonate; this represents the removal in solution of about 140 tons from every square mile of chalk exposed in the drainage area involved." Higher up the river the proportion of calcium carbonate is probably just as high, in fact Druce states that some Thames-side meadows contain limestone fragments.

The apparent anomaly of chalk-down plants growing in Thames water-meadows is therefore explained by the basic nature of the silt left behind after flooding. In the higher reaches examples include Burnt Orchid, *Orchis ustulata*, and Clustered Bellflower, *Campanula glomerata*. Traveller's Joy, *Clematis vitalba*, is plentiful in hedges by the river right down to Kew Bridge and even beyond.

It might be expected that the number of calcicoles would decrease as soon as the Thames left the chalk country, but this is not obviously the case. Many occur in the Windsor meadows, and from Staines, on the Middlesex side, Mr. D. H. Kent lists the following: Traveller's Joy, Wild Mignonette, Spindle Tree, Common Buckthorn, Salad Burnet, Wayfaring Tree, Clustered Bellflower, Downy Oat, *Helictotrichon pubescens*, and Upright Brome, *Bromus erectus*. Some of these species are not strictly confined to calcareous soils but taken collectively they are very significant. Even as far down as Hampton Court he lists eight downland plants, including Small Scabious, *Scabiosa columbaria*, and Upright Brome. On the Surrey side of the river Dropwort, *Filipendula vulgaris*, is widespread. Nottingham Catchfly grows near Teddington. It is possible that some of these are relics of a time when the lime content of the soil was higher than it is at present.

CHAPTER 7

CHALKLANDS NORTH OF THE THAMES

THE THAMES between Reading and Goring forms a natural boundary between two very different types of chalk country. The Berkshire downs considered in the last chapter stretch away to the south-west and merge into those of Wiltshire. Characteristically these are open, treeless, sheep-grazed pastures. The Chilterns, on the other hand, which extend to the north-east, are heavily wooded except on the steeper slopes. They include some of the finest beechwoods in England, and although many of these are on superficial deposits over the chalk, they add welcome variety to the flora. Moreover, the downland turf itself, in my experience, is less uniform, and this, speaking very generally, is probably attributable to less intensive grazing. Although the area of chalk exposed at the surface is perhaps less than on Salisbury Plain and its outliers, the flora is more attractive.

THE CHILTERNS

On the higher ground of the Chilterns the chalk is often covered with patches of Clay-with-Flints, brickearth and gravels, and the vegetation usually indicates these very clearly to the observant eye. This, however, is not always the case in beechwoods. The beech, *Fagus sylvatica*, forms magnificent woods on well-drained soils other than on chalk, and the accumulation of leaves creates its own environment to suit certain plants irrespective of the underlying rock. On the other hand, the fine escarpment facing west, and later north-west, which extends from Whitchurch and Goring on the Thames to Stokenchurch,

Princes Risborough, Wendover and Tring and beyond, provides a steep slope on which only a thin soil covers the chalk-rock. Here many of the finest chalk flowers are to be found.

Two of the most characteristic rare flowers of this escarpment are the Candytuft, *Iberis amara* (Plate 18, p. 83), and Large Autumn Gentian, *Gentianella germanica* (Plate 25, p. 114). Both of these occur in greater quantity than anywhere else in Britain. Both favour rather bare and very chalky soils. The Candytuft grows on open places on the hill slopes and also in clearings in the woods and cultivated fields. On the Chilterns it is certainly native, but in most other districts it is either an obvious introduction or doubtful. The Large Autumn Gentian is likewise at home on the open slopes and is occasionally found in woods.

The beechwoods are the homes of rare orchids. One of these, the Spur-lipped Coralroot, *Epipogium aphyllum*, has been described as our rarest British plant. It has been found in this country only in three small areas, two on the Chilterns, and the other near Ludlow, and is so intensely scarce that you could search unsuccessfully for years. It is a curious and fascinating plant, living like the Bird's-nest Orchid, *Neottia nidus-avis*, and Yellow Bird's-nest, *Monotropa hypopitys*, on the decaying remains of dead leaves. Flowers appear only at long intervals, and even when the exact locality at which they have been found is known, it may be very many years before search is rewarded with success. It has been seen in at least three places, many miles apart in the woods of the Chilterns, and on several occasions. The recorded dates range from May to August, so evidently it has an exceptionally long flowering season.

The Chiltern wood borders are the place to look for the Military Orchid, *Orchis militaris*. At one time this was not extremely rare, and up to about a century ago there are records of it being seen in considerable numbers. Moreover, the records extend from east of Tring across the Thames into Berkshire; and they were from places well scattered over the Chilterns (Distribution Map, p. 222). Then it disappeared from one district after another, until by about 1914 it seemed to be extinct. Whatever the reason for its going—and there are quite a number of theories—there must have been some factor which affected it over a wide area. In May, 1947, I rediscovered the Military Orchid! In a way it was just luck. The excursion was intended as a picnic, so I had left my usual apparatus at home and took only my note-book. But I selected our stopping places on the chalk with some care, and naturally wandered off to see what I could find. To my delight I stumbled on the orchid just coming into flower. The following week-end I returned to make a careful survey of the colony and to take the first opportunity given to any British botanist for well over thirty years of studying the particular conditions under which the Military Orchid lives in our country. It was on this second visit that I took the colour photograph used for Plate 26 (p. 115)—the first to be taken of this plant in England.

Careful plotting showed that there were 39 plants in the colony and that 18 of them had thrown up flowering spikes. Of these, the 5 most exposed had the flower-stems bitten right off—almost certainly by rabbits. The plotting also revealed that the plants most in shade either failed to flower or put up only pale, small spikes. Trees on one side of the colony had been cut down in the early days of the war, as I estimated from the growth of bushes round their stumps, and it is likely that this had stimulated germination of dormant seeds of the orchid. Analysis of a sample of the soil revealed that the free carbonate of lime amounted to no less than 50·2 per cent—an astonishingly high proportion.

It was interesting to compare this locality with the marshes near Brunnen in Switzerland, where I saw the Military Orchid in May, 1930. Whereas on the Chilterns it was growing on a shallow chalk soil under almost the driest possible conditions, in Switzerland it thrived in very wet marshy meadows. It is probable, however, that the soil-water there was basic, although I made no tests at the time.

The plants on the Chilterns varied greatly in size. The smallest was only about four inches tall with two flowers—a miserable, depauperate little plant. The largest—the one which is illustrated—was 14 inches (35 cm.) tall with no less than 26 flowers. This must be about the finest Military Orchid seen in England; for most of the herbarium specimens (dating from the time when it was plentiful) are only some 7 to 9 inches in height.

The flowers are extremely beautiful; in saying this I think I can fairly say that I have not allowed the rarity of the plant to bias my judgment. The pointed sepals are folded together to form a hood over each flower and are a pale ashy-grey on the outside. The flowers open at the bottom of the spike first and therefore the buds at the top appear slightly pinkish-grey from the colour of the sepals, which act

Brian Perkins

EARLY GENTIAN, *Gentianella anglica*; a local species found in southern England. Surrey; June

Brian Perkins

LARGE-FLOWERED CHALK-EYEBRIGHT, *Euphrasia pseudokerneri*. Various species of Eyebright are common on chalk and limestone. Surrey; September

as wrappers. It is the resemblance of the hood to an ancient helmet which has led to the plant being called the Soldier or Military Orchid; the name is a very apt one. The lip, which projects beneath the helmet, has two lobes on each side and one very small pointed terminal one: it is spotted and flushed with a colour which is usually described as pink but which is far less red than is shown in most of the published colour pictures. It is a colour which is very difficult to match, but perhaps comes nearest to the one described as "roseine purple" of the old R.H.S. colour chart. In 1955 a second fine colony of the Military Orchid was discovered in Suffolk—far from previously known habitats.

The Monkey Orchid is now less rare so far as numbers are concerned. The best known locality is a tiny area of down on the Chilterns, and for many years this was a secret shared by a considerable number of botanists who visited it annually. They kept the secret so well that in 1943 a paper was published in a scientific journal recording its "rediscovery" although, in fact, the plant had never been lost! Unfortunately the numbers have been reduced considerably by the ploughing of the lower part of the habitat, and increase of the downland scrub. As the bushes were fast making the down unsuitable, a party of public-spirited botanists now make an annual visit in winter to clear away the scrub, and there are already indications that the orchid may be increasing. There are old records from several parts of Kent but for a time the Monkey Orchid was thought to be extinct in the county. Then in 1952, a single plant reappeared, and flowered in each of the next three years. Shortly afterwards it was refound in greater numbers in another part of the county, and here Mr. H. M. Wilks has taken active steps to conserve it and his efforts seem likely to be successful. In Sussex and Berkshire the orchid appears to be extinct, and there are doubtful records from Surrey.

The Monkey Orchid flowers about a week earlier than the Military Orchid. It shares with this species, the Lady Orchid, *O. purpurea*, and the Man Orchid, *Aceras anthropophorum*, the possession of coumarin in the leaves. On account of this the drying foliage emits a strong and very pleasant smell resembling new-mown hay. The resemblance of the lip to a monkey is clear. Like the Man Orchid, it is chiefly a plant of the open downs, while the Military and Lady Orchids are generally characteristic of woods and wood borders.

Before leaving the orchids there is one more species which should be mentioned. The Green-flowered Helleborine, *Epipactis leptochila*, is, as far as my own experience goes, far more common in the Chilterns than anywhere else. In the beechwoods within easy access of Henley-on-Thames it is quite a common plant. It flowers a little earlier than the allied Broad-leaved Helleborine, *E. helleborine*, from which it differs in having yellow-green flowers, with longer and more pointed sepals and petals and in other characters.

In the same district the Cut-leaved Self-heal, *Prunella laciniata*, has recently been discovered in two places. It will be discussed in a later chapter (see p. 113).

The beechwoods of the Chilterns are not only more extensive than those of the North and South Downs, but they also differ somewhat in their associated flora. For example, the handsome grass Wood Barley, *Hordelymus europaeus*, is relatively frequent. I have seen it in various places between Tring and Henley forming fine colonies in the lighter parts of the woods. Similarly the Lesser Wintergreen, *Pyrola minor*, with its lovely cream-coloured bells of flowers, is fairly frequent in isolated patches in the extensive woods of the Chilterns. On the whole of the North and South Downs I can remember only one record for this plant, though in Surrey, Kent and Sussex it occurs on sandy or boggy soils in a few places. There is thus a great contrast in behaviour. Then again in some of the Chiltern woods there is a display of Hawkweeds, *Hieracium spp.*, such as we never see on the North and South Downs. In these three respects the resemblance of the flora is to that of the beechwoods of the Cotswolds rather than to the chalk hills farther south.

Within a limited area roughly bounded by High Wycombe and Amersham, Watford and Harefield, the Coralroot, *Cardamine bulbifera*, is locally common. It also occurs just across the Thames in Berkshire. It is a plant with a surprisingly short flowering season, being at its best for less than a week during May. I have never seen fully-formed fruit of Coralroot, which must be uncommon, and the plant evidently depends mainly for reproduction on bulbils, which form in the axils of the leaves. The woods where it grows are on chalk, but it does not follow that the soil is always chalky. In fact I have seen it in some places on soil which was almost certainly somewhat acid.

East of the Colne there are small areas of chalk in Middlesex; the best and most famous of these is near Harefield. Here, within 16 or 17 miles of London, chalk flowers persist, and Mr. D. H. Kent has been successful in refinding many of those recorded by Blackstone (see p. 27) over two centuries ago. The Military Orchid was seen in this district at the beginning of this century.

Hertfordshire and Bedfordshire

The escarpment of the Chilterns is continued across Buckinghamshire and a small corner of Hertfordshire, near Tring, into Bedfordshire. One locality for the Pasque Flower, *Pulsatilla vulgaris* (Plate X, p. 51), in this district has received a good deal more than its fair share of publicity. It is not only well known to local country people and to visitors, but on at least two occasions has been the subject of letters to Sunday newspapers. There are several places where the plant is more plentiful. A little beyond Tring are the last of the big beechwoods and, farther east, I remember only comparatively small copses and belts of beech. It is perhaps for this reason that the Military Orchid has never been found farther east on these hills than Aldbury.

Just east of Tring is thus the approximate position of a change in the character of the flora. Not only does it mark the end of the fine Chiltern beechwoods, but also the beginning of certain plants of a more eastern distribution. A good example is the Great Pig-nut, *Bunium bulbocastanum.* This plant has been found in Britain only in contiguous parts of Hertfordshire, Buckinghamshire, Bedfordshire and Cambridgeshire, and it occurs locally in great abundance. Yet it is as adaptable to quite a wide range of different habitat conditions. I have seen it equally at home in the dense downland turf and in arable fields, on shallow chalk soils and in deep marl. As a weed in cereal crops its deep " bulbs " are so much below the surface of the soil that they are hardly disturbed by ploughing. In downland turf it is apparently able to compete with the grasses. From near Cambridge almost to Tring there are areas where the plant is to be seen in countless thousands, and yet it has never spread beyond these limits.

Purple Milk-vetch, *Astragalus danicus,* which is absent from the Buckinghamshire Chilterns, has a number of localities on the chalk to the east of them. Field Fleawort, *Senecio integrifolius,* becomes more frequent. These are plants which are chiefly associated with the drier chalk areas.

Along the hills which extend north-east from the Chilterns the best places for chalk flowers are, as usual, on the hill slopes. These are found on the steep escarpment which, in contrast to that of the North Downs, faces north. Much of the chalk on the flattish top is covered with other soils. The escarpment in places forms fine promontories which project into the lower ground to the north, while intervening bays form great sheltered amphitheatres. Pitstone Hill and Ivinghoe Beacon and the slopes between them are of great interest. Near Dunstable the best places are Dunstable Downs and Blow's Downs on the higher ground, and the much quarried country east of Castle Hill, Totternhoe. The famous philosopher and economist, John Stuart Mill, was one of the first to point out that the Box, *Buxus sempervirens*, was to be found on the hills between Dunstable and Tring. Here, as at Great and Little Kimble farther west, it is usually regarded as having spread from trees which were originally planted; but the matter is not beyond doubt.

Beyond Dunstable the north-facing escarpment forms a magnificent range from Sundon through the Barton and Pegsdon Hills almost to Hitchin. Here I have seen Purple Milk-vetch and Field Fleawort in abundance, while at one spot Mountain Stone Parsley, *Seseli libanotis* (see p. 69), Pasque Flower, *Pulsatilla vulgaris*, and Spotted Catsear, *Hypochoeris maculata*, all grow together. The flowers of the latter are often eaten off by cattle. In two localities on the range Upright Cinquefoil, *Potentilla recta*, is naturalised. Elsewhere in the district there was until recently a fine colony of Lizard Orchids, *Himantoglossum hircinum*. It has been known in the vicinity since 1938, and in 1947 I saw 23 plants. When the photograph reproduced on Plate 27 (p. 122) was taken in 1946 there were even more, but it seems likely that the orchids suffered from the severe weather early in 1947 and from the drought which followed. Ploughing then destroyed the colony.

Cambridgeshire

East of Hitchin there is no continuous chalk escarpment, though in a few places such as Therfield Heath, near Royston, there are slopes sufficiently steep to have discouraged ploughing. In general, however, the chalk is heavily cultivated and it is only on earthworks and in narrow strips by tracks and round quarries that the old downland turf still remains. This destruction of the native plants doubtless took place at a rapid rate in the eighteenth century, but it was in the early

J. E. Lousley

Yorkshire Broomrape, *Orobanche reticulata*. Restricted to Magnesian Limestone

PLATE XVIII

R. H. Hall

Miller's Dale, showing Raven's Tor (Carboniferous Limestone)

part of the nineteenth century that successive Enclosure Acts resulted in loss on a grand scale. It led to the complete extinction of some of the recorded plants and greatly reduced the number of localities of others.

Professor Babington of Cambridge was able to observe the closing stages of the worst of this destruction at first-hand. Referring to the Cambridgeshire chalk country, he wrote :

> " Until recently (within 60 years) most of the chalk district was open and covered with a beautiful coating of turf, profusely decorated with Pasque Flower, Purple Milk-vetch, and other interesting plants. It is now converted into arable land, and its peculiar plants mostly confined to small waste spots by roadsides, pits, and the very few banks which are too steep for the plough. Thus many species which were formerly abundant have become rare ; so rare as to have caused an unjust suspicion of their not being really natives to arise in the minds of some modern botanists. Even the tumuli, entrenchments, and other interesting works of the ancient inhabitants have seldom escaped the rapacity of the modern agriculturalist, who too frequently looks upon the native plants of the country as weeds, and its antiquities as deformities."[1]

This was published in 1860, and at this distance of time it is difficult to appreciate the magnitude of the change which took place over the chalk of the adjoining parts of north Hertfordshire and Essex and southern Cambridgeshire.

It is in the records of the rarer plants that the destruction of the downland flowers can be traced. An example is the Early Spider Orchid, *Ophrys sphegodes* (Plate 31, p. 142), which has already been referred to in Chapter 5 (p. 69). Gibson still knew it on chalky banks near Hildersham in 1842, and it is believed that he found it on the baulks left between arable fields. These were destroyed by more intensive cultivation. Babington found it on a baulk near Abington on 24 May, 1837, but three years later he found that someone had " dug up all the plants." There were vandals even in those days ! But these records seem to have been the very last chapters in the story, and although the Early Spider Orchid was probably never plentiful

[1] Babington, C. C., *Flora of Cambridgeshire* (1860), p. xiv. English names have been substituted in the quotation.

Fig. 7

Chalklands north of the Thames. Upper Cretaceous (Chalk) hatched where at the surface and stippled where covered by Glacial Drift

in Cambridgeshire, it is fairly safe to say that the last known localities were merely those which had dodged the plough longest.

The history of the Pasque Flower is rather similar. It still persists on earthworks and other places where it has been protected from the plough. But many of its haunts have been lost and the baulks between fields where it was known to botanists of a century ago have long been destroyed. The Purple Milk-vetch can now be found at very few of the spots given in the old floras. Field Fleawort—which Relhan called Cambridge Ragwort—may well be another example of a flower which was once much more common.

The ploughing up of the downland has not been all loss. In the chalky arable fields which took its place many interesting weeds characteristic of this part of East Anglia are to be found. Perhaps the most general of these are three small-flowered Fumitories, *Fumaria micrantha*, *F. parviflora* and *F. vaillantii*. There are also rare Poppies. The Rough Round-headed Poppy, *Papaver hybridum*, with dark crimson petals, each with a purplish-black patch at the base, seems to be more common than it was a century ago. On the other hand, Lecoq's Poppy, *P. lecoqii*, with its headquarters for Britain here, is much rarer. The Larkspur, *Delphinium ambiguum*, which was for a time rather widespread in chalky fields, is now almost if not quite gone in such places. The Greater and Lesser Bur-parsleys, *Caucalis latifolia* and *C. platycarpos*, are both now very rare, though I saw a fair quantity of the latter in 1947 and 1948. Such changes are due to improved cultivation and cleaner seed. On the credit side we have Madwort, *Asperugo procumbens*. This had not been recorded in Cambridgeshire for over two centuries until refound on the chalk about 1927. In a field, which adjoins one where Professor Babington made a special study of the Fumitories many years earlier, it varies in quantity from season to season according to the weather and the crop. It is an annual which completes its life-cycle in a very short period, and usually a few plants appear in May and a much larger number after the late summer rains. During the dry middle of the summer I have found it completely burnt up.

Fortunately a considerable number of rare downland plants still occur on the small patches which escaped the ploughing. One of these is Mountain Everlasting, *Antennaria dioica*, which is common enough on the wetter limestone of the north and west, but exceedingly scarce and erratic in appearance in the south and east of England. It was found on a heath near Royston about 1841, and a note made about the same time says that there was only a square yard of it. Later it was noticed in two places in the same district, and in 1882 it is known to have flowered freely. After this I can trace no further records for 65 years until, in 1947, it was rediscovered by Mr. Donald Pigott. During the 1939-45 war a large part of the down had been ploughed but the place where it grows had been left alone.

Another remarkable survival is the Tuberous Thistle, *Cirsium tuberosum*, which owes its protection to a very ancient trackway. It is restricted to a very small area where it was discovered by Dr. W. H. Mills in July, 1919. Between the two world wars it spread out into the adjoining chalky fields, but when these were again taken into cultivation early in the second war, the Thistle once more became limited to the edge of the trackway. Along hedge-banks and field borders on the Gog Magog hills there are two pretty bulbous plants: the Grape Hyacinth, *Muscari atlanticum*, and Common Star-of-Bethlehem, *Ornithogalum umbellatum*. They are both grown in gardens but the first is almost certainly native and the second has been there for a very long time. Another very beautiful plant which is one of the features of these hills is the lovely blue-flowered Perennial Flax, *Linum anglicum*. It has been known from Newmarket for three centuries, but even on the Gogs, which is the place where most people go to see it, the plant is local. From north Essex it is to be found in scattered localities on the chalk and limestone right up the eastern side of England to Durham, and then, rather strangely, it reappears on the limestone to the west in Westmorland and also in Kirkcudbrightshire.

It is on the Gogs that the Mountain Stone Parsley, *Seseli libanotis*, and Great Pig-nut, *Bunium bulbocastanum*, grow within a few yards of one another. In the downland turf by the Roman Road over the Gogs, and on the Devil's Ditch near Newmarket, there is a very rare little sedge, *Carex ericetorum*, which is not easy to find. These are the only two places where I have seen it in Cambridgeshire, but in Breckland, shortly to be discussed, it is certainly more plentiful, and it has been discovered on the limestone farther north (see p. 171). On chalk in this county I was shown Spiked Speedwell, *Veronica spicata* (Plate XI, p. 58), in 1947, in a place which may well be the same as one where John Ray found it in the seventeenth century. The flowers are of a most intense blue, and although there are several localities for it in Norfolk and Suffolk (Distribution Map 11, p. 221), the plant is much

PLATE 21

Brian Perkins

COMMON TEASEL, *Dipsacus fullonum*, growing with Wild Parsnip, *Pastinaca sativa*, on the North Downs.
Surrey; August

Robert Atkinson

ORCHIDS OF A HAMPSHIRE BEECH-WOOD. The rare Narrow-leaved Helleborine, *Cephalanthera longifolia* (right) and the common Large White Helloborine, *C. damasonium* (left), growing with a barren plant of Broad-leaved Helleborine, *Epipactis helleborine*, and two Common Twayblades, *Listera ovata*, with their flowering stems eaten off. June

more scarce than its western subspecies, *V. hybrida* (see p. 118). In a few places I have seen the spring Cinquefoil, *Potentilla tabernaemontani*, but it is here usually much smaller than in the limestone districts of western England with their heavier rainfall.

Some mention must be made of the Boulder Clay, which in places contains a considerable proportion of lime. It is a glacial deposit derived from rocks which have been crushed by ice and contains a heterogenous mass of material. Where it overlies the chalk it often contains boulders of chalk and flint, and the flora includes a number of calcicoles. Boulder Clay occurs widely over England and, although it is only marked on the " drift " (and not on the " solid ") editions of the geological maps, it is of considerable importance to the botanist. The best known areas are to the north-west and south-east of the Cambridgeshire chalk, around Hardwick, Caxton and Eversden, and from Saffron Walden and Quendon towards Haverhill respectively.

The most characteristic flower of the Boulder Clay is the Oxlip, *Primula elatior*. In very general terms this has flowers rather like those of a Primrose, *P. vulgaris*, carried at the end of a long stalk like those of the Cowslip, *P. veris*. A hybrid between the last two species is not uncommon in some parts of the country, and this hybrid or False Oxlip is sometimes confused with the true Oxlip, which is restricted to the Eastern Counties. In many of the woods on the Boulder Clay the latter occurs in the greatest abundance—a most beautiful sight when in flower in April. It sometimes hybridises with Cowslip and also with the Primrose. In Britain the species is restricted to this particular kind of clay.[1] Another characteristic plant of these woods is the Crested Cow-wheat, *Malampyrum cristatum*, with handsome red and yellow flowers recalling those of the Field Cow-wheat, *Melampyrum arvense* (see p. 76). It is strangely local in its occurrence and prefers the edges of woods and open rides. After coppicing it sometimes appears in great quantity, only to decrease as the bushes grow up again.

Sulphur Clover, *Trifolium ochroleucon*, is locally abundant on field borders and roadsides on the Boulder Clay, though it also occurs on chalk. In the cultivated fields a number of uncommon weeds are probably more frequent here than anywhere else in England. These include Slender Tare, *Vicia tenuissima*, Warty Spurge, *Euphorbia platyphyllos*, and a rare Brome-grass, *Bromus arvensis*.

[1] Miller Christy, *Journal of Ecology*, *10:* 200-210 (1922) and *12:* 314-16 (1924).

Breckland

Commencing near Chippenham, a few miles beyond Newmarket, and extending through Mildenhall to north of Brandon, east of Thetford, and nearly to Bury St. Edmunds, is a fascinating area known as "Breckland." Here a layer of sand overlies the chalk, and this has given the district a wild and unique character. Many rare plants are to be found, and a holiday spent at any of the towns mentioned will provide plenty of interest for the botanist.

Over a great part of the Breck the wild flowers are sand-loving species and often plants which avoid lime. But here and there the sand is thin, and chalk is very close to the surface. It is in such spots that the vegetation is most varied and that most of the rarer plants are found. These places can usually be recognised by the presence of chalk-pits which have been dug there because it is more economical to dig chalk where the sand is thin rather than where it is deep. Round these pits the sand looks the same as elsewhere, but it contains an appreciable percentage of calcareous matter. Many of the plants are lime-lovers.

Some of the plants I have seen in such places are certainly calcicoles, such as Burnt Orchid, *Orchis ustulata*, Purple Milk-vetch, *Astragalus danicus*, Spring Cinquefoil, *Potentilla tabernaemontani*, Spiked Speedwell, *Veronica spicata*, and a Meadow-rue, *Thalictrum babingtonii*. All these are true chalk plants in Cambridgeshire, which has just been discussed. But I strongly suspect that a good many other species which grow here are likewise calcicoles although there is less certainty about them. Examples are Grape Hyacinth, *Muscari atlanticum*, and Common Star-of-Bethlehem, *Ornithogalum umbellatum*, which both occur over considerable areas of Breckland sand. Similarly the rare sedge, *Carex ericetorum*, which I have only seen here and in Cambridgeshire and Yorkshire on limestone soils, may perhaps not be restricted to them as my experience would indicate. Then Spotted Catsear, *Hypochoeris maculata*, which is always on chalk in the Eastern Counties and on limestone in the north-west, does occur in Cornwall in a place which may not be calcareous. Again, the dainty little Spanish Catchfly, *Silene otites*, which I have seen on chalk in north Norfolk, grows on sand near Thetford quite near plants which avoid limestone. Thus about these there is an element of doubt, but I feel fairly sure in my own mind that in Breckland they are chalk- rather than sand-lovers. The same probably applies to other rare species.

The influence of man has produced some interesting changes in Breckland vegetation. Thus the enormous artificial mound known as Castle Hill, Thetford, has a number of calcicoles, including *Thalictrum babingtonii*. The chalk débris round the entrances to the underground workings started by prehistoric man in search of flint at Grime's Graves, near Weeting, has a flora very different from the surrounding sand. The various embankments such as that of the Devil's Ditch nearly all have chalk flowers. Where the Breck has been ploughed plants of the usually chalk-loving Fine-leaved Sandwort, *Minuartia hybrida*, are common. Round the edges of fields I have found Maiden Pink, *Dianthus deltoides*, and the large flowers of Field Mouse-ear Chickweed, *Cerastium arvense*. Both of these are usually chalk plants elsewhere.

Norfolk and Suffolk

In the counties of Norfolk and Suffolk chalk is by far the most important rock formation, and yet so much of it is covered by other deposits that it is only in relatively few places that it is important to the botanist. There are only the tiniest patches of anything approaching downland and these are mostly by chalk-pits or along roadsides. Perhaps the largest stretches are Ringstead Downs and Massingham Heath. On the latter there were formerly chalk grassland plants growing between anthills on which the calcifuge Ling was to be seen. But Massingham Heath was ploughed up during the second world war. A little over a mile to the west there is an excellent chalk flora, including Spanish Catchfly, Maiden Pink and a rare grass, *Phleum phleoides*, but the best ground extends only for a hundred yards or so. To the south there are good calcicoles near Castle Acre, and Swaffham is the centre of other scattered chalk exposures.

Lincolnshire and Yorkshire

Much the same must be said of Lincolnshire. Chalk is the formation of the Wolds, but in many places it is covered with Glacial Drift. Elsewhere it is mostly under cultivation. There may be small areas of downland turf left, but as I have never botanized in this part of the county I cannot say. In any case, most of the recorded stations of calcicoles are on the limestone farther west, and the chalk of Lincolnshire is of little importance to the botanist.

In east Yorkshire there is the most northerly exposure of chalk in England, occupying an area which has been estimated at as much as 400,000 acres. It extends from the Humber north to the Vale of Pickering and includes the magnificent cliffs of Bempton and Flamborough Head. Although much broken up by cultivation and superficial deposits, there is an interesting ground, especially towards the north.

Many of the common plants are the same as those of the southern chalk—Common Rock-rose, Hairy Violet, Fairy Flax, Common Birds-foot Trefoil, Dropwort, Salad Burnet, Clustered Bellflower, Marjoram, Hoary Plantain, and so on. Some of the scarcer species are those with an eastern distribution, found also farther south, like Perennial Flax, *Linum anglicum*, and Purple Milk-vetch, *Astragalus danicus*. But the southern botanist will notice that many of the plants with which he is familiar on the South and North Downs are absent, while others, such as Bee Orchid, *Ophrys apifera*, are much rarer, or even rare and here doubtfully native, like Traveller's Joy. The Beech is quite common, but here, as in all the glaciated parts of England, it is suspected of having originated from planted trees. Deadly Nightshade, *Atropa belladonna*, is very frequent and exceptionally fine. In general, Yorkshire chalk lacks many of the attractive southern plants and has very few additional northerners by way of compensation.

This chapter concludes the review of the English chalk. While there is a list of common plants to be found in all districts, yet each area considered has special characteristics. People interested in flowers will always find plenty to see in any of the places discussed, and the fortunate chance that so much of the best English chalk is near to favourite holiday resorts will make it familiar to most readers. Some of the limestone areas to be reviewed in the following chapters are much more difficult of access.

CHAPTER 8

LIMESTONES OF SOUTH-WEST ENGLAND

MOST OF the older limestones are harder than the chalk. For this reason much of the scenery of places to be described in the following chapters is more rugged. The gently undulating country of the chalk downs has its counterpart on the Oolite and Permian, but steep slopes and inland cliffs are more characteristic of the older limestones.

In addition to hardness there are differences in chemical composition. While much of the Upper Chalk is almost pure calcium carbonate, other limestones often contain a large percentage of other substances. Therefore the soils formed over them are frequently less calcareous than on the chalk. This tendency is increased in regions of heavy rainfall in the west and north. The larger amount of rainfall passing through the soil carries off the soluble calcium carbonate more rapidly and leached areas are more common.

The very striking contrasts between the floras of the chalk and older limestones may be partially due to differences in the physical and chemical qualities of the rock. But climatic conditions are undoubtedly of greater importance. Heavy precipitation and humid atmospheric conditions allow the growth of species which could not thrive on the dry chalk of south-east England. Lower temperatures in the north exclude some of the southern species but suit others adapted to a harder climate. The mild winters and early springs of the western coast result in special flowers being found which could not grow elsewhere in our country.

Where two kinds of calcareous rock outcrop close together it is usual to find that there is little, if any, difference between their flowers.

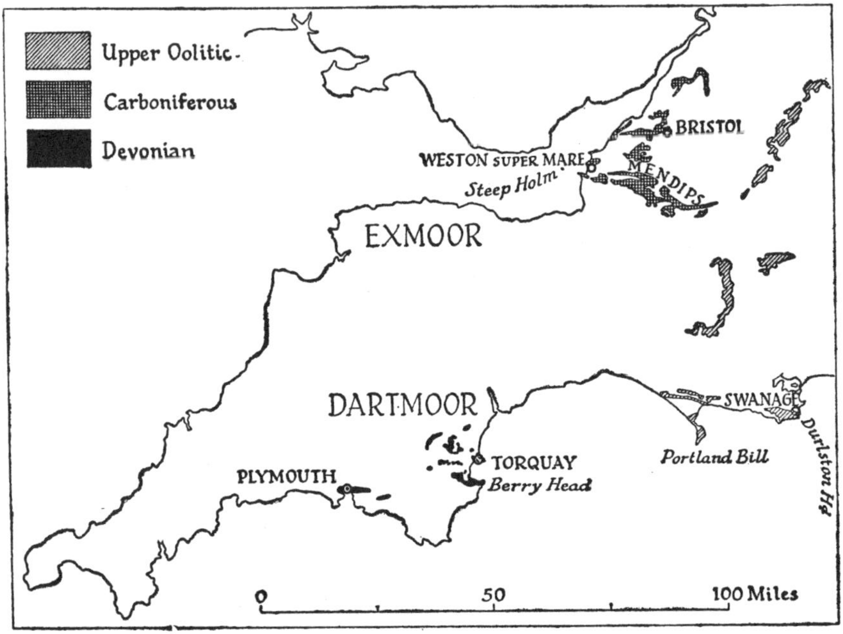

FIG. 8
South-west England

A good example is the Dorset chalk and oolite. Climate is the important factor to remember in reading the following chapters. In addition to the chalk already considered, the following limestones occur in south-west England :

Oolite—Dorset coast (see also Chapter 9).
Devonian—Torquay, Berry Head and Plymouth.
Carboniferous—Mendips and Avon Gorge.

Their floras are at their best in spring and early summer. The more humid atmosphere is indicated by the greater abundance of ferns as compared with the chalk districts.

DORSET

The presence of the sea adds a delightful variety to the flora of limestone districts just as it does to the chalk. Thus the oolite downs, which stretch for some 11 miles west from Swanage and Durlstone Head along the Dorset coast, are rich in botanical interest. Here the Early Spider Orchid, *Ophrys sphegodes*, is abundant over a limited area, and it was here that the photograph reproduced in Plate 31 (p. 142) was taken. On these downs Early Gentian, *Gentianella anglica*, is often plentiful but it varies greatly from year to year. Sometimes people fail to find it at all and suppose that it has become extinct, but a season or two afterwards it is found again in its old haunts in quantity.

The next important limestone district to the west is the Isle of Portland. In spite of generations of quarrying, this peninsula—for in spite of the name it is joined to the mainland—is a paradise for the botanist. It may be just good fortune; but all my visits here have been in perfect cloudless weather when the glorious blue of the sea and sky contrasted with the dazzling rock and showed up the beauty of the plants to perfection. Under such conditions botanizing on Portland is hot and thirsty work, and I have marvelled that plants could thrive on the dry soil which is often so shallow over the rock.

On the limestone cliffs there are many attractive maritime plants. The first to flower is Danish Scurvy-grass, *Cochlearia danica*, with mauvish blooms which open in March and April. In early summer two Spurreys, *Spergularia marina* and *S. rupicola*, make a good show. In late summer the yellow flowers of Samphire, *Crithmum maritimum*, and the reddish bracts of Portland Spurge, *Euphorbia portlandica*, brighten the cliffs.

The Portland Spurge is not a great rarity—it is, for example, quite plentiful on the mainland cliffs of Dorset. But the Portland Sea-lavender, *Limonium recurvum*, is not known to occur anywhere else in the world. It has been known to grow here since 1832 and is extremely scarce. Fortunately for the continued existence of the plant, it is not easy to distinguish from the Rock Sea-lavender, *L. binervosum*, which is more plentiful, and a great many people go to Portland and find stunted forms of the wrong plant.

The shrubs include Wayfaring Tree, Dogwood and Privet. Traveller's Joy and Madder, *Rubia peregrina*, scramble about on the rocks. On Ivy there are parasitic plants of Ivy Broomrape, *Orobanche hederae*. This has already been mentioned in connection with the Isle of Wight and it becomes plentiful in the west of England. The usual common plants of chalk turf are also here on the limestone. They include Common Rock-rose, Salad Burnet, Squinancywort, Horse-shoe Vetch, and a number of orchids such as Autumn Lady's-tresses, *Spiranthes spiralis*. In one place, on rock ledges, I have seen a scarce little Corn Salad, *Valerianella eriocarpa*.

When I first visited Portland in 1932 there were two or three fields which had not long gone out of cultivation. They had probably been ploughed during the first World War and then, as their productivity fell and the demand for food decreased, the farmer had left them to go wild. In these fields there was a lot of Slender Tare and Pheasant's Eye, and with them Cut-leaved Self-heal, *Prunella laciniata*. This was rather scarce in its normal form with pretty, cream-coloured flowers, but it was accompanied by quite a number of plants with purple flowers and cut leaves. The latter are believed to be hybrids with the Common Self-heal, *P. vulgaris*, which is abundant in the vicinity. (See also p. 113.)

The Isle of Portland was once the home of a curious industry. A substitute for arrowroot was manufactured from the underground parts of Cuckoo-pint, *Arum maculatum* (Plate 23, p. 106), and sold under the name of Portland Sago. It is said that enough was made to send to London for sale ; if so, the Cuckoo-pint must have then existed in much greater quantities than it does to-day. In any case a visitor in 1857 was able to find only two people who made it, and they had so little that they were unwilling to part with sufficient for a trial.

Torquay and Berry Head

To the west of Portland there are other places where a limestone flora is developed, but it is not until we come to the Devonian exposures about Torquay and Brixham that they are of outstanding importance. There they form the lovely cliffs of Wall's Hill and Anstey's Cove at Babbacombe, Daddyhole Plain in Torquay and Berry Head, near Brixham. Although overrun by hordes of holiday-makers every year, these still remain exceedingly interesting places to the botanist. In addition to the common limestone flowers, and some maritime species, there are a number of rarities not easily met with elsewhere.

The craggy limestone cliffs drop down to the sea in broken steps forming slopes or ledges on which flowers find a home together with occasional bushes or stunted trees. Ash is perhaps the most common

John Markham

CUCKOO PINT, *Arum maculatum*, in fruit.
The fallen leaves are those of the Whitebeam, *Sorbus aria*. Hertfordshire; September

Brian Perkins

RARE CUCKOO PINT, *Arum neglectum;* a scarce plant of partially shaded places on calcareous and other soils near the south coast. Plant from Sussex photographed in Kew Gardens; June

of the latter, but near Anstey's Cove there are a good many dwarfed trees of a rare species of Whitebeam, *Sorbus porrigentiformis*. At the top of the cliffs there is a band of broken ground merging into downland turf and then, above this, the flattish top where acid conditions tend to develop over the limestone. This leads to a queer association of calcifuges and calcicoles, of a type which will be met again and again in the wetter western parts of Britain. At Wall's Hill it is evidenced by the lime-avoiding Common Gorse and Bracken, growing mixed up with the chalk-loving Traveller's Joy and Dropwort. On the top of Berry Head I saw the same four plants growing together with the addition of the calcifuge Fine-leaved Heath, *Erica cinerea*.

On the limestone the Small Meadow-rue, *Thalictrum minus*, is fairly common. The flowers are rather small and inconspicuous, but the delicately divided leaves somewhat recall the fronds of the Maidenhair Fern, *Adiantum capillus-veneris*, which is also to be found on this coast. When I first found the Small Meadow-rue at Wall's Hill as a boy I thought there were two species present differing in the size and shape of the leaflets. Some botanists still think this may be the case at Berry Head, but it seems more likely that they are just forms of the same variable species. Another attractive plant which is locally plentiful here is the White Rock-rose, *Helianthemum apenninum*. It is much more shrubby than the common yellow-flowered species, and has small silvery leaves and very fugacious (early-falling) white petals. May is probably the best month to see it in flower, but a few blossoms appear throughout the summer and I have seen them as late as September.

On all these headlands there is plenty of Autumn Squill, *Scilla autumnalis*, with attractive purplish-blue flowers which appear in August and September. More locally, and varying a good deal in quantity from year to year, there is the little annual Small Restharrow, *Ononis reclinata*. This eluded me on all my earlier visits, and when I eventually found it I was obliged to adopt subterfuge in order to study the flower. The place was crowded with holiday-makers, and if I had stopped to look at the Restharrow in the ordinary way it would have attracted attention and perhaps endangered the plant. So I just sat down on the grass a little way away and endeavoured to act like all the other people. I ate chocolate and talked to my companion, and eventually edged along a few feet until we were seated just by the flower we wanted to look at. Then for the first time I realised what a beautiful little thing it is. Covered with viscid hairs which glisten in the sunlight, with racemes of lovely pink flowers hanging from short stalks, it was very different from what I had expected. Previously I knew it only from pictures and some half-dead plants I had seen in the Channel Isles years before. *Ononis reclinata* at its best proved to be a very lovely flower.

The Small Haresear, *Bupleurum baldense*, is equally rare. Apart from the Channel Isles, where it is plentiful, I know it elsewhere only in Sussex (see p. 69). It is fairly widespread on this Devonian limestone but extremely inconspicuous and difficult to find. After a wet spring the plants are often two or three times as large as in dry seasons, but even at their best they seldom exceed four inches in height. Honewort, *Trinia glauca*, is another local rarity (see p. 114). But perhaps the Goldilocks, *Crinitaria linosyris*, has an even more remarkable British distribution (see Distribution Map 6, p. 218) than the rarities already mentioned. It is to be found in Devon only on one short stretch of cliff and stops immediately the limestone comes to an end. Elsewhere I have seen it in small patches in Somerset and Carnarvonshire (and Glamorgan, see p. 146), and it also occurs on a limestone headland in Lancashire. Thus, it extends in a few widely-spaced colonies along the west coast of Britain. How it spread from one habitat to another is a mystery. Wind would hardly serve to disperse the seeds between the widely separated limestone headlands to which it is limited. It is one of our latest flowering plants and botanists in the north regard it as a mid-October flower, but I have seen the yellow heads fully open in Devon in the first week in September, and in Somerset even earlier. On account of the narrow foliage one of my friends calls it the Hair-leaved Goldilocks to make quite sure that there is no confusion with the woodland Buttercup, *Ranunculus auricomus*, which is also known as Goldilocks.

Stonecrops are a feature of the Devon limestone. All the cliffs have masses of the common Yellow Stonecrop, *Sedum acre*, which adds a delightful splash of colour in early summer. But in addition there are two more local species. The White Stonecrop, *Sedum album*, is abundant at Berry Head and may well be native there, although in many of its British stations it is a mere escape from cottage gardens. The Rock Stonecrop, *S. forsteranum*, is a larger species with yellow flowers and is to be found at Wall's Hill and near Berry Head.

Apart from the rarer plants, the botanist will notice that the Devon limestone flora differs considerably from that of the south-eastern chalk. This is mainly due to the presence of certain plants of western distribution in Britain and the absence of others confined to the eastern side of England. Thus the Ivy Broomrape, *Orobanche hederae*, and Madder, *Rubia peregrina*, are abundant. Both these plants are relatively common in the west but become rarer as one goes east. Then there is the curious Wall Pennywort, *Umbilicus rupestris*, which is not particular as to the kind of rock it grows on, but has a distribution rather similar to the last two species. The very fleshy round leaves have suggested its other apt name of Navelwort. Rustyback Fern, *Ceterach officinarum*, and Portland Spurge are western plants. Other species like Pellitory-of-the-Wall, *Parietaria diffusa*, attain an abundance with which the eastern botanist is unfamiliar. Yet others like Herb Robert, *Geranium robertianum* var. *hispidum*, occur as special varieties or forms.

PLYMOUTH

Of other patches of limestone in south Devon none equals the small area at Plymouth for interest and importance. To-day much of it is built over and the botanist must search for his treasure in the few open spaces still left. The amazing thing is that in spite of constant threats most of the rarities still persist.

The famous Hoe is now a well-tended public promenade with close-cut lawns and beds of garden flowers, and yet two plants are still be be found there which are believed to be relics of the long use of Plymouth as a naval base. One is a thistle, *Carduus pycnocephalus*, which grows as a weed. It is closely allied to the common Slender-headed Thistle, *C. tenuiflorus*, which has already been mentioned in connection with several coastal chalk places. From this it may be known most easily by the stem immediately below the flowers being without the strong spiny wing of the common species and by the heads being larger, but fewer in each cluster. Both thistles grow together on the Hoe. The rare one, *C. pycnocephalus*, was first noticed there in 1868 and this is the only place in Britain where it can be regarded as permanently established. Its native home is in the countries around the Mediterranean and there is little doubt that it came to us in some way connected with the Navy.

The other special plant of the Hoe is a red-flowered Bladder

Campion, *Silene vulgaris* subsp. *macrocarpa*. It may be known from the common Bladder Campion, *S. vulgaris*, by the very narrow hairless leaves as well as the dull red colour of the flowers. Like the thistle it is a Mediterranean plant, and as both are common in Malta it is a fair deduction that both may have been accidentally brought by the Navy from that island. Although it was not noticed at Plymouth until 1921, it is quite possible that it had been there much longer and passed over as a colour form of the common species.

When Sir Francis Drake played his famous game of bowls on the Hoe there must have been a great many limestone plants which have since been destroyed. It is a pleasant thought that their place has to some extent been filled by two rare and interesting plants perhaps brought in by chance by the Navy which he did so much to establish. It is even more pleasing that an enlightened City Council should take action to prevent a thistle from being eradicated from its pleasure grounds! As a result of representations from botanists the Parks and Recreation Committee of Plymouth City Council, in September, 1938, requested the City Surveyor to take the necessary steps to ensure the preservation of *Carduus pycnocephalus* in its two principal stations.

Other exposures of limestone round the town have interesting plants. In at least two places Field Eryngo, *Eryngium campestre* (Plate 16, p. 73), is still to be found. One of the places where it grows is believed to have been the one where John Ray found it on 7 July, 1662. At the other spot it grows on the top of a cliff which has Maidenhair Fern on its limestone face.

Mendips

It is nearly 90 miles from Plymouth to the Mendips, and in between there are the great forests of Dartmoor and Exmoor. These are typical acid soil districts where the vegetation is mainly composed of calcifuge species—Ling, Heath, Whortleberry, Tormentil and the like. There is little variety in the flowers and a day spent on the moors will generally produce only a relatively short list of species. They contrast sharply with the Mendips, which rise abruptly from the low-lying levels of north Somerset and extend as a great limestone ridge noted for the richness of its flora.

PLATE XIX

R. H. Hall

Woolly-headed Thistle, *Cirsium eriophorum*; Dovedale

R. H. Hall

Nottingham Catchfly, *Silene nutans*; Miller's Dale

North of Wells the Mendips are about six miles wide, rising to over 1000 feet in Blackdown, and much of the higher ground is covered with acid soil. But on the exposed limestone rock, and especially on the slopes and cliffs, in such places as Cheddar Gorge and Burrington Combe, there is a magnificent variety of calcicoles. The northern slopes are fairly well wooded but those facing south are often made up of bare rock or loose stones with only a very shallow layer of soil. West of Cheddar and Axbridge (which is the most convenient centre for exploring this district) the ridge runs through Wavering Down to the steep, stony Crook Peak. Then, across the Lox Yeo River, the Bleadon Hills and Purn Hill have a wealth of interesting plants which extend to beyond the little church at Uphill and along the steep-sided promontory of Brean Down. The small island of Steep Holm out in the Bristol Channel is an extension of the Carboniferous Limestone of the Mendips, while there are other small areas at Weston-super-Mare and to the north between Swallow Cliff and St. Thomas's Head.

Cheddar Gorge is undoubtedly the best known of all the Mendip plant localities. Every year it is visited by hundreds of thousands of tourists from all parts of Britain, and throughout the summer the mile and a half length of road which runs between mighty cliffs is thronged with people. Nevertheless it remains a first-class place for the botanist, thanks to the fact that the choicer flowers find sanctuary on the higher, inaccessible rock-ledges. From these their seeds drop down to places within the reach of visitors below, and Nature is constantly replenishing the stock which thoughtless people destroy. When I first knew Cheddar in 1923 there were few private cars and still fewer coaches and, although even then it was popular with tourists, the plants by the road were much more plentiful than they are to-day.

The beauty of the Gorge is to a considerable degree due to the strong contrasts in the colour of the vegetation. The dark green leaves of the Yew and Ivy on the almost perpendicular cliffs throw up the lighter green shivering foliage of the Ash and the lovely silvery leaves of the Whitebeams, *Sorbus spp.* To these are added in autumn the black berries of the Dogwood and Privet, and the feathery fruits of Traveller's Joy. Near the village the Wallflower, *Cheiranthus cheiri*, has escaped from gardens on to the cliffs, while Red Spur Valerian, with its rich red flowers, extends a long way up the Gorge. These are the main contributors to the colour scheme, but every month in the

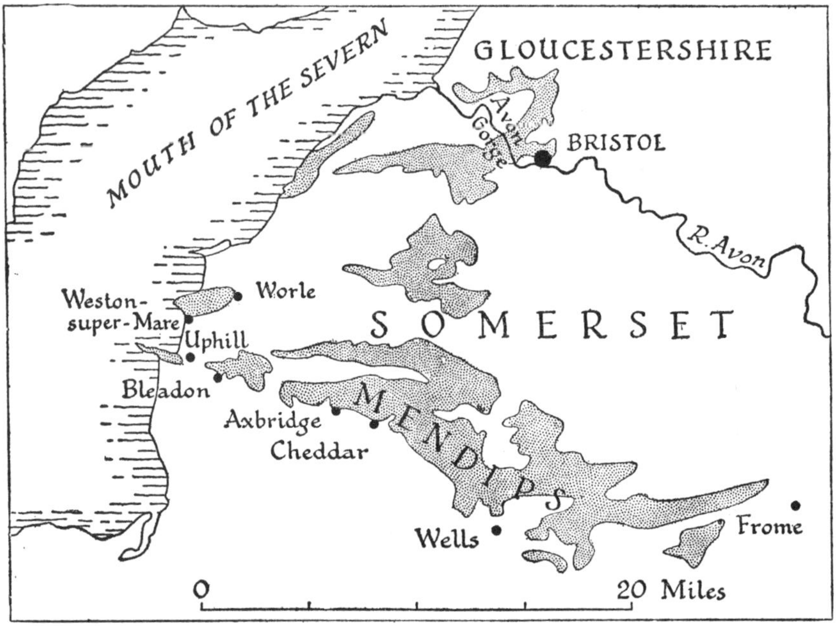

FIG. 9
The Carboniferous Limestone of the Mendips and Avon Gorge

year has its special features, and every few yards of the cliffs show a change in the flowers which make them so attractive.

The special rarity which has derived its popular name from the village is the Cheddar Pink, *Dianthus gratianopolitanus.* It has been known from " Chidderoks " for some two and a half centuries, and the Mendips still remain the only British locality for the plant. It is most attractive and well up to the standard of most Pinks grown on rockeries, and it is not surprising that selfish visitors have done their best to destroy it by stealing the roots. When I was a boy some of the villagers used to offer growing plants for sale, and I have little doubt that many of these were taken from the cliffs and not obtained by propagation in their gardens. On recent visits I am pleased to say that I have seen no signs of this nefarious trade being carried on, and it is to be hoped that a more kindly attitude towards our wild flowers has brought it to an end. Even to-day, after repeated reports that the Cheddar Pink has been threatened with extirpation, it grows sufficiently near the highway for a close-up view to be obtained through field-glasses.

Another plant which appeals to tourists is the yellow-flowered Welsh Poppy, *Meconopsis cambrica.* It grows on the screes and rocky slopes and I used to find it right down on the roadside. It is an attractive flower but it is difficult to see any sense in picking such a delicate blossom. One can, however, understand people gathering the ferny leaves of the Small Meadow-rue, *Thalictrum minus*, to go with the lovely flowers of the Ox-eye Daisy, *Chrysanthemum leucanthemum*, which occurs here in exceptional abundance.

Two plants with very fleshy leaves which are common here have already been mentioned in connection with the south Devon limestone (pp. 108, 109). They are Rock Stonecrop and Wall Pennywort. Other plants as plentiful as in Devon include Ivy Broomrape, Pellitory-of-the-Wall and Madder. The last is usually found by the sea, but it is scattered about the Somerset copses and wood borders inland on the limestone from Brent Knoll to Bristol.

These flowers are particularly characteristic of the south-west of England, but on the Mendips there is also a group of plants which are more common in the north. One is a fern, the Limestone Polypody, *Thelypteris robertiana*, which is quite plentiful on screes. Another, the Mossy Saxifrage, *Saxifraga hypnoides*, has here its most southerly station in Britain and it is necessary to go over 40 miles north to the Welsh border before finding it again. Even more interesting are two plants which show a strange partiality for places where lead has been mined. On the higher ground of the Mendips they are to be found on the edges of ancient pits and on spoil heaps which remain as relics of Roman activities. This association of Spring Sandwort, *Minuartia verna* (Plate 45, p. 194), and Alpine Penny-cress, *Thlaspi alpestre*, with old lead-mines is as well marked here as it is in Derbyshire, Yorkshire and elsewhere.

At one place high up on the top of a limestone cliff there is a colony of Cut-leaved Self-heal, *Prunella laciniata*, which now spreads over several acres. It was found here by Mrs. E. S. Gregory in 1899 and was at first taken for a white-flowered variant of Common Self-heal, *P. vulgaris*, with divided leaves. It was not until 1906 that J. W. White published it as an addition to the British flora. Since its discovery the plant has increased enormously, and recently intermediates which are probably hybrids between *P. laciniata* and *P. vulgaris* (see

p. 106) have become plentiful. It was not until at least seven years after she first detected the plant that Mrs. Gregory noticed a single small patch bearing bluish-purple flowers. Searching the field in a deluge of rain in June, 1946, I found that similar blooms, and other puzzling intermediates, had become very much more numerous since my previous visit in 1933. The inference is that during half a century Cut-leaved Self-heal has been hybridising freely with the common species, so that now the typical species with cream-coloured flowers is less plentiful than the hybrid offspring. It is at its best in late June and early July, but mutilated plants often put up late flowers again in the autumn.

Away from the tourist-haunted Gorge (which is best visited in the early morning or late evening when the crowds are absent) it is a relief to seek the quiet of some of the neighbouring woods. One of the choice plants to be found is Blue Gromwell, *Lithospermum purpuro-caeruleum.* This is a rarity with only a few localities rather widely scattered about the limestone of England and Wales (Distribution Map 10, p. 220), but in the Mendips there is probably more of it than in all the rest of Britain put together. There is also one of our rarest sedges, *Carex depauperata.* This grows along a hedge-bank which is often severely trimmed just about the time it flowers in May. Elsewhere in our islands there are a few plants in Surrey and it was formerly known near Charlton in Kent. There is a more recent record from near Holyhead and it may have grown in Cranborne Chase.

The broken ridge of limestone which runs west from Axbridge has several unusual features, but the characteristic which has always impressed me is its windyness. This might be expected where the 300 feet high Brean Down runs into the sea, but I have been astonished by the strength of the wind on hills several miles inland.

One of the most characteristic rare plants of the ridge is Honewort, *Trinia glauca,* which is remarkable amongst the Umbelliferae for having its male and female flowers separated on different plants (dioecious). The tighter male umbels can be distinguished at a glance from the longer-rayed females. The leaves are pale green, very glaucous and much divided, and their bases persist to form a fibrous jacket round the stem half hidden in the turf (Distribution Map 7, p. 219). But the plant so many botanists come to these hills to see is a grass which is not known to grow elsewhere in Britain. Dillenius's Hair-grass, *Koeleria vallesiana,* was first collected by a German botanist,

Robert Atkinson

LARGE AUTUMN GENTIAN, *Gentiana germanica;* a local flower chiefly found on the Chiltern Hills, Oxfordshire; September

J. E. Lousley

MILITARY ORCHID, *Orchis militaris;* taken by the author on the occasion of his rediscovery of this very rare orchid which was regarded as extinct in Britain. S. England; May

J. J. Dillenius (1684-1747), who made his home in Britain. His discovery was not published until 1905, a few months after Dr. G. Claridge Druce had recognised his specimen in an old herbarium and refound the grass at Uphill. The publication of a modern drawing of the plant side by side with one made nearly two centuries earlier followed one of the most remarkable discoveries in the history of British field botany. Dillenius's Hair-grass has handsome thrift-like leaves with fibrous bases which persist to form a protective and characteristic covering to the rootstock. In this it resembles Honewort with which it sometimes grows.

On two of the hills in this district the White Rock-rose, *Helianthemum apenninum*, is to be found. Elsewhere in Britain it occurs only in a few places on the Devonian limestone (see p. 107 and Distribution Map 3, p. 217). The pretty white flowers are remarkable for the sensitive movement of the stamens in response to being touched or knocked. The hybrid between the Common Rock-rose, *H. chamaecistus*, and the White Rock-rose is rare but easily recognised from its associates by the sulphur-colour of the petals. Closer examination reveals other diagnostic characters and I have seen it growing in the same place year after year.

The limestone island of Steep Holm out in the Bristol Channel is really a detached part of this same ridge. It is inaccessible to many botanists, and I have only once been able to arrange for permission to land. But the flora of about 220 species is very interesting.

The best known Steep Holm plant is the Wild Paeony, *Paeonia mascula*, which grows in two patches on the edge of a precipice. It was not discovered until about 1803, and 31 years later was nearly eradicated by a party of "scientists." If it is really native it seems remarkable that early botanists visiting the island overlooked such a conspicuous plant, and for this, and other reasons, it is thought that the Paeony was planted after the monks had left the island, and for some reason which is not easily explained. The other special plant found here is a Plantain, *Plantago sabrinae*.

About Weston-super-Mare some of the best of the limestone country has been spoiled by building. At one time there were two places where Hair-leaved Goldilocks, *Crinitaria linosyris*, could be found near the town, but it disappeared from both of them about 1856. To the great delight of local botanists, a new place on limestone rocks in Somerset was discovered early in the present century when there were about a hundred plants. So far as I could judge on my recent visits, the Goldilocks has not increased during the last 40 years, and there is much less of it than in south Devon (p. 108) or in North Wales.

The Avon Gorge

The remainder of this chapter concerns the Bristol limestone, which is perhaps the richest in all Britain in the variety of its flora and in its botanical associations. The hills (of Carboniferous Limestone) flank the city to the west and extend from Penpole Point, through King's Weston, Henbury, Durdham and Clifton Downs to the Avon, and thence through Leigh Woods, Failand and Cadbury Camp to Clevedon. The Avon divides the Gloucestershire from the Somerset limestone, and from the famous Clifton Suspension Bridge a magnificent view may be had of the fine cliffs, which attain a height of some 300 feet and are clothed with characteristic limestone vegetation.

The precipice near the bridge is known as St. Vincent's Rocks and was the subject of pilgrimage by most of our famous early botanists. In spite of extensive quarrying in past years, and of the disturbance caused when the bridge was constructed, the general vegetation is not very different from the time when William Turner (c. 1510–1568), the "Father of English Botany," found a root of Honewort, *Trinia glauca*, "at Saynt Vincentis rock a little from Bristow." Indeed it is surprising how few of the plants found by the long series of important visitors in the past four centuries have disappeared, though some of them are now exceedingly scarce. There was no road or railway through the Gorge in the times of Johnson, Parkinson, Merrett, Ray, Dillenius, Banks or Curtis, but the flora is very much the same as when they came here and to the botanist this is holy ground. It is hoped that the reader will treat it with the respect it deserves.

The ways of botanists have not changed a great deal through the ages. Just as to-day we carefully consult the records already printed before visiting a new place, so our forerunners looked up such books as were available to them. Information about the exact spots where interesting plants could be found was passed on by letter or word of mouth, as is done by modern flower-hunters, and so each visiting botanist was supplied with information about what had already been found and he did his best to add fresh records. There is no better example of the manner in which knowledge of the flora of a district has been built up through the centuries than the Avon Gorge. Almost every competent visitor has added fresh plants to the list until, in recent times, additions have of necessity become less frequent. Sometimes mistakes have been made and then time has been spent on putting them right. One can sympathise with Gerard, who wrote in his Herbal of 1597 : "Bastard Mewe, or *Meum*, groweth in the waste mountaines of Italie, and the Alps, and (as it hath been told me) upon Saint Vincents rocke by Bristow, where I spent two daies to seeke it, but it was not my hap to find it, therefore I make some doubt of the truth thereof." Parkinson was given the same information, but there is little doubt that barren plants of Honewort in the early flowering stage were mistaken for the continental *Meum mutellina.* One can only hope that Gerard's two days' search was rewarded with other interesting plants and that he did not count them as wasted !

Undoubtedly Clifton Suspension Bridge is the best place to get a general view of the Avon Gorge (Plate XV, p. 74). Looking downstream, the high ground above the crags to the right is Clifton Down, continuing on to Durdham Down. The cliffs on this, the Gloucestershire side, are broken by the " Great Fault " where the displacement of the strata brings Millstone Grit, shales and Dolomitic Conglomerate to the surface, and the gradual slope is made use of for the Bridge Valley Road which descends the cliff. The brief change from limestone at the fault can be picked out immediately by the different vegetation. From a distance the White Birches, *Betula pendula*, are conspicuous—at closer quarters one finds a wealth of Blackberries, *Rubus spp.*, which are scarce on the cliffs either side, and also such small calcifuges as Birds-foot, *Ornithopus perpusillus*, and Ciliate Pearlwort, *Sagina ciliata.* Looking to the left from the bridge there is a good view of the well-known Leigh Woods on the Somerset side.

Most of the trees, shrubs and climbers on the limestone are those familiar on the chalk. Holly, Yew, Wayfaring Tree, Hazel, Dogwood, Spindle, Ivy and Traveller's Joy are here, adding a variety of colouring to the cliffs at all times of the year. But Ash largely takes the place of Beech, which is so characteristic of the south-eastern downs, and the White Beam, *Sorbus aria*, is accompanied by related species which do not occur in the east. Ferns are relatively plentiful : Hartstongue, *Phyllitis scolopendrium*, is common, while there is a good deal of Rustyback, *Ceterach officinarum*, and Wall-rue, *Asplenium ruta-muraria*, on the walls and rocks. No doubt the humidity of the air facilitates the germination of their spores and development of their fronds. The frequency of Madder, scrambling up amongst the bushes like an enormous Cleavers, and of Ivy Broomrapes, are other signs of a western flora.

Many of the choicest rarities have retreated to inaccessible ledges on the cliffs. The most conspicuous of these is perhaps the Bloody Cranesbill, *Geranium sanguineum* (Plate 39, p. 174), which is a glorious sight in June. The flowers are as large as a half-crown, and as the plant grows in big patches and blooms profusely it can be seen from a distance. The Western Spiked Speedwell, *Veronica hybrida* (Distribution Map 11, p. 221), is a scarcer but almost equally beautiful plant. It grows about eighteen inches high and has dense spikes of flowers of a glorious intense blue. Fortunately the places where it grows are extremely difficult to reach and most of the plants are absolutely safe from marauders.

Other interesting plants grow on the screes, which are like miniature rock-gardens in early spring. Some of these are in good flower almost before winter has passed, but I hardly realised how precocious they could be until 3 March, 1946, when I happened to have a few hours to spare after visiting Bristol for a broadcast. On this day snow rested on the tops of all the hills, and yet Rock Pepperwort, *Hornungia petraea* (Distribution Map 2, p. 216), had formed fruits as well as flowers, and Bristol Rock Cress, *Arabis stricta*, and Spring Cinquefoil, *Potentilla tabernaemontani*, were almost in bloom.

Rock Pepperwort is a tiny Crucifer with very small, narrow, white petals, and divided leaves with a faint odour of cress. Under the lens it is seen to be clothed in short, scattered hairs of which those on the stem are star-like. Bristol Rock Cress is also a Crucifer and one of our rarest and most local British plants. It is almost restricted to the two sides of the Avon Gorge. The flowers are cream-coloured, and the rosette of deep green leaves is clothed and ciliated with stiff hairs. Spring Cinquefoil is a much more widespread plant, both here and in Britain generally. Individually the flowers are not unlike those of Tormentil, *Potentilla erecta* (a plant of acid soils), but they are a little larger and produced freely from a mat of stems which hardly rises above the surface of the ground. The general effect is very attractive and I gladly give *Potentilla tabernaemontani* (obtained from a botanic garden) a place on my London rockery, where it has flowered as early as the first days of January. It is so true a calcicole that J. W. White wrote in his Bristol Flora that " Its localities form the links of a geographical chain connecting the limestone outcrops of the district."

Less conspicuous, but interesting on account of its restricted distribution, the Dwarf Sedge, *Carex humilis*, is just as precocious in its flowering. The flowering spikes appear in March and April half hidden in the foliage.

The Avon Gorge is the home of Round-headed Garlic, *Allium sphaerocephalon*, which is now one of our very rarest British plants on the score of numbers of individuals. Elsewhere it occurs only in Jersey (where it is part of the French rather than the British flora), and in the Gorge it is restricted to two or three small colonies. One of these is fortunately practically inaccessible. The flowers are dark purplish-red in tight heads which terminate tough leafless stems about eighteen inches to two feet in height. Small boys scrambling about the screes and rocks find these a great temptation and some plants get torn up by the roots in wanton destruction. In the places which can be reached it is to be feared that Round-headed Garlic is a doomed plant.

In addition to the native species the rocks owe a good deal in the way of interest and beauty to a number of introduced plants which have made their home there. The Wallflower, *Cheiranthus cheiri*, and Snapdragon, *Antirrhinum majus*, have long been thoroughly established on St. Vincent's Rocks. There are also masses of Alexanders, *Smyrnium olusatrum*, which is suspected of ancient introduction from its use as a pot-herb, and Red Valerian, *Centranthus ruber*. A more recent arrival is the beautiful purple-flowered *Buddleja davidii*, which is such an attraction to Red Admirals and other butterflies. It is now abundant on waste ground in Bristol (as in many other towns) and has established itself from wind-borne seeds in various places on the rocks of the Avon Gorge. A well-drained soil with lime seems to be the habitat it requires.

Across the Avon on the Somerset side, Leigh Woods cover a stretch of rugged country and come right down to the river. They have suffered too much interference at the hand of man to be regarded as a natural bit of woodland, but are interesting on account of the wide variety of trees represented. Hence, as White points out, Leigh Woods offer " a foliage of singularly varied tint, from that of the darkest Yew to the pale light green of Lime and Oak, or silver of the Whitebeam." The local Small-leaved Lime, *Tilia cordata*, is abundant, and here sometimes reaches a height of 60 feet. When coppiced the strong stump-shoots bear monster leaves which disagree with the book characters and deceive even experienced botanists. In addition to the Whitebeams, *Sorbus aria*, there are a few trees of the allied *Sorbus bristoliensis* recently described by the late Mr. A. J. Wilmott of the British Museum (Natural History).

There is considerable difference between the flowers of the two sides of the Avon Gorge, and I think this may be partly explained by contrasts in gradient and direction of exposure. The rocks on the Gloucestershire side are steep and face west, while those of Leigh Woods are more gradual with a deeper soil which faces east. Whatever the cause, the fact remains that Rock Pepperwort is strangely rare on the western side, while Fingered Sedge, *Carex digitata*, which is found in some quantity in Leigh Woods, is rarer on the Gloucestershire side. Similarly with a number of other rarities ; those which like rocks and open spaces are most plentiful on the Bristol side of the Gorge. An example is Curtis's Mouse-ear Chickweed, *Cerastium pumilum*, which grows to perfection only in damp, mild springs and is usually daintily flushed with a characteristic reddish hue. This is only to be found in small quantity below the woods, but on the opposite side it is often abundant on the rocks and by path-sides.

The Bristol limestone has a unique flora so rich that some species have had to be omitted on account of space. It includes plants which are to be found nowhere else on the mainland of Britain, and nature has provided a terrain which has preserved them from destruction in spite of the proximity of a large city to the finest habitats. Every effort must be made to hand on the legacy intact for the study and enjoyment of future generations.

CHAPTER 9

THE JURASSIC LIMESTONES

THE ROCKS of the Jurassic system extend for nearly 300 miles across England from Portland Bill in Dorset to north Yorkshire. They are exposed as a varied series of sands, clays and limestones, and they change in character so frequently that it is difficult to match up the particular beds of one county with those of others. Where they give rise to calcareous soils the flora is often of great interest.

In Britain the Jurassic system includes Lias and the Oolites. The former is mainly a clay formation, but in the south the Lower Lias includes alternations of shale and limestone. On the coast of Glamorgan and in Somerset and Dorset these are exposed and have a calcicole flora.

The Oolites are of far greater botanical importance. They include limestones of many types. Some of them, like the famous Portland and Bath building stones, are made up of small rounded grains resembling the roe of a fish. Hence the name " oolite " or egg-stone from the Greek *oos*, egg, and *lithos*, stone. Others are thin bedded limestones, like the Stonesfield " Slate." Some are very impure, though many such give rise to excellent soils of which the Cornbrash is a notable example.

Besides the varied nature of the Jurassic rocks there is the complication of drift. Towards the north this becomes increasingly common and important. In Yorkshire and Lincolnshire much of the Oolite is covered with glacial Boulder Clay which has been brought down by the ice. This in turn may be locally calcareous. Besides these complications it is necessary to remember that the calcium carbonate may have been leached out of the soil. Only the places where the limestone flora is best developed can be covered in a limited survey.

The Oolite includes the following four areas of special interest to botanists:

1. Parts of the Dorset coast, including Portland Bill. Because this district is particularly noted for maritime plants, it has been described in the last chapter (see pp. 104-106).
2. The Cotswolds and their extension eastwards into Oxfordshire —mostly upland country.
3. The Oolite district about Stamford, extending into Rutland, Northamptonshire and Lincolnshire—mostly agricultural country.
4. The hinterland of Scarborough and Whitby in the North Riding—the limestone edges of hilly northern moors.

The Lias flanks the Oolite on the west throughout the whole of its course.

On account of its geographical position the Jurassic forms a link between the limestone floras of the west and east and also between those of the south and north. There is a gradual transition in species of restricted distribution from the southern and western types of Dorset, to the eastern types of Stamford, and the northern of Yorkshire. Two rare plants are in Britain almost restricted to the Oolite—Downy Woundwort, *Stachys germanica*, and Perfoliate Penny-cress, *Thlaspi perfoliatum*. The Wasp Orchid, *Ophrys trollii*, only occurs elsewhere on the Carboniferous Limestone near Bristol. Pasque Flower, *Pulsatilla vulgaris*, Woolly-headed Thistle, *Cirsium eriophorum* var. *britannicum*, Yellow Star-of-Bethlehem, *Gagea lutea*, and Purple Milk-vetch, *Astragalus danicus*, are more frequent on the Oolite than on other formations.

Two other special features must be pointed out. In the first place, the habitats described in this chapter are not well-known holiday districts. Apart from the Cotswolds, which are fairly popular with walkers and motorists, and the district near the Yorkshire coast, most of the Oolite country is quiet, and the scenery, though pleasing, has very few outstanding features. Secondly, this chapter deals with inland districts where maritime plants are absent. In these two respects there is a great contrast with the south-west limestones, and the comparison is not entirely to the disadvantage of the less well-known Oolite.

Robert Atkinson

LIZARD ORCHID, *Himantoglossum hircinum;* the largest and one of the rarest of our downland orchids. Bedfordshire; July

Brian Perkins

GOG MAGOG HILLS, CAMBRIDGESHIRE

The downland turf has long been ploughed except on the golf-course and the broad verges by this ancient track. August

The Limestones round Bath

After leaving the Purbeck and Portland cliffs there are no places of exceptional interest to the botanist on the Jurassic south of the Bath area. In the intervening country there are a few stations for rare calcicoles, such as the Germander Whitlow-grass, *Draba muralis*, in a quarry near Beaminster, but the first important plant is the handsome Woolly-headed Thistle (Plate XIX, p. 110), which is so abundant locally on the Lias and Oolite about Bristol and Bath.

There are few finer plants in the British flora than this. The height is often as much as five feet, with a stout woolly stem, and leaves eighteen inches long with narrow segments ending in stout spines. The flowers are reddish purple in heads some two or more inches across, protected by spiny webbed bracts so that it is almost impossible to pick them without drawing blood. "Friar's Crowns," the earliest botanists called them. No doubt the thistle is a nuisance to the farmer like its allies, but since the roots do not creep it can be eradicated by persistent use of the scythe. It has been shown that our British *C. eriophorum* belongs to a special subspecies which Petrak named *britannicum*, to be known from the eight or so other continental subspecies chiefly by the characteristic form of the bracts (phyllaries). Our own particular plant does not cross the Channel and its nearest neighbour in France stretches right across Europe to overlap the area of the Russian subspecies.

Fond as I am of the sight of this handsome thistle, I feel that any one who makes use of its prickly buds and stems for culinary purposes can hardly be begrudged his prize; but the same cannot be said of the Spiked Star-of-Bethlehem, *Ornithogalum pyrenaicum*. This is locally plentiful in open woods and on banks from near Frome to the hills about Bath, and in June it puts up spikes of greenish flowers bordered with white inside. It is not particularly beautiful, but I deplore the trade in the young flower-buds which are sold as "Bath asparagus." The unexpanded spikes are cut off and tied up in bundles and are said to be very little inferior to the cultivated vegetable. To what extent the traffic continues I do not know, but it seems to me that there is less of the plant in the woods near Bath than one would expect from accounts given in books.

Another member of the Liliaceae which is perhaps more frequent in the woods about Bath than anywhere else in Britain (and it ranges

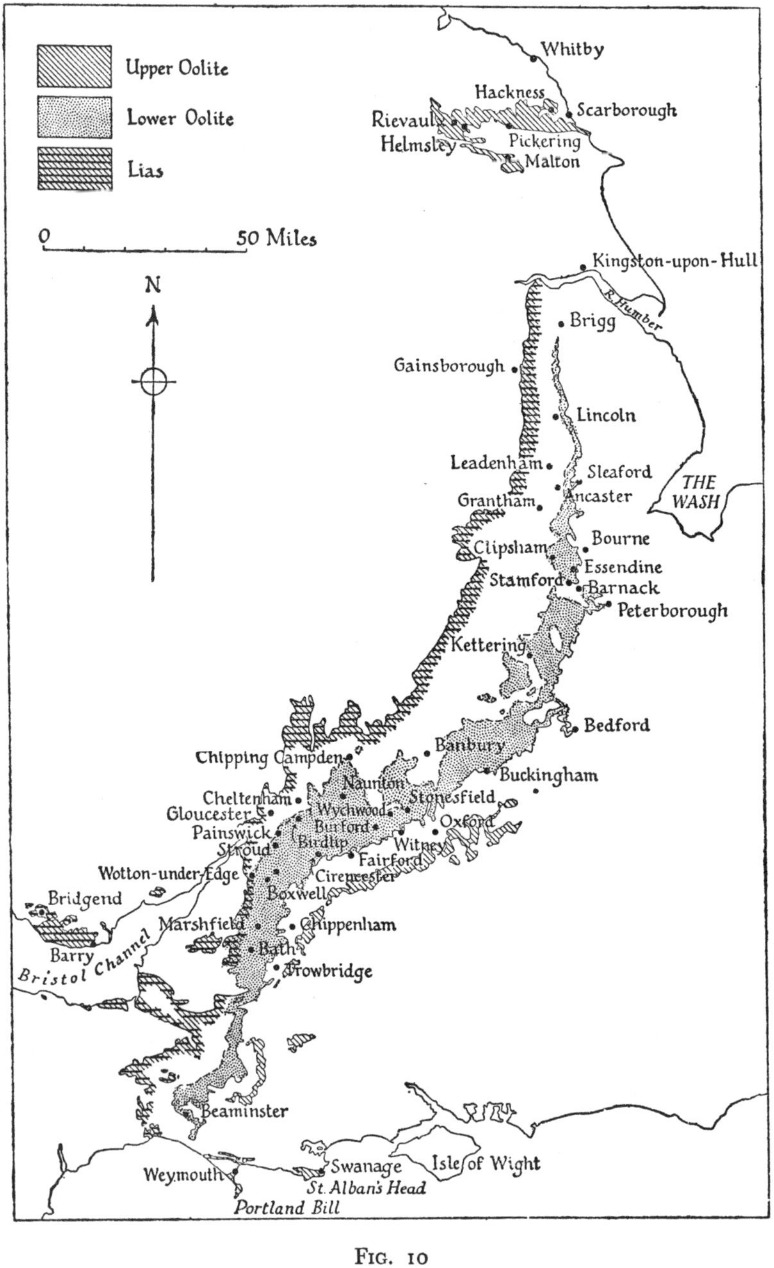

FIG. 10
Jurassic exposures of England and Wales

widely over limestone and other soils) is the Yellow Star-of-Bethlehem, *Gagea lutea*. Its yellow stars appear in March and April, but only a very small proportion of the plants flower. This has been my experience in all the places where I have seen it, and often many thousands of young plants may be seen to every mature specimen in bloom. It seems that many individuals of *Gagea* are fated to remain almost permanently in a juvenile state and then only the practised eye can distinguish them from young Bluebells by the number of nerves on the hooded-ended leaves. These juveniles cannot be true seedlings, for ripe seed seems to be seldom produced in this country, and I think they arise by offset bulbils from the parent bulb. Yellow Star-of-Bethlehem grows in a few places on the chalk but it thrives best on the calcareous red soils produced over limestone.

The flora of woods on the Oolite is sometimes very similar to that of copses on the North Downs. This was shown in a very striking manner when I listed down the trees and shrubs in the place where I used to know Hairy Spurge, *Euphorbia pilosa*. Although the woodland is in part planted it consists predominantly of calcicole species. The Spurge has been recorded from here for over three centuries, but in recent years it has got scarcer and scarcer and is probably now extinct. At any rate the single plant I photographed in 1937 could not be found when I looked for it nine years later.

Immediately north of Bath there is a lot of pleasant Oolite country. The sides of some of the valleys are composed of limestones, the rest being of the intervening clays. However, extensive spreads of calcareous downwash cover the slopes and hence there is no anomaly in calcicoles growing on soil over the clay outcrops. As an example of the open type of valley, one near Marshfield in Gloucestershire may be instanced. Here the soil is only slightly calcareous and there is a fine display of the Woolly-headed Thistle accompanied by Stemless Thistle, *Cirsium acaulon*, and a good deal of Bee Orchid, *Ophrys apifera*, and Pyramidal Orchid, *Anacamptis pyramidalis*. Along the edges of the field there is the pretty Meadow Cranesbill, *Geranium pratense*, growing here, as on the Wiltshire chalk (see p. 85), in the driest situations. But the real reason why I like visiting this particular valley is to see a scarce alien pea which rejoices in the name *Tetragonolobus maritimus*. It is rather like an outsized Common Birds-foot Trefoil, *Lotus corniculatus*, with the wings of the flowers cowslip-yellow, the standard primrose-yellow, and the small keel whitish. The plant was found at Marshfield in

1924 but the owners of the land said that they had then known it for about twenty years. In 1946 I estimated that it was spread over about four acres and that it had increased considerably since my previous visit eight years earlier. This is, I think, its best locality, but *T. maritimus* also occurs on the Berkshire and Hampshire chalk and in a few other places.

The Cotswolds

The term Cotswolds (or Cotteswolds) is applied to the whole range of Oolite hills from where they rise from the valley of the Avon, near Bath, to 54 miles to the north-east, where they sink into the Midland Plain near Chipping Campden. In places they are as much as 30 miles broad, but most of the finest places for scenery and plants are on, or near, the steep western escarpment, where the limestone is near the surface. Here jagged promontories are formed jutting out into the Lias of the Severn valley.

When ecologists or field botanists refer loosely to the Cotswolds in the course of conversation they usually think of the lovely beech woods about Birdlip, Cranham and Painswick in the centre of the range. Here the general flora is very similar to that of woods on the North and South Downs. One of the most obvious differences is the abundance of a fine Hawkweed, *Hieracium exotericum*, which, as J. W. Haines has written, forms " ladders of gold " on the steeper banks with the abundance of its yellow flowers in June. Also there is a good deal of the waxy blooms and thick leaves of Lesser Wintergreen, *Pyrola minor*, and graceful spikes of Wood Barley, *Hordelymus europaeus*, are found as frequently as under some of the beeches of the Chilterns. As a link between some of the northern limestones, where it is fairly plentiful, and the Bath district and Mendips, where it is rare and untypical, the Angular Solomon's-seal, *Polygonatum odoratum*, occurs in several spots. It flowers best when the woods have been cut, and I have seen whole beds of this charming flower within a few yards of a busy road.

But the queen of this part of the Cotswolds is the Red Helleborine, *Cephalanthera rubra*. It is one of the most elusive of British orchids, and many wild flower hunters have spent a surprising amount of time and money in its quest. One of my friends even received a cable from

Brian Perkins

A CAMBRIDGESHIRE CHALK-PIT showing the shallow layer of soil above the chalk. The Woolly-headed Thistle, *Cirsium eriophorum*, is plentiful in the foreground. August

Brian Perkins

FIELD FLEAWORT *Senecio integrifolius;* a local flower of chalk and limestone.
Cambridgeshire; June

a lady in Monte Carlo who was anxious to fly over to see it! Records for the Red Helleborine, spread over the last century and a half, extend over a great many of the beechwoods from Nailsworth to Birdlip, but it has seldom been seen in quantity and flowering is extremely erratic. Probably plants still exist in quite a number of places, but blooms appear only when the trees are not too dense to exclude the light. Even then they often get picked before the botanist sees them.

I have only seen flowers on a few occasions, and one colony has hardly bloomed since 1936, although plenty of leaves appear every year. The foliage is a little narrower and more pointed than is usual in the Large White Helleborine, *C. damasonium*, but the difference is so slight that in the absence of the handsome red flowers I could not distinguish it from the common species with confidence. Fortunately for its continued existence, the Red Helleborine spreads underground so that little colonies forming rough circles of tufts of barren leaves are formed. If this were not the case it would probably soon become extinct.

Although this district is best known for its beechwoods, the Oolite grassland is also of interest. It has a general resemblance to that of the chalk described in earlier chapters. The close grazing of sheep leads to the formation of similar short, dense turf. Where there is less grazing, taller coarser grasses such as Tor Grass form rough herbage. The most obvious difference in the larger flowers between the Cotswolds and south-eastern England is in the frequency of the Meadow Cranesbill, *Geranium pratense*, which is hardly known on the North and South Downs.

There are also differences in the orchids. Musk, *Herminium monorchis*, and Frog, *Coeloglossum viride*, are both finer and more plentiful than they are in the south-east. Wasp Orchid, *Ophrys trollii* (Plate 33, p. 146), has its headquarters here. It is closely allied to the Bee Orchid, *O. apifera* (Plate 6, p. 15), of which, indeed, some botanists treat it only as a variety or a form. The differences in the flowers should be quite clear if the two coloured plates are compared. In the Wasp the lip is drawn out into a long, sharp-pointed triangle with the tip not reflexed and with elongated dark brown blotches on a yellow background. The Bee Orchid, on the other hand, has a round lip with a small reflexed tip and very different (though variable) markings. So far as I know, the true *Ophrys trollii* in this country is restricted to Gloucestershire and perhaps the extreme west of Oxfordshire, though a variation of *O. apifera* with a pointed lip has sometimes done duty for it elsewhere. A clearly defined geographical range such as this is one of the qualifications of a species. I have seen the Wasp Orchid growing near Bristol and in two places on the Cotswolds accompanied by Bee Orchids. Here it was remarkably uniform, and showed no tendency to form intermediates towards its near ally.

This part of the Cotswolds is most easily explored from Stroud, Gloucester or Cheltenham. Farther south there is an area which is far less accessible, and unless you have the use of a car or bicycle its investigation will involve very long walks in country which tourists seldom visit. I have always had the feeling that fresh and unknown treasures might reward the labour of a botanist who searched this district diligently, and this theory is encouraged by the fact that it was not until 1897 that the Alpine Woundwort, *Stachys alpina*, was found for the first time in Britain in an out-of-the-way place near Wotton-under-Edge. This plant is rather like a stout Hedge Woundwort, *S. sylvatica*, but clothed with white hairs, and with blunter leaves with less sharp teeth. According to Cedric Bucknall, who discovered it, Alpine Woundwort was first found in undergrowth where a wood had been cleared, but two of the places where I have seen it are in hedgebanks and the third out in the open in limestone grassland. The locality is said to extend over about two square miles, and it seems remarkable that the plant, which is nearly a yard in height, was overlooked for so long. In the only other British locality—a steep limestone bank in Denbighshire—it was discovered even more recently, although hundreds of cars pass within a few yards of it every day!

In contrast, the Box trees at Boxwell have a very long botanical history. John Ray gives the record as far back as 1695, on the authority of John Aubrey, in the second edition of the famous Camden's *Britannia*. When I visited the place in June, 1946, I found an almost pure wood of *Buxus sempervirens* stretching for over half a mile on the north side of the valley, with other Box trees in mixed woodland near. Fringing the carriage drive to Boxwell Court some of the trees are trimmed into a neat hedge, but the great majority are obviously self-sown and some of them grow out of solid limestone rock. Having regard to the antiquity of the place names, and the early botanical records, there can be no real doubt that the Box is native here and in other places a little way away towards Alderley. Apart from Box Hill in Surrey, it is the largest colony of the tree in Britain.

It is over 30 miles from Wotton-under-Edge to the north Cotswolds where the Oolite makes a curve northwards. The change is essentially one from a soft landscape relieved with plenty of trees to bleak open country. I have never botanized on the steep west-facing escarpment of this part of the Cotswolds but, judging from the plants recorded, it must have an interesting limestone flora. The same applies to Bredon Hill, an isolated Oolite outlier between Tewkesbury and Evesham. The places I do know are on the undulating plateau. One very famous spot is near to the boundary of Worcestershire—so near that the botanists of that county regard it as their own although they have plenty of other[1] enclaves set in this part of Gloucestershire. (Botanists still base their records on boundaries set out over 100 years ago.) It is a piece of ground which seems to have been quarried all over many centuries ago and left studded with pits and mounds now grassed over. This rough land is grazed by cows, and most of it is short downland turf full of the usual attractive common plants.

But the botanist does not travel 90 miles from London on a bitterly cold April morning to see common plants. On such a day, when snow threatened, the Pasque Flower, *Pulsatilla vulgaris*, was just coming into flower. It was similar weather when I visited it near Cirencester several years earlier, and these localities must about represent its western limits in Britain (Distribution Map 1, p. 216). The story runs that the places where it grows mark the limits of the invasion of the Danes and that it sprung up where their blood had been spilled—hence the name " Dane's Blood." It may be left to historians to decide whether the known distribution is in keeping with the legend but I fancy that it will be found not very wide of the mark. The finest of our British anemones grows with the Field Fleawort, *Senecio integrifolius* (Plate 30, p. 127), and the slender little Fine-leaved Sandwort, *Minuartia hybrida*, is found close by. In late summer the Woolly-headed Thistle makes a fine show there.

The plant which was the main object of my long April journey was already in full flower and even forming fruit. Perfoliate Pennycress, *Thlaspi perfoliatum*, is a very local species and (with the exception of railway sides in Wiltshire, Buckinghamshire, Middlesex etc., restricted

[1] For botanical purposes enclaves are regarded as forming part of the surrounding county.

to the Gloucestershire Oolite and the adjoining counties. Except to the botanist, it is a very ordinary looking little Crucifer. The flowers are small and white, in a close head, and are succeeded by notched fruits rather like those of the Shepherd's Purse, which is such a nuisance as a garden weed. The leaves are waxy grey-green (glaucous) and those on the stem have lobes which project round it. In these pits (I dare not indicate the locality more precisely) the Perfoliate Penny-cress is small and only a couple of inches or so high, but on more recent workings half a mile away it grows six inches tall.

The district just described is a northern tongue of the Oolite. To the south the main mass round Cirencester and Northleach is the headquarters of the rare Downy Sedge, *Carex filiformis*, which grows here in dry limestone turf which has evaded the plough. It was first found in Britain in the last year of the eighteenth century, in wet meadows by the Thames at Marston Meysey in Wiltshire, where I saw it in 1936. In Surrey and in Middlesex I have seen it in similar damp places, and it is in wet pasture at Otmoor in Oxfordshire. These habitats seem a surprising contrast to the dry limestone turf of the Cotswolds until one remembers that they are all fed with water which drains down from calcareous districts (see p. 87). It is probable that *Carex filiformis* demands a fairly high lime content in the soil and, provided this is present, it is immaterial whether it is wet or dry. Another plant worth noticing is Cut-leaved Germander, *Teucrium botrys* (see p. 62), which grows on a bank above a railway tunnel. I have looked for it twice without success, but as it is said to vary a good deal from year to year, it seems likely that I chose the wrong seasons.

The Oxfordshire Limestones

Oxfordshire appears to be one of the most calcareous counties in the whole of England. The northern part is on Oolite and Lias which give rise locally to calcareous soils. In the south there is the chalk of the Chilterns, which had already been considered (see pp. 88-93). Looking at the geological map, it is easy to forget that there is also a considerable amount of drift and much variation in the soils originating from the Oolite and Lias, so that limestone plants are in fact more or less absent from considerable areas.

The western side of the county is a continuation of the Cotswolds

It has similar walls, stone-built villages and similar wild flowers. The Downy Sedge, *Carex filiformis*, so named on account of the very downy fruits, is found just within the county on a patch of downland turf by a roadside. Here it grows with such representative limestone plants as Hairy Violet, Common Rock-rose and Wayfaring Tree. Dr. Druce says there is also a profusion of Purple Milk-vetch, *Astragalus danicus*, Horse-shoe Vetch, *Hippocrepis comosa*, and Chalk Milkwort, *Polygala calcarea*. The flora of this place is just a relic sample of the floral riches of Burford Downs before they were enclosed and the ancient turf with its rarities broken up under the plough. We can picture in our minds the scene in about the year 1760 when the Reverend John Lightfoot came riding out from Oxford, where he was engaged in botanical work. By the road from Burford to Cirencester he records Pasque Flower, " in great plenty." In the same place there was Field Fleawort and Purple Milk-vetch. On the road from Witney to Burford, " a little beyond the fourth Milestone on the right Hand," he got Perfoliate Penny-cress growing with Early Spider Orchid, *Ophrys sphegodes*. Doubtless there were other interesting plants also, but none of these is to be found there now.

Some four miles north of Witney is the Forest of Wychwood—the relic of an immense Royal demesne. On " solid " geological maps it is marked as Oolite and indeed it is the *locus classicus* of the hard flag-like limestone which William Smith called " Forest Marble." Nevertheless large areas of the woodland are on clays, while some of the higher ground is covered with High Level gravels where the flora is almost like that of a heath. The limestone flora is best developed in open parts where the rock is nearest to the surface of the ground. Such places are the home of Meadow Clary, *Salvia pratensis*, which extends eastwards from here for several miles. It is one of our most beautiful English wild flowers, with large blossoms of glorious blue, very like those of garden Sage. Apart from the old locality in Kent (see p. 58), Oxfordshire is the county where it has the oldest botanical history, having been known for well over two centuries. In addition to the Wychwood district it still occurs in abundance on the side of a busy road near Middleton Stoney. When I saw it there in 1935, with motors dashing past, I could not help wondering whether the plant suffered more from the dust thrown up from the faster modern transport than from the slower eighteenth-century vehicles on the then unmetalled surface of the road. At Finstock, on the borders of Wychwood, my friend, Dr. R. C. L. Burges, showed me the pretty white-flowered variation which has been known there for many years.

The Forest is also a home of Green-leaved Houndstongue, *Cynoglossum germanicum*, which is one of the rarest and most elusive of Oxfordshire limestone flowers. The locality is an old one but very few modern botanists have had the luck to stumble on it, though A. W. Graveson was able to produce a photograph as evidence of his good fortune a few years ago. The Green-leaved Houndstongue is recorded from as many as nineteen British vice-counties, but so far as I am aware the limited district in Surrey mentioned on page 64 is the only one where it is to be found regularly in real quantity.

Another erratic plant is Downy Woundwort, *Stachys germanica.* It has been found over a wide area of the Oolite from Minster Lovell and Wychwood in the west to just east of the Cherwell, but in most localities it comes and goes in a most baffling manner. Every now and then, following disturbance of the ground or cutting down of bushes, fine colonies of Downy Woundwort appear and then often for many many years no more plants are seen at that place. Perhaps years afterwards, the news goes round among botanists that it is back in its old haunts! *Stachys germanica* may fairly be claimed as Oxfordshire's own peculiar rarity. There are a few records for other counties, but they have all been of a temporary nature and it is only on this stretch of Oolite that the species can be regarded as undoubtedly native.

Perfoliate Penny-cress is again to be found in the district immediately east of Wychwood. Here it is getting towards the eastern limit of its main area in Britain. In one place I have seen it in an old quarry in the Lower Oolite which was worked by the Romans. The rejected slabs of limestone lie about in heaps all along the side of the valley and afford a most interesting habitat for rare plants. Here in spring the red-flushed Curtis's Mouse-ear Chickweed, *Cerastium pumilum*, and the rare and usually coastal grass, *Poa bulbosa*, discovered in 1938 by J. P. M. Brenan, are to be found. In summer there are many attractive limestone flowers, including Narrow-leaved Everlasting Pea, *Lathyrus sylvestris*, which sprawls over the hillocks. A mile and a half south-east of this quarry is one of the best places in the district for the Yellow Star-of-Bethlehem, *Gagea lutea* (see p. 125). I saw about fifty blooms there in March, 1946, which is an excellent score for this shy-flowering plant.

NORTHAMPTONSHIRE

Throughout the Cotswolds and Oxfordshire the Great Oolite can be traced by the characteristic stone buildings and walls and by the quarries from which the material for their construction has been obtained. The same applies in its course across the north of Buckinghamshire and the adjoining parts of Northamptonshire, though its influence on the vegetation is much obscured by the presence of drift.

The limestone of Northamptonshire is at its best in the extreme north of the county. Over the greater part of the area coloured for Oolite on the map very few rarities are to be found, though where it runs over the Bedfordshire border near Rushden there is a good colony of the richly coloured Crested Cow-wheat, *Melampyrum cristatum.* In the north there is a rich district roughly bounded by the triangle enclosed by lines drawn between Stamford, Peterborough and Wakerley, and extending north across the county boundary into Rutland. Within this triangle there are fine old woods such as Bedford Purlieus and Wakerley Great Wood, and quarries and patches of aboriginal turf at Helpston, Barnack, Southorpe, Collyweston and many roadsides. Some good ground—such as Wittering Heath—has been destroyed, but much remains and the district deserves to be better known to botanists than appears to be the case.

One very fascinating place—I must not specify its location precisely—consists of some 60 acres of alternating pits and mounds where ancient quarrying operations dug out limestone. Working has long since stopped, and a close limestone turf formed over the earth to produce " as fine a place for variety of rare Plants as ever I beheld." Dr. Bowles wrote these words three centuries ago[1] and, even if changes in the flora have led to a loss of a few of the rarities, his words ring very true to-day.

Perhaps the chief glory of this place is the Pasque Flower. The local schoolmaster told me that there was far less of it in recent years owing to selfish people carrying off roots in their cars. Nevertheless I have never seen so much anywhere else, though I must admit that Dr. Bowles' statement that " there are tens of thousands of these plants " might seem an exaggeration to-day. When I was there in June, 1948, most of the plants had put up their lovely feathery fruits, but there were still a few blooms of this Eastertide flower to be seen (see

[1] In How, William, *Phytologia*, p. 82, 1650.

also p. 86). Purple Milk-vetch forms large patches on many of the slopes, but it is necessary to go in May to see it at its best. Yet I suppose it is the orchids which appeal to people most. Man Orchid, *Aceras anthropophorum*, is quite plentiful—almost as much so as on the North Downs. Having regard to its great rarity over the intervening chalk, it is surprising to find so much on limestone so far north. Bee Orchid, *Ophrys apifera*, and Sweet-scented Orchid, *Gymnadenia conopsea*, are fairly common.

All the plants mentioned in the last paragraph are also to be found in other old quarried areas in the district. Other flowers which are still there but which I did not notice include Perfoliate Yellow-wort, *Blackstonia perfoliata*, Tall Broomrape, *Orobanche elatior*, and probably Squinancywort, *Asperula cynanchica*.

Many of the interesting plants of these old pits can also be found in and about old quarries on both sides of the Great North Road (A.1), but the best woodland is to the west. Small-leaved Lime, *Tilia cordata*, is the tree which many people go to Bedford Purlieus to see. Here, as in a number of other woods in the neighbourhood, it is undoubtedly native and easily recognised when in bloom by the fact that the flowers are upright, whereas in our other Limes they hang down. The Purlieus are only a couple of miles off A.1 at Wansford and are well worth a visit, judging from the recorded species. There are said to be large beds of Lily-of-the-valley, *Convallaria majalis*, the sinister purple blooms of Deadly Nightshade, *Atropa belladonna*, the Woolly-headed Thistle, and the rather dingy-flowered Everlasting Pea, *Lathyrus sylvestris*. It was here that Dr. G. C. Druce found the pretty grass known as Mountain Melic, *Melica nutans*, which is frequent farther north. Nearby John Gilmour found Wall Bedstraw, *Galium parisiense*. In this wood, and also Wakerley Wood five miles to the west, the Caper Spurge, *Euphorbia lathyrus*, has put in a very erratic appearance (cf. p. 55). Between Wakerley and King's Cliffe, a good many interesting limestone plants have been found, including Crested Cow-wheat, *Melampyrum cristatum*, and Downy Woundwort, *Stachys germanica*. The latter has not been seen for many years.

Rutland and Lincolnshire

North of Stamford the Jurassic rocks include important limestones, including the famous Lincolnshire Limestone. The Northamptonshire Oolite just described is botanically very similar to that of Rutland just across the Welland. Over the whole district the best flowers are to be found where there is old turf which has never been broken by the plough, resting on limestone. The tops of quarries, broad verges by roads and ancient tracks, golf courses, and similar places avoided by agriculture, are suitable spots. Stamford is the centre for some of the best country.

Near the Great North Road are two old limestone workings of great interest. At the most southerly of these Perennial Flax, *Linum anglicum*, is still plentiful in the place known to the old botanists who passed this way to the north. With it grow Sulphur Clover, *Trifolium ochroleucon*, and Tall Broomrape, *Orobanche elatior*. Bloody Oaks Quarry on Roundstone Hill is probably the most northerly place in Britain for the beautiful lapis-lazuli flowers of Chalk Milkwort, *Polygala calcarea*. Other interesting calcicoles in the district include Small Meadow-rue, *Thalictrum minus*, Wild Liquorice, *Astragalus glycyphyllos*, and Purple Milk-vetch. The latter grew even on the verges of A.1 about Stretton. Crested Cow-wheat is on the edges of at least three woods. Clipsham Quarries, where stone was cut for the new House of Commons, have an interesting calcicole flora.

The escarpment of the Lincolnshire Limestone continues almost due north right through the county after which it is named. Characteristic pleasant undulating country is to be seen from the North-Eastern main line just north of Essendine. The feathery-fruited Traveller's Joy and yellow-flowered spikes of the Dark Mullein, *Verbascum nigrum*, are indicators of the calcareous content of the soil. On one steep little hillock in the district there is a fine flora, including Pasque Flower and some of the largest Bastard Toadflax, *Thesium humifusum*, I have ever seen.

Lincoln Edge runs north to the west of Sleaford. Good limestone plants are to be found near Ancaster and Leadenham, and doubtless elsewhere. But there is little natural grassland remaining on limestone in Lincolnshire, and habitats of special interest are small and scattered.

Yorkshire

Across the Humber the Oolite covers a very small area near North and South Cave, and then jumps a large stretch of country. It reappears on a big scale in the North Riding, reaching the coast near Scarborough and Whitby and forming much interesting ground inland. South of the Vale of Pickering, the Howardian Hills between Castle Howard and Coxwold include good localities for limestone plants. Here for example, the Bloody Cranesbill, *Geranium sanguineum*, Wild Liquorice and Purple Milk-vetch have been found. North of the Vale calcareous beds outcrop round the edges of the Moors, while their higher ground has vegetation characteristic of acid soils over large areas.

Two of the best districts are the vicinity of Rievaulx Abbey and Helmsley, and the Forge Valley and Hackness, near Scarborough. In old steep-sloped woods by Slip Gill, near Rievaulx, the Small-leaved Lime, *Tilia cordata*, is regarded as native, while the elusive Lady's Slipper Orchid, *Cypripedium calceolus* (see p. 179), was formerly found in the neighbourhood. In the Scarborough district there is the best British locality for the May Lily, *Maianthemum bifolium*. It has spikes of small white flowers which are in some years produced only in very small numbers. In other years it flowers freely. On these calcareous hills can be found Wood Vetch, *Vicia sylvatica*, sprawling over undergrowth and rocks, and the blue-flowered Wild Columbine, *Aquilegia vulgaris*, by paths in the less frequented woods. Beds of Lily-of-the-valley, *Convallaria majalis*, the purple bells of Deadly Nightshade, *Atropa belladonna*, and Woolly-headed Thistle occur. Most of the commoner orchids of the south of England grow in the district —such as Bee and Fly, *Ophrys apifera* and *O. insectifera*, Birds-nest, *Neottia nidus-avis*, and Autumn Lady's-tresses, *Spiranthes spiralis*. But in addition there are northern plants like Baneberry, *Actaea spicata*, and Stone Bramble, *Rubus saxatilis*, which will be considered in a later chapter. These are full compensation for limestone flowers of the south of England which fail to reach this Yorkshire end of the Oolite chain. If Traveller's Joy is missed in the hedges, and the yellow spikes of Dark Mullein on the roadsides, it emphasises a simple example of plant geography.

The flora of the North Riding calcareous soils is thus a meeting-place for flowers with different types of distribution in Britain. Some southern and some northern plants already mentioned are associated with Perennial Flax, which is found near Scarborough. Curiously enough, the name of one of its Yorkshire localities is Box Hill! This plant, of eastern distribution in Britain (Distribution Map 6, p. 218), follows up the chalk and limestone from East Anglia, though it has another locality in north-west England which must be regarded as an exception to the rule. In addition there are rare plants of more scattered distribution such as Yellow Star-of-Bethlehem, *Gagea lutea*, and Narrow-leaved Helleborine, *Cephalanthera longifolia*.

CHAPTER 10

LIMESTONES OF WALES AND THE WELSH BORDER

SOME OF the limestone areas of Wales and the Borderland are as well known to the tourist as to the botanist. Others are difficult of access and seldom visited except by people in search of uncommon flowers. No less than six of the geological systems provide habitats for calcicoles of greater or less importance :

Jurassic.—Limestone outcrops in the Lower Lias of the Glamorgan coast.

Rhaetic.—Calcareous beds of White Lias of the Glamorgan coast.

Carboniferous.—Provides important fine scenery and habitats for limestone flowers in (*a*) the Wye Valley, (*b*) South Wales, including Gower and Tenby, and (*c*) North Wales, including the Great and Little Orme and hills near Llangollen.

Silurian.—Hills and outcrops of Woolhope, Wenlock and Aymestry Limestones in the border counties and elsewhere.

Ordovician.—Provides small scattered exposures of limestone and also the basic volcanic soils of Snowdon, Cader Idris and the Breidden Hills.

Pre-Cambrian.—Scattered very small outcrops of no special botanical interest.

Of these the third is of by far the greatest importance and forms the main subject of this chapter.

The Carboniferous Limestone is much older than the Chalk and Oolites, and by contrast to these younger rocks it is massive and hard. It weathers relatively slowly and, following solution along the cracks, often forms vertical cliffs. Thus craggy precipices and gorges with more or less inaccessible sides often provide beautiful scenery and at the same time sanctuary for rare and attractive plants. The value of this protection has already been remarked on in connection with Cheddar and the Avon Gorge. In addition to saving flowers from destruction by holidaymakers, the steepness of much of the Carboniferous Limestone has protected it from the plough. On this rock the botanist makes for natural landscape features, in contrast to the old quarries and roadside verges of the Jurassic regions described in the last chapter. The habitats described in this chapter are arranged in a clock-wise sequence round Wales.

The Wye Valley

There are two places in the lower part of its course where the "sylvan Wye" breaks through the Carboniferous Limestone to form some of the most beautiful scenery in Britain. That beauty is in great measure due to the lovely colourings of the woods which clothe the precipices and slopes. The more interesting plants are mostly those of limestone woodland. Patches of natural turf or even exposed rocks are relatively scarce.

The lower limestone area extends for about three miles north of Chepstow and includes the rocks below the Castle, Piercefield Cliffs, and the Wyndcliff on the western bank of the river, and Tutshill and Lancaut rocks to the west. These places between them have produced a most interesting list of wild flowers. Formerly the richest flora was to be found at the Wyndcliff, but in recent years this has been turned into a tea-garden with well-kept paths and a charge for admittance. Some of the choice plants still linger and doubtless others are to be found in the adjacent woods, but the place is too crowded to encourage a thorough search. The Mossy Saxifrage, *Saxifraga hypnoides*, under such conditions, might well be a garden outcast, and no botanist has seen the small white flowers of the Toothed Wintergreen, *Orthilia secunda*, for many years. I have, however, seen the Mountain and Fingered Sedges, *Carex montana* and *C. digitata*, and the Mountain Melic, *Melica nutans*, but these are humbler plants which the tourist ignores.

Across the Wye, the Martagon Lily, *Lilium martagon*, grows in hundreds in coppiced woodland. Dr. W. A. Shoolbred, who practised in Chepstow for many years and had an unrivalled knowledge of the flowers of the district, regarding it as native and I am inclined to agree with him. The lovely hanging purple flowers of this Lily are to be found in several spots, and certainly at the one where I know it there seems no likely reason why it should have been planted. On the other hand, one must take into account the ease with which the plant has become naturalised in woods and copses in other parts of England.

In the Wye Valley a Spurge, *Euphorbia stricta*, has its main British localities. It is a dainty, much branched plant of rather a yellowish-green and quite the prettiest of all our Spurges. The only place where I can depend on finding it is by a stream off the limestone, but when conditions are right—probably after coppicing—it is said to come up in quantity in the calcareous woods. Its erratic appearance may be compared to that of the Caper Spurge, *E. lathyrus*, which has been found in two woods in this district and also higher up the river.

The second place where the Wye cuts through the Carboniferous Limestone is at Symond's Yat, some 15 miles north of Chepstow. Here the river comes right up to the base of the great wooded hills and then swings north again in a five-mile loop to pass the base of the Yat only a quarter of a mile from the spot where it first approached. On the east side, in Gloucestershire, there is the Yat itself with extensions to Huntsham Hill and the Coldwell Rocks. On the west, in Herefordshire, the Great and little Doward, with Lord's Wood between them, drop down to the water. The trees, which add so much to the scenery, are very much the same as those in the woods near Chepstow.

Here the Beech forms almost pure woods over small areas, and the dark-leaved Yew contrasts with the silvery leaves of the Whitebeams, *Sorbus spp.*, as on the chalk. Holly, Dogwood, Field Maple and Privet are other common trees and shrubs adding their quota of harmonious colouring. But in addition there are rarer species. The two native Limes, the Large-leaved and Small-leaved, *Tilia platyphyllos* and *T. cordata*, grow out of the cliffs on both sides of the Wye. In a quarry below the steepest end of the Great Doward I have seen several trees of a Wild Pear closely related to the scarce *Pyrus cordata*. There are also several rare Sorbi, including *Sorbus vagensis*, which A. J. Wilmott described as new to science from Symond's Yat. The upper woods on the hills have a deeper layer of soil over the limestone, and the trees and flowers are not always those characteristic of calcareous soils.

At Symond's Yat and the Dowards the wild flowers are mostly woodland species. The Green and the Stinking Hellebores, *Helleborus viridis* and *H. foetidus*, both occur on the Great Doward. Their flowers resemble those of the garden Christmas Rose and appear almost equally early in the year. In these woods there are also three rare sedges. The Fingered Sedge, *Carex digitata*, and the Mountain Sedge, *C. montana*, are fairly plentiful by the sides of paths, but the Dwarf Sedge, *C. humilis*, is extremely rare. It grows in a very small patch of limestone turf high up on one of the hills, and when I saw it in 1935 it covered an area of only about two yards square. The story of how it was first discovered here is an interesting one. A botanist named Abraham T. Willmott, who lived at Ross-on-Wye, visited Bristol in 1851 and saw plenty of the Dwarf Sedge in the Avon Gorge. He was particularly impressed by the similarity of the Carboniferous Limestone and, as he called it, " the correspondence of the surface of the rocks " of the Dowards to those at Clifton. Therefore on his return home he made a special search for the sedge and was rewarded by the discovery of the tiny patch which is still the only one known in the Wye Valley. Other Bristol plants which also grow here include Bloody Cranesbill, *Geranium sanguineum*, Rock Pepperwort, *Hornungia petraea* (this I failed to find), Wall Pennywort, *Umbilicus rupestris*, and Narrow-leaved Bitter-cress, *Cardamine impatiens*. It is a little remarkable that Spring Cinquefoil, *Potentilla tabernaemontani*, which is so abundant on carboniferous rocks in several other districts, is not to be found on the Dowards, but in Herefordshire is restricted to Silurian limestones.

The Wye Valley can be recommended with confidence not only as a delightful place for a holiday but also as one of the best districts for studying the woodland plants of calcareous areas. It was with good reason that W. H. Purchas claimed that of all the rocks in Herefordshire the Carboniferous limestone is " by far the richest as to the number of plants it produces."[1] It should, however, be made clear that there are other limestones both within the county and just beyond its borders, though they extend over much more restricted areas. Thus parts of the Malvern Hills are calcareous and there are basic rocks at Stanner to the west. In the upper parts of its course there are places

[1] Purchas & Ley, *A Flora of Herefordshire*, vi (1889).

where the Wye flows over limestones, but although all these produce rare and interesting flowers they are unimportant in comparison with the areas already described.

South Wales

Carboniferous Limestone outcrops round the South Wales Coalfield. It extends in a narrow strip running east from Kidwelly in Carmarthenshire to near Abergavenny, where it turns south past Pontypool and behind Cardiff runs westwards to beyond Porthcawl. Interrupted by Swansea Bay, the rock outcrops extensively in the Gower Peninsula and again about Tenby in Pembrokeshire. It thus gives rise to two contrasting kinds of flora—one of the steep inland cliffs above the mining villages characterised by a certain number of upland species, the other of coastal cliffs with maritime plants. Both floras are exceedingly interesting and beautiful, and I think their charm is enhanced by the contrast with the industrial areas through which one has to pass to reach them.

The best place I know on the inland part of the limestone is a magnificent stretch of cliff high up above Crickhowell. Here there is a shrub allied to the Whitebeam and known as *Sorbus minima.* It grows freely on the precipitous rock and spreads freely from seed, and yet this cliff and another about two miles to the west are the only places in the world where it is known to grow. There was once a threat that the area would continue to be used as a military training ground where live shells would be employed. Energetic protests from botanists, supported by Members of Parliament, prevented this unique little shrub from any risk of being blown out of existence. On the same cliffs I have seen *Sorbus porrigentiformis,* another scarce tree allied to the Whitebeam, and Miss E. Vachell also showed it to me at a place near Cardiff which is on the same kind of limestone.

The Crickhowell cliffs have Beech growing at over 1000 feet above sea-level in what is probably its most westerly station in Britain as a native plant. They produce both the Large- and Small-leaved Limes, and they have other good things like the little Rock Pepperwort (which I was too late to see myself) and Limestone Polypody, *Thelypteris robertiana.*

It is surprising how rich this Breconshire limestone is in rare Sorbi. The Rock Whitebeam, *Sorbus rupicola,* which may be known from the

Robert Atkinson

EARLY SPIDER ORCHID, *Ophrys sphegodes;* an orchid which flowers in March and April and has become extinct in many counties. Dorset; May

John Markham

CHEDDAR GORGE, SOMERSET

The steep rocks of the Carboniferous Limestone are a sanctuary for rare and beautiful flowers. September

common Whitebeam, *S. aria*, by its narrower leaves with a tapering base, fans out its branches on the cliffs. And in addition to the other two rare species already mentioned, *Sorbus leyana* has its only known locality on a single short rock-face in the Merthyr Tydfil district. When I visited it in 1948 I found that a number of the trees were dead. Others had their leaves so eaten by caterpillars that they were almost unrecognisable.

To the south the Carboniferous Limestone outcrops again on and near the coast from Southerndown to beyond Porthcawl. It forms the humps of Ewenny and Ogmore Downs. The Mountain Sedge, *Carex montana*, grows here near the roadside in a more open place than the Symond's Yat localities discussed above. Chalk Violet, *Viola calcarea*, is found near it, but in 1935 I thought it far less uniform and even less convincing as a distinct species than the Box Hill plant. Wall Germander, *Teucrium chamaedrys*, grows on limestone rocks where it has been known for a century.

The lower beds of the Lias consist of alternating layers of hard impure limestone and shale, whilst the Rhaetic Beds, which extend east from Southerndown, are locally calcareous. They form limestone cliffs along parts of the coast of south Glamorgan, and are quarried for lime and cement at Bridgend. The flora has a good deal in common with that of similar soils in Somerset on the other side of the Bristol Channel. Blue Gromwell, *Lithospermum purpurocaeruleum*, is frequent, just as it is in parts of the Mendips (see p. 114). Woolly-headed Thistle, *Cirsium eriophorum* var. *britannicum*, is abundant, as it is on the Lias near Bristol (see p. 123). Madder scrambles about the cliffs and over bushes, as at the Avon Gorge (see p. 118). Although the traveller from Somerset to Glamorgan has to make a very long journey by land, the direct distance across the Channel is only about 12 miles.

But the Welsh Lias has some plants to offer which are not to be seen on the opposite coast. As Miss Vachell wrote[1]: "Near Nash Point, at a height of approximately 200 feet, the cliffs are bright in spring with the yellow flowers of the Sea Cabbage (*Brassica oleracea*) and the magenta blooms of the Hoary Stock (*Matthiola incana*) which, in such an inaccessible position, might well be considered native." A mile away there is a most interesting colony of the rare Tuberous Thistle, *Cirsium tuberosum* (see pp. 81 and 98). When this was dis-

[1] E. Vachell, in *Glamorgan County History*, I: 129 (1936).

covered a century ago it set in train a long argument about the correct identification of the Glamorgan plant. The trouble was caused by the ease with which this species hybridises with other thistles both here and in Wiltshire, where it was first found. Because of this it is often very difficult to find pure specimens of the Tuberous Thistle and hence botanists in this country had trouble in getting to know just what the species really was. Now that it has been seen in more places (Distribution Map 8, p. 219), the arguments of past generations seem almost unnecessary, but I must admit that I saw more of the hybrids than of the pure plant in the South Wales locality !

Another very special rarity of the Lias is the Maidenhair Fern, *Adiantum capillus-veneris*. I very much doubt if it is still to be found at populous Barry Island, but it grows at a number of places along this coast. At the one where I have seen it a white streak of calcareous matter runs down the cliff. Opinions may differ as to whether the Maidenhair Fern is a calcicole, but from my own experience of it on widely scattered places on the coast I am inclined to think that it is, and that the presence of calcium carbonate in quantity is just as important as freedom from severe frosts in determining where it can grow.

A little to the west is the Gower Peninsula with its fine cliffs of Carboniferous Limestone. At week-ends it becomes the playground of Swansea, from which it is only a short bus or cycle ride, but nevertheless the coast remains unspoiled and a paradise for the naturalist. Except in the places where sand has accumulated—and there is a lot of it at Oxwich Burrows—nearly the whole of the south coast is limestone, which is eventually extended on the western side into the long promontory known as Worm's Head.

The plant for which Gower is most famous is a small Crucifer, Yellow Whitlow-grass, *Draba aizoides* var. *montana*, which grows nowhere else in Britain. It is best known on some old ruins, but I have also seen it on the cliffs, where it occurs for several miles. Like the Maidenhair Fern, it is fortunate that some of the colonies are inaccessible, for otherwise such an attractive plant might soon be exterminated. It has tight little rosettes of leaves rather like those of some of the smaller rockery plants and the heads of yellow flowers appear very early in the year. Just how early they first open I do not know, but at the time of my earliest visit in mid-April they were well past their best and fruits were forming.

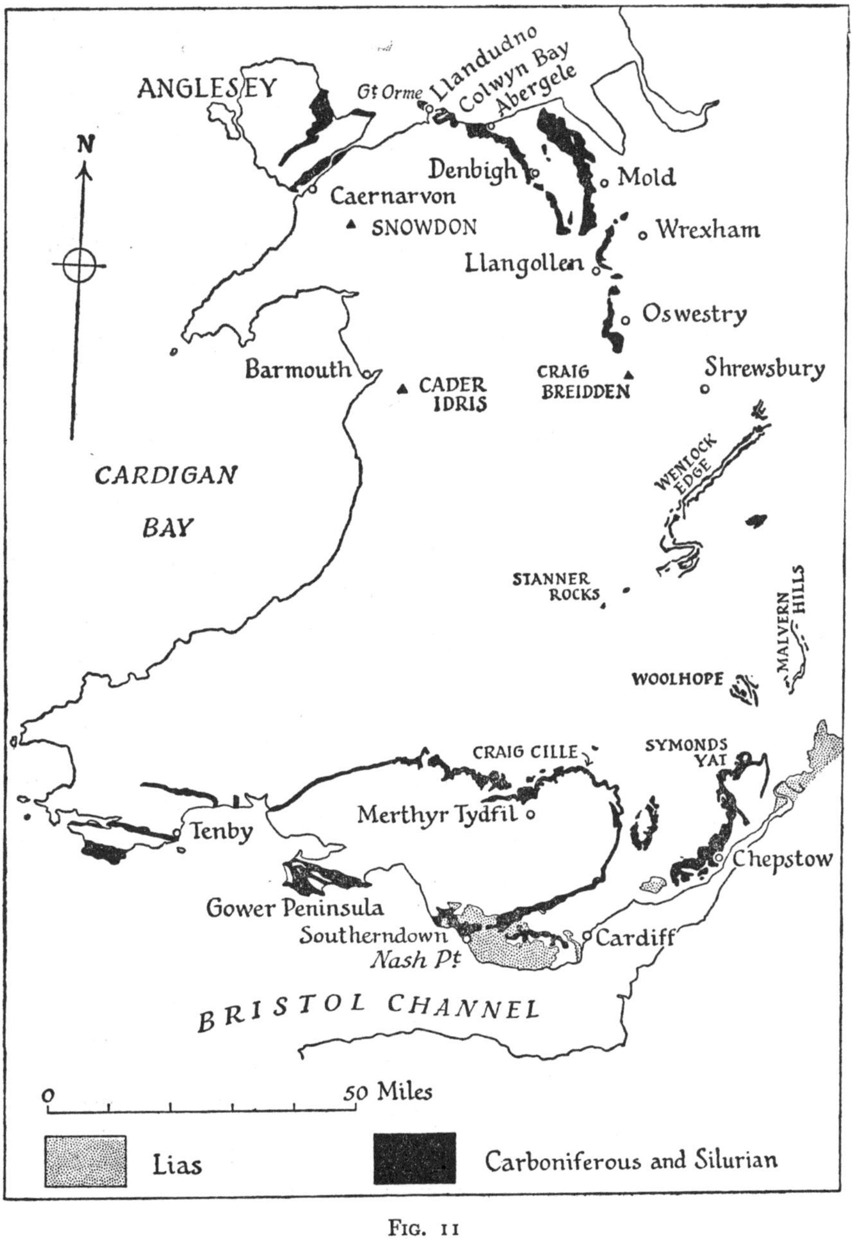

FIG. 11
Wales and the Welsh Border

The limestone cliffs where the Yellow Whitlow-grass grows rise up from the sea in a series of narrow steps which form a delightful natural rock-garden. In the spring they are blue in places with the flowers of the Vernal Squill, *Scilla verna*, which is like a miniature Bluebell with erect instead of hanging bells. These contrast with the bright yellow blooms of the Spring Cinquefoil, *Potentilla tabernaemontani*, and the paler yellow of the Hoary Rock-rose, *Helianthemum canum*. The last may easily be known from the Common Rock-rose, *H. chamaecistus*, by the very much smaller flowers and the greyish appearance of the leaves due to white hairs, and absence of stipules. Hoary Rock-rose is a very local plant (Distribution Map 3, p. 217), but in the places where it occurs it is nearly always abundant. In one place where I saw *Draba aizoides* it was accompanied by exceptionally large plants of Rock Pepperwort. A little later in the year patches of Bloody Cranesbill, *Geranium sanguineum*, add their quota of bright colour to parts of these cliffs.

I suppose early spring is the best time of the year to visit the Gower limestone, and yet I have a feeling that too many botanists go in April to the neglect of later months. As some evidence for this there is the Western Spiked Speedwell, *Veronica hybrida*, which flowers in July and August. It is a handsome and conspicuous plant (see p.118) and there are fairly old records for these cliffs, and yet it was not until 1945 that Glamorganshire botanists could be sure that it grew there. Having regard to its occurrence in the Avon Gorge and in various places in North Wales, it is a flower one would expect to find in Gower. Small Restharrow, *Ononis reclinata*, now known elsewhere only in South Devon (see p. 107), is another plant recently refound. Specimens were collected from the Gower cliffs in 1828 and it was not seen again for a hundred and twenty-five years.

For many years I expected that someone would find Hair-leaved Goldilocks, *Crinitaria linosyris*, in Gower. It grows in Somerset and North Wales (see pp. 115 and 151) on the Carboniferous Limestone, and there are plenty of suitable habitats on this coast. My expectation has proved to be well justified. When I visited the Gower cliffs with Miss E. Vachell and Mr. D. McClintock in 1948 for the purpose of checking what I had written for this chapter, we were fortunate enough to discover the Goldilocks. There were only a few plants, but they grew in a wild place far from houses in limestone turf and are undoubtedly native.

The limestone woods of this peninsula are also of interest. I have

Robert Atkinson

WASP ORCHID, *Ophrys trollii;* allied to the Bee Orchid (Plate 6) but restricted to a small area of limestone in western England. Gloucestershire; June

PLATE 34

John Markham

MALHAM COVE, WEST RIDING, YORKSHIRE

A magnificent amphitheatre of cliffs of Carboniferous Limestone long famous for its flora. July

seen Stinking Hellebore near Park Mill, and Gladdon and Caper Spurge at Nicholaston. The last seems to be much more regular in appearance than in most of its other native habitats, and I think the reason is that it favours the open edge of the woods, where it extends out on to the sand-dunes and is therefore not dependent for light on periodical felling of the trees. Blue Gromwell, *Lithospermum purpuro-coeruleum*, is found in the same wood and in other bushy places in the neighbourhood.

In southern Pembrokeshire there are considerable outcrops of Carboniferous Limestone, particularly on the coast near Tenby. Here it occurs about the town and forms part of Caldey Island, and then extends as a long ridge from Giltar Point until it meets the Old Red Sandstone near Manorbier. Vernal Squill is abundant and there is some quantity of Small Meadow-rue, *Thalictrum minus*, with many common limestone plants.

The chief object of my visits to these limestone cliffs has been to see the very rare Sea Lavender, *Limonium transwallianum*, in the place from which H. W. Pugsley described it as new to science in 1924. It looks very like the Rock Sea-Lavender, *Limonium binervosum*, but has flowers only half the size in short, dense spikes, and leaves less dilated towards their ends. It has since been found in other places in Pembrokeshire and in the Burren district of Ireland. I do not know whether the special Tenby Daffodil, *Narcissus obvallaris*, is on limestone or not, but Madder, *Rubia peregrina*, and Ivy Broomrape, *Orobanche hederae*, are certainly among the flowers which grow here on that rock.

North Wales

Throughout the whole of Central Wales limestone flowers are scarce. From the Tenby district to the Menai Straits acid soils are the rule, and the traveller becomes accustomed to mile after mile of peaty moorland and heath. There are small outcrops of volcanic rocks giving rise to basic soils on a number of the mountains, and especially on Cader Idris and in Snowdonia—such as the well known " hanging garden " of the Glyders—but these are outside the scope of this book. There are also calcareous areas in the coastal dunes, but the only lowland place with a really rich limestone flora recorded is a little hillock on the outskirts of Barmouth. Here there were a number of nice plants, including Western Spiked Speedwell, *Veronica hybrida*, and Vernal Squill, *Scilla verna*, forming an interesting link between South and North Wales.

But this is a trivial affair in comparison with the Carboniferous limestone of Anglesey and Caernarvonshire. On the Bangor side of the Menai Straits there was a fairly rich flora until perhaps fifty years ago, when it was spoiled by the extension of the town. In Anglesey the best limestone is three or four miles north of Beaumaris. Here there is a ridge extending from Marian-dyrys, where there is limestone turf by the roadside and round quarries, to Arthur's Seat a little to the west. Bwrdd Arthur (as the Welsh call it) is a very fascinating place for the botanist. From the road there is a short slope up to a wall of limestone rock about ten feet high. This forms a circle with a flat top, to which a track gives access, enabling the farmer to use it for grazing. In June the ledges on the low cliffs are covered with flowers of brilliant colours in which yellows predominate. Clumps of Hoary Rock-rose are mixed with the less compact but larger flowered Common Rock-rose. Kidney Vetch, Mouse-ear Hawkweed and Lady's Bedstraw are other abundant yellow flowers here. There are big patches of Bloody Cranesbill, *Geranium sanguineum*, and bushes of the excessively prickly and dwarf Burnet Rose, *Rosa pimpinellifolia*. Both in Anglesey and near Llandudno the last two grow on limestone and also on sand-dunes within a few miles. Near Arthur's Seat there is a small colony of Rock Pepperwort.

The larger area of Carboniferous Limestone marked on the map across the centre of the island is disappointing. I have noticed a few calcicoles here and there by the roadsides, but most of the rock on the lower ground is covered with unsuitable soils.

But the limestone flora of Anglesey is only a curtain-raiser to that of the Carboniferous ridge which begins at the Great Orme and extends with only short gaps through Denbighshire to Denbigh and Ruthin. Llandudno is the usual centre for exploring the riches of this area, and the town nestles under the massive headland of the Great Orme on the one side and the hills running from the Little Orme through Gloddaeth to Deganwy on the other. To many botanists this Creuddyn Peninsula, as it is called, is the limit of their knowledge of the limestone of North Wales, but there is plenty of less well known but almost equally interesting country farther east. From Bryn Euryn, near Colwyn Bay, and Llysfaen to Cefn-yr-Ogof, near Abergele, and then along by Cefn Rocks and Henllan to Denbigh and beyond, there is a chain of fine limestone habitats. In Flintshire a broader range runs southwards from Prestatyn. Many places on these hills have such a profusion of wild flowers that it is a pity they are not better known.

Most readers will already know the Great Orme's Head (Plate XVI, p. 75). On three sides there is a toll motor road giving grand views of the coast, and above this steep cliffs rise to the plateau, which attains a height of 679 feet above sea-level; on the fourth side there is the town of Llandudno. The botanist can therefore approach it in two ways. On the first day a walk round the four mile long road with careful examination of the cliffs affords an ample programme. A second day can be devoted to the old quarries and the plateau approached by way of the tramway.

The botanical season on the Orme is a very long one, but to see the full beauty of the flowers here it is necessary to come well before the usual holiday times. My own earliest visit was in the first week in May, and I am not sure that even this was quite early enough to see the spring plants at their best before the shallow soil over the limestone had been baked by the sun. At this time of the year many of the rarities are of course not yet out, but their absence was more than compensated for by an abundance of charming plants of which I had only previously seen the last lingering blossoms. There were sheets of Spring Cinquefoil, *Potentilla tabernaemontani*, of which the bright yellow flowers contrasted with the blue of Vernal Squill, *Scilla verna.* On the Little Orme Mr. J. E. S. Dallas told me there are three parallel bands of this last little gem growing where the rocks are steepest. During the short flowering period these show up from a distance as blue bands across the hill. On my early visit a few last flowers of Hairy Violet, *Viola hirta,* on the Great Orme showed that there had been an earlier display of blue of a different sort, while the rather pale flowers of Hoary Rock-rose were already open. Another early plant in greater abundance than I had previously see it was Rock Pepperwort. Though too small to add conspicuous colour to the display, the daintiness of this little plant is extremely attractive. White was added to the show by the masses of flowers produced by tufts of Spring Sandwort, *Minuartia verna.*

The Marine Drive on the north side of the Orme divides the limestone cliffs above the road from rocks of a different kind with a contrasting flora below. Maritime plants ascend well up on the limestone. Amongst the earliest to flower is the Sea Cabbage, *Brassica oleracea*, of which the yellow blooms are also to be seen in abundance in a quarry on the Little Orme. A white-flowered Crucifer which grows by the road is Common Scurvy-grass, *Cochlearia officinalis.* Although most frequent by the sea, this fleshy-leaved plant seems to thrive on the limestone, for it is also found inland on that rock at Cheddar. The pink flowers of the Thrift, *Armeria maritima*, and the white Sea Campion, *Silene maritima*, are very little later, and are followed towards the end of summer by the yellow Umbellifer, Samphire, *Crithmum maritimum.* Some of these maritime plants get quite a long way from the sea. Mr. Dallas told me that he has seen Yellow Sea-Poppy, *Glaucium flavum*, inland here in a limestone quarry, just as it occurs away from the shore in Sussex, Kent and the Isle of Wight (see p. 50).

On these cliffs above the road there are also patches of Bloody Cranesbill and a profusion of Hawkweeds, *Hieracium spp.* These yellow-flowered Composites, with blooms somewhat like those of the Dandelion, are a puzzling lot not only to the tyro but also to the experienced botanist. Several rare ones occur on the Orme and it happens that one of these is quite easily identified. *Hieracium cambricum* has narrow glaucous leaves with long teeth on each side, and is only found in Wales and chiefly on the limestone about Llandudno.

On the top the cliffs are exposed to the full force of the wind and it is interesting to see its effect on the shrubs. Common Buckthorn, Juniper, Privet, Hawthorn and Wild Cotoneaster, *Cotoneaster integerrimus*, all grow with prostrate, woody, knotted stems hardly rising above the rocks and with very few leaves. The Cotoneaster is the special plant which many people come to the Orme to see. I have found it in two places well over a mile apart in recent years, but it was once more common. Probably grazing by sheep has prevented its regeneration from seed and they, rather than unscrupulous botanists, are to be blamed for its present rarity. Where protected from the wind, it grows into a bush some five feet tall, but here the plants show signs of dying from old age, if one can judge from the amount of dead, or almost dead, wood they now show.

Our native *Cotoneaster integerrimus* has small pinkish-white flowers and almost round leaves which are white with short, dense hairs underneath. Until the present century its identification never caused the slightest difficulty, but now a number of allied shrubs have become so thoroughly naturalised that many people mistake the foreigners for the rare plant of our Floras. On the Orme the usual shrub they name in error is *Cotoneaster microphyllus*, which is abundant in places at the Llandudno end. Here it is probably bird-sown from fruits brought from the public gardens. This Himalayan species grows almost flat on the rocks and has numerous small white flowers which are very attractive to bees. The evergreen leaves are only about a third of an inch long and shining green above, whereas the deciduous leaves of the native plant are three times as long. The Chinese *Cotoneaster horizontalis* is rather similar to *microphyllus*, growing flat on the rocks with branches spreading out to form flat sprays, and leaves only a trifle larger, but the flowers are pink and the leaves only very slightly hairy below. The shrub which is really most like *integerrimus* is *C. simonsii*, a native of Assam, but this has densely hairy young twigs and the leaves have long scattered hairs on both surfaces. These are all naturalised in various places on the limestone in North Wales. On one hill, Cefn-yr-Ogof, on the Abergele side of Llanddulas, I have seen all three aliens growing close together. But I think the native Cotoneaster has never been found off the Great Orme, and even there not all recent records are reliable.

To see all the rarities of this great limestone headland it is necessary to make quite a number of visits at different times of the year. In June I have seen the great yellow flowers (nearly two inches across) of the Spotted Catsear, *Hypochoeris maculata*, but it seems to be restricted to one limited part of the Orme. In July and August there are lovely blue spikes of the Western Spiked Speedwell, *Veronica hybrida*. This is much more widespread and so abundant in places that it attracts the attention of people who are not specially interested in flowers. Late September or even early October is the time to go for Goldilocks, *Crinitaria linosyris*. I have seen this in two places on the Orme and it is known elsewhere in the district.

With the exception of the Cotoneaster and the Hawkweed, which are special rarities of the Orme, all the plants so far mentioned for the headland have been discussed earlier. In other words, they are species which occur farther south and in many cases have a distribution in Britain along the west coast. Some indication of the northern element in the flora is given by the greater abundance of Mountain Everlasting, *Antennaria dioica*, which here and in Anglesey is much more constant and plentiful than in southern counties. A more definite sign is the

Dark-flowered Helleborine, *Epipactis atrorubens*, which grows in the chinks of the Carboniferous Limestone. This orchid is met again in the north of England and it is also found on limestone rocks in Scotland and Ireland. Early in the summer it may be recognised by the oval shape of the leaves, and in July the rich red colour of the flowers, with their characteristic rugged bosses, make identification easy. The Dark-flowered Helleborine is nearly always seen growing out of narrow chinks in the limestone (Plate 41, p. 178) but sometimes, in the Peak District and Yorkshire, for example, it favours screes.

Facing the Great Orme and on the other side of Llandudno, there is another series of hills extending from the Little Orme's Head to Gloddaeth. Here some of the limestone flowers are better grown and more plentiful than they are on the more popular headland.

Likewise many of the Orme plants are abundant on the hills which run eastward from Colwyn Bay almost to Abergele, where they turn south. The nicest hill on this range is, I think, Cefn-yr-Ogof, where the three Asiatic Cotoneasters (see above) grow in great abundance with interesting native plants.

Some six miles south-east of Abergele there is another good patch of limestone on both sides of the river Elwy, and extending on through Galltfaenan and Henllan to Denbigh. In one place in this area there is a colony of Western Spiked Speedwell and the woods contain a good deal of the Small-leaved Lime, *Tilia cordata*, and some Herb Paris, *Paris quadrifolia*. But the specially exciting plant here is Blue Gromwell, *Lithospermum purpurocaeruleum* (see also pp. 82 and 114).

This was first discovered by John Ray, the greatest of early English naturalists, when he stayed at Denbigh on Saturday and Sunday, 17 and 18 May, 1662. He described it as " an elegant plant " and gave the locality in such clear terms that even now it is easy to find from his published note. And yet I must admit that the Blue Gromwell caused two friends and myself to search very hard on the evening of 12 June, 1947. Perhaps it was because we were tired after a hard day's botanizing—or maybe we were just stupid—but although we went straight to the right place it was over three hours before we saw our plant. In the meanwhile we had decided to search elsewhere and spent valuable time in the failing light without success. At last we decided to abandon our botanical pride and inquired at a farm-house whether a plant with brilliant blue flowers which appeared in April and May grew in the neighbouring woods. The farmer's wife knew it at once and took us straight to the spot. We were pleased to observe that she was proud of the rarity in her keeping and intended to take care that no harm came to it. At this place the Blue Gromwell grows, not on a sunny wood border as I had expected from my previous experience, but well within the wood amongst hazels and in considerable shade. It produces flowers very sparingly, and it is likely that it is less flourishing than it was before the trees and shrubs reached their present height.

From Denbigh Castle Hill the Carboniferous Limestone is discontinuous as it runs south-east by Ruthin. Just west of Wrexham a narrow outcrop runs south for some 20 miles and on the way forms magnificent cliffs near Llangollen. Here on the Trevor Rocks and precipices above Tan-y-graig on the Eglwys Mountain there is an interesting limestone flora, though the choicer plants are in small quantity and difficult to find. Of these the Dark-flowered Helleborine and the Rock Pepperwort have already been discussed in connection with the Great Orme, where they are more plentiful. The Limestone Polypody, *Thelypteris robertiana*, and Rigid Buckler Fern, *Dryopteris villarii*, are two ferns found sparingly. The latter is particularly interesting as it is only known elsewhere in Britain in a limited area in north-west England, where it is locally plentiful, and in Snowdonia, where it is extremely rare.

The extension of this outcrop south of Llangollen does not seem to be well known botanically. A careful search might well reveal uncommon plants in new localities.

So much for the Carboniferous Limestone of Wales, but before this chapter closes brief mention must be made of a few areas where calcicoles occur on older formations. The most famous of these is on the Ordovician rocks of Breidden Hill in Montgomeryshire. Here igneous rocks give rise to basic soils on which some of the limestone flowers abound. This steep, well-wooded hump between Welshpool and Shrewsbury has long been a mecca for botanists. To them it is still a " mine of wealth " (as the Rev. W. W. How described it in 1859), but it must have been even more attractive before the plantations of firs and larches grew up and before quarrying destroyed some of the best ground. The naturalist who now climbs to the rough column of stones erected to the memory of Lord Rodney on the 1200-feet high top may be disappointed in his finds. Nevertheless most of the rarities are still there.

The gem of Craig Breidden is Rock Cinquefoil, *Potentilla rupestris*, which was first recorded in 1688. Thanks to the removal of plants to cottage gardens and the attacks of unprincipled collectors, it became so rare that it was regarded as probably extinct until a few plants were found again about 25 years ago. Western Spiked Speedwell, *Veronica hybrida*, Sticky Catchfly, *Lychnis viscaria*, Bloody Cranesbill, *Geranium sanguineum*, and Welsh Stonecrop, *Sedum forsteranum*, are other rarities which have been found on these precipitous crags.

The Silurian system includes the Woolhope, Wenlock and Aymestry Limestones. Those of the Wenlock series are exposed along the fine Edge of that name which runs from Much Wenlock to Craven Arms and has a fairly good limestone flora. But the Silurian limestones as a whole have relatively little botanical importance. Although more extensive than those of the Ordovician and Pre-Cambrian systems, they are equally dwarfed by the Carboniferous as providing calcareous habitats in Wales and the border counties.

PLATE 35

John Markham

BRACKEN, *Pteridium aquilinum*, ON LIMESTONE

This fern grows abundantly on shallow soils over limestone in districts where rainfall is high. Taken above Gordale Scar, Yorkshire; July

John Markham

LIMESTONE PAVEMENT, INGLEBOROUGH, YORKSHIRE
Lily-of-the-valley, *Convallaria majalis*, in the foreground. July

CHAPTER 11

THE DERBYSHIRE DALES

Some of the best of the Carboniferous Limestone is to be found on the Pennines, where it forms magnificent scenery. The cliffs and slopes which are the foundation of the beauty are the homes of uncommon and interesting flowers.

In this chapter the extreme south of the Pennine Range will be considered—the region of the Derbyshire Dales. The limestone here extends particularly over an area of some 25 by 15 miles from near Wirksworth and Ashbourne in the south, through Matlock and Buxton, almost to the lower slopes of Kinder Scout in the north. This area is sometimes inaccurately referred to by botanists as the Peak District,[1] but properly the term should be restricted to the high, mostly acid ground which is just beyond its northern limits. I prefer to refer to it as the Derbyshire Dales, though even this description has its objections, since the west parts of Dovedale and the whole of the Manifold Valley are within the county of Staffordshire.

To a southern botanist like myself this big stretch of limestone is particularly exciting as the nearest place where a number of northern species can be seen. Lovely flowers such as Mountain Pansy, *Viola lutea*, Jacob's Ladder, *Polemonium caeruleum*, and Globe Flower, *Trollius europaeus*, have taken advantage of the high ground of the Pennines to extend south with trees like Bird Cherry, *Prunus padus*, and shrubs like the Soft-leaved and the Glaucous Roses, *R. villosa* and *R. dumalis*. Hoary Whitlow-grass, *Draba incana*, and Melancholy Thistle, *Cirsium heterophyllum*, grasses like Mountain Melic, *Melica nutans*, and Wood Fescue, *Festuca altissima*, a rare sedge, *Carex ornithopoda*, and a fern, the

[1] Partly because the special sheet of the 1-inch Ordnance Survey covering the whole area is entitled *The Peak District*.

Green Spleenwort, *Asplenium viride*, are less conspicuous examples. Apart from the presence of particular species, the flora has a definitely northern facies which is refreshing to people who are more familiar with the chalk and limestones of the south. Ash takes the place of the Beech in the woods, and plants like Common Lady's Mantle, *Alchemilla vulgaris*, which such botanists are apt to regard as rare, are here extremely common.

On the contrary, some of the abundant plants of the South and North Downs are absent or rare. Orchids are surprisingly scarce. Whitebeam, *Sorbus aria*, is only found at a few places, though the allied Rock Whitebeam, *Sorbus rupicola*, of the north and west, is more common. Wayfaring Tree is probably absent, and Traveller's Joy is found only near gardens where it has almost certainly been introduced. Such common downland plants as Squinancywort, Stemless Thistle, Blue Fleabane and Yellow-wort are extremely rare. Other abundant chalk flowers like Dropwort, Clustered Bellflower and Common Gromwell, *Lithospermum officinale*, and even the characteristic grass, Upright Brome, *Bromus erectus*, are local and scarce.

If the Derbyshire Dales are characterised by northern plants coming south into the Midlands in quantity, it cannot be said that the southern flowers use the same district to push north. Their road in this direction is the Magnesian Limestone, which runs to the east of the Pennines and is to be considered in the next chapter.

The area in which the Dales are found may be described roughly as a great tableland rising in height towards the north. Out of this tableland steep-sided winding valleys, with limestone exposed on their cliffs and slopes, wander in all directions. Most of them have streams or rivers running through them—the best known of these being the Derwent in the east and the Dove in the west. The area is one of heavy rainfall, particularly on the high ground around Buxton, and this has the effect of accelerating the process known as "leaching." Rain, charged with the acid carbon dioxide, dissolves the calcium carbonate of the limestone and leaves behind a residue which produces an acid rather than a basic soil. These residues have tended to accumulate on the flattish top of the tableland, and here they give rise to soils on which rather acid heathy vegetation develops. On the slopes these tend to wash down as they form, leaving the limestone rocks exposed and clothed with plants characteristic of calcareous habitats. It will be evident that it is on the limestone precipices such as High Tor, Matlock, or on steep rocky slopes such as those which are so well-known in Dove Dale and Miller's Dale, that one must expect to find the most characteristic calcicoles.

In addition to extensive leaching there are intrusions of other rocks in the Carboniferous Limestone which lead to complications. The most interesting of these are the bands of dark basaltic lava known as " Toadstone " which may be seen in some places along the sides of the valleys. Here there is an immediate and striking change in the vegetation, and acid-loving plants take the place of the calcicoles of the surrounding limestone. Chert, which is siliceous in character, forms a thin overlayer in some valleys and also gives rise to a calcifuge flora.

Scattered over most of the area are spoil-heaps from the lead-mines. As in the Mendips (see p. 113), the ore was mined here on a considerable scale by the Romans and some of the heaps have remained undisturbed from their times—others are of later date. Even the older mounds seldom get completely grassed over, and many of them have two species of plants which are specially associated with places where lead has been mined. The most widespread of these is Spring Sandwort, *Minuartia verna* (Plate 45, p. 194). As far back as 1688 Ray recorded the locality as "In Derbyshire on the barren earth they dig out of the shafts of the lead mines near Wirksworth," and it is quite common in such places all over the Dales area. It does occur sometimes where no lead has been mined, but it does not follow that the ore is not present at these places.

The other lead associate is a much rarer plant—a special kind of Alpine Pennywort distinguished as *Thlaspi calaminare*, and known in Britain only from Derbyshire and Rhum. It is to be found in many places from Wirksworth to Matlock, and north of this at Alport by the River Bradford. The Alpine Pennyworts are critical and it takes an expert eye to distinguish *T. calaminare* from all the forms of the much more widespread *T. alpestre*. The fruiting spikes are shorter and denser and the fruits are cut off almost square at the ends with long styles. It is also said that *T. calaminare* flowers earlier. This may be generally true, for I saw it in three places with young fruits formed one year as early as 19 May, but it is useless as a character, as flowers can still be found as late as August in some summers.

As compared with the chalk and limestone districts discussed in earlier chapters, the flowers of the Derbyshire Dales bloom late. This applies particularly to the northern valleys and is mainly due to the high altitude. To see the finest displays of colour, the visitor should go in June or even July—a full month later than on the South or North Downs. The best centres to stay at are Matlock, Buxton and Ashbourne, and although the whole of the area can be explored by using public transport from the first-mentioned centre, it will be convenient to discuss the more important Dales in sequence according to their proximity to these three towns.

Matlock

The last time I stayed in Derbyshire was at a hotel which had bedrooms with lovely views of the High Tor, Matlock, towering up above the River Derwent. The huge cliff was clothed with the trees and bushes characteristic of limestone scenery and growing out of chinks in the rock where it seemed unbelievable that their roots could find sufficient nutriment. The very dark green leaves of the Yew and Holly and those of the Wych Elm, *Ulmus glabra* (far more abundant than in the south), contrasted with the shivering paler foliage of the Ash, which was the dominant tree in so many of the woods in the neighbourhood. Rock Whitebeam, *Sorbus rupicola*, grew only on the very steepest cliffs, and its silvery leaves contrasted with the greens of the trees already mentioned and harmonised with the white of the limestone.

In short evening walks on both sides of the Derwent valley I saw many interesting plants, including the Spring Sandwort and *Thlaspi calaminare* in several places. In the woods there were two northern grasses. Mountain Melic, *Melica nutans*, was common. It is a very ornamental plant, easily distinguished from the Wood Melic, *M. uniflora*, by the much larger spikelets which nod on their stalks and are arranged on an unbranched stem. Wood Fescue, *Festuca altissima*, grows in one rocky wood and is equally graceful, though a much taller grass, forming loose clumps. Where I saw it, it was associated with Wood Barley, *Hordelymus europaeus*. Lily-of-the-Valley, *Convallaria majalis*, is to be found at Matlock and in some of the other Dales, as is also Giant Bellflower, *Campanula latifolia*, another species more common in the north than the south of England. About Matlock Bath, the rocks are covered with masses of White Arabis, *Arabis caucasica*, a garden

PLATE 37

John Markham

Wooded Limestone Pavement, Ingleborough, Yorkshire

Ash, *Fraxinus excelsior*, Sycamore, *Acer pseudo-platanus*, and other trees growing up from the cracks in the pavement where they have been protected as seedlings from grazing animals. July

John Markham

BANEBERRY, *Actaea spicata*, in fruit. A rare plant of Limestone in northern England. Yorkshire; July

plant which has become thoroughly established here and is still extending its area.

A favourite walk or drive from Matlock is through the steep-sided wooded valley called the Via Gellia, which is about three miles to the south-west. Although this is not a place where special rarities are to be found, it is an excellent introduction to the Dales. Near the road and stream along the bottom of the valley there is thick woodland in which Ash and Wych Elm are dominant. In this Mr. R. H. Hall showed me Herb Paris, *Paris quadrifolia*, and the round-headed Lesser Teasel, *Dipsacus pilosus*. Here and there in the woods are rocky screes made up of boulders of various sizes, in which we saw plenty of Mountain Melic and Stone Bramble, *Rubus saxatilis*. The latter is a small creeping plant related to the Blackberry, but seldom as much as a foot in height, and usually with only three leaflets to each leaf. The fruits are bright red when ripe, and pleasant, if somewhat sharp, in taste, and thus very refreshing on a hot, thirsty August day. The screes extend above the wood into a belt of scrub-land where Elder and Hazel are dominant. Above this is a somewhat leached area with plants which are not particular about growing on calcareous soils.

Some six miles north-west of Matlock is the valley of the Bradford, of which the best part is between Alport and Youlgreave. The special plants of the lead spoil-heaps here have already been mentioned. About the village of Alport there is Dark Mullein, *Verbascum nigrum*, with yellow corolla and purple stamens. In the south of England we regard it as a common chalk plant, but as far north as this it is a rarity. On rocks in Lathkill Dale nearby I have been shown the fern Rustyback, *Ceterach officinarum*, which, although so common in the south-west of England, is scarce in the north. Growing with it was Fine-leaved Sandwort, *Minuartia hybrida*. High up in this valley is a colony of Jacob's Ladder, *Polemonium caeruleum*, one of the showiest of our northern wild flowers. The flowers are of a rich blue against which the yellow projecting stamens show up to advantage, and the leaves are divided into some 12 or 14 narrow leaflets (pinnate). Often cultivated in cottage gardens as Greek Valerian, the plant is sometimes found in places where it is doubtfully wild, but in the Derbyshire Dales and in Yorkshire (see p. 183) it grows high up in remote places where there can be little question of its status. From the high screes, which seem to be its proper home, it gets carried down the valleys by streams, and no doubt this explains why it is also to be found by the Bradford near Alport and by brooks near Ashbourne.

North of Eyam, in the Hope Valley, as at Castleton and the Winnats, there are other exposures of Carboniferous Limestone which I have not yet visited. Judging from the records, they have many of the commoner plants of the Derbyshire Dales, and some of the rarities.

Monsal Dale to Buxton

For about nine miles from Monsal Dale to Buxton the River Wye runs through a steep-sided gorge with some of the finest scenery and best botanizing in central England. The main railway line from St. Pancras to Manchester, and its branch to Buxton, share the valley, and passengers on these lines can get some idea of the country from brief glimpses they obtain as the trains rush in and out of cuttings and tunnels. To the walker the railway is so well concealed that it hardly mars the scenery.

The main valley forms a series of Dales known as Monsal Dale, Miller's Dale, Chee Dale, Wye Dale and Ashwood Dale. Off these lead a sequence of smaller valleys, of which the most interesting to the botanist are Cressbrook or Raven's Dale, Tideswell Dale, Monk's Dale, Great Rocks Dale and Cunning Dale to the north, and Deep Dale, leading to Back Dale, in the south. In the following paragraphs these will not be mentioned by name when the scarce plants are discussed. The series as a whole differs from the other Dales in its higher altitude. Many of the better habitats are very near the one-thousand-foot contour and northern plants accordingly tend to be more numerous. There is no doubt that from the point of view of the botanist it is along this series of Dales that the most attractive ground is to be found, and it is a great pity that so many naturalists merely pay a hasty visit to one particular stretch and ignore the remainder.

The special plant which brings many botanists here is the Birds-foot Sedge, *Carex ornithopoda*. It is restricted to limestone in Britain and, apart from this valley, grows mainly only in north-west England in the district where Yorkshire, Westmorland and Cumberland meet. The name is a remarkably apt one, for the young spikes in outline show a close resemblance to the foot of a bird. It is allied to the Fingered Sedge, *C. digitata* (which R. H. Hall also found here in 1947), and indeed specimens collected in 1801 were confused with this species, and not recognised as an addition to the British flora until three-quarters of a century later. I have seen Birds-foot Sedge in two places in these Dales—one in the main valley and the other in a small Dale some two miles away. It flowers in May, but the wiry little plants can be recognised at all times of the year, and I have found fruits by careful searching as late as August.

At one place the sedge is associated with Hoary Whitlow-grass, *Draba incana*, with leaves and stems covered with greyish hairs, and the small white flowers succeeded by pods which are curiously twisted. This little Crucifer is more common farther north, but it is found in several places in the Dales. On limestone rock ledges in the district there is also the Germander Whitlow-grass, *D. muralis*, which is much earlier-flowering and quite dried up by July and August, when *D. incana* is at its best. Another Crucifer is Rock Pepperwort, *Hornungia petraea*, which Mr. Hall tells me varies greatly in quantity from year to year, so that botanists who come in a good spring for the plant get a false idea of its abundance.

One of the localities for Rock Pepperwort is on a rock in the smaller dale, where Bird's-foot Sedge grows. Here I saw Dark-flowered Helleborine, *Epipactis atrorubens*. Mr. Hall had known the plants for years and visited them most seasons, but it was not until July, 1946, that we first saw them in flower. Another nice plant was Small Meadow-rue, *Thalictrum minus*.

In this and other dales in this series there is a good deal of Bloody Cranesbill (I prefer this old and thoroughly English name to the "Blood-red Cranesbill" of some ultra-delicate writers). *Geranium sanguineum* (Plate 39, p. 174) is handsome enough to be commonly grown in gardens, and yet is widespread as a native on limestone cliffs and also sometimes occurs on the chalk. The flowers may be as much as an inch and a half across and are usually deep magenta in colour. They show to advantage against the deeply divided leaves, which turn a delightful shade of red in autumn. In this species the stamens mature one or two days earlier than the stigmas, and it is possible that this is connected with changes in the colour of the petals following pollination. In Johnson's 1633 edition of Gerard's *Herbal* these changes are described in the following picturesque words: "The floures are . . . of a perfect bright red colour, which if they be suffered to grow and stand untill the next day, will be a murry colour; and if they stand unto the third day, they will turne into a deep purple tending to blewnesse, their changing is such, that you shall finde at one time upon one branch floures like in forme, but of divers colours." I do not know how accurately this description fits the facts (" murry " is the colour of the mulberry—purple-red), but the question does not appear to have been recently investigated. A rare gall, *Eriophyes geranii*, has been found on Bloody Cranesbill in this dale.

Another feature of this little dale was the abundance of Roses. I noticed Burnet Rose, *Rosa pimpinellifolia*, and Field Rose, *Rosa arvensis*, as well as Dog Rose, Soft-leaved Rose, and Glaucous Rose; here they were abundant and variable.

Higher up the valley we saw Dropwort, *Filipendula vulgaris*, one of the most handsome of British wild flowers and, in my opinion, superior to its much more widely admired relation, the Meadow-sweet, *F. ulmaria*. Old-fashioned gardeners would appear to have very similar views, for a fine large form of Dropwort is sometimes grown in country districts. The flowers are creamy white, often flushed with red outside, and are gathered into a loose head. The leaves are made up of very numerous small sharply cut leaflets, pinnately arranged, while the root-fibres are enlarged into the drop-shaped tubers which have given the plant its name. On the southern chalk the plant is often abundant, but although it goes north on the limestone to the north of Scotland, it becomes much more local on the way. In Derbyshire it is rare but in the Dales where I have seen it Dropwort is a much larger and finer plant than on the drier chalk downs. The same applies to other localities in the north. It is said that the swollen roots, when dried and reduced to powder, can be made into a sort of bread not to be despised in times of scarcity. It would be necessary to gather an immense number of plants to produce a sufficient quantity to be of any real use, and it is to be hoped that it will never be necessary to try the experiment in this country!

Near the Dropwort there was a colony of Melancholy Thistle, *Cirsium hetrophyllum* (Plate 40, p. 175). This is not particularly a lime-stone plant, and I think it grows equally well on a wide range of soils, provided an adequate supply of moisture is available. Nevertheless it is so frequent on the Carboniferous Limestone of Derbyshire and Yorkshire that it must have a place in this book. The leaves are cottony-white on their lower surface, and the bare, spineless stem stands bolt

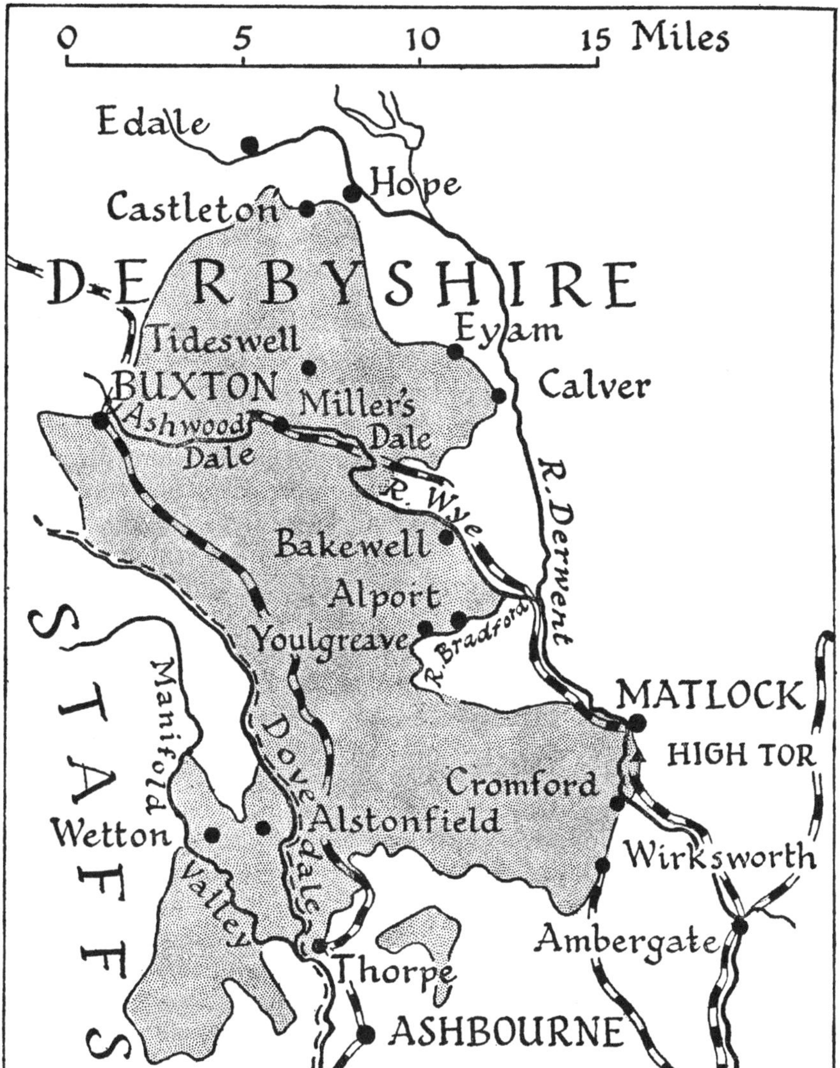

FIG. 12
Carboniferous Limestone of Derbyshire and Staffordshire

upright with a single purple flower head (rarely two or three) at the top.

The main series of dales is in no way inferior to the side valley just described. There are banks in Miller's Dale where a show of bloom to equal the best we have in the south may be seen. Even from the road, limestone plants can be seen growing as luxuriantly as anywhere in Britain.

One small cliff which I examined will serve as an example. Here there was Nottingham Catchfly, *Silene nutans* (Plate XX, p. 111), a plant which is scattered about the chalk and limestone from Dover to Kincardineshire, but always very local. The name Catchfly has been applied to the genus on account of the viscid hairs which clothe the upper part of the stem and on which small insects are often caught.

On the ledges on the same cliff was Long-stalked Cranesbill, *Geranium columbinum*, which is less common on limestone than on chalk. The rather pale purplish-rose flowers are carried on long stalks from the axils of the very finely divided leaves. Growing with it were Spring Cinquefoil, *Potentilla tabernaemontani*, Hairy Rock-cress, *Arabis hirsuta*, with its racemes of strict, narrow pods, and Basil Thyme, *Acinos arvensis*.

All along Miller's Dale there are abundant Hawkweeds, *Hieracium spp.*, of several different sorts, brightening the rocks with their golden flowers. Mossy Saxifrage, *Saxifraga hypnoides*, is scattered about in the damper spots. We also saw Alpine Currant, *Ribes alpinum*, a bush five feet or so in height. The male and female flowers are on different plants (dioecious), and thus only some of them have bunches of bright red fruits in late summer. These look very like those of the garden Red Currant and taste rather similar though somewhat insipid. In wet copses on the limestone in this valley there are colonies of the handsome Globe Flower, *Trollius europaeus*. It is a plant of mountain districts and is rather like a big Buttercup with globe-like yellow flowers. Higher up towards Buxton, in Ashwood Dale, London Pride, *Saxifraga umbrosa*, is abundantly naturalised on damp rocks.

The main road to Buxton runs through the well-wooded Wye and Ashwood Dales, where the more interesting plants are high up on crags which are not readily accessible, or in the smaller lateral dales.

Dovedale

Compared with the rugged dales near Buxton, Dovedale seems soft and unduly civilised. The best part both for scenery and plants extends from Milldale, near Alstonfield, for about three miles south to near Thorpe. All along this stretch the sides are steep and well wooded. To see the choicest plants the botanist must leave the well-trodden track by the Dove and climb some 500 feet to the crags. But even if this strenuous exercise is avoided, the beauty of the view, and the sight of some of the finest general vegetation in Derbyshire, will more than justify a visit. On the first occasion I went to Dovedale it was cold and May snow rested on the higher ground; on the second it was a wet August day; and yet I count both trips as well worth while.

It is perhaps seldom realised how much of the beauty of this Dale is due to the Ash. This tree is dominant throughout the popular stretch of the valley, and it is the peculiar shade of greyish green of its foliage, and the rounded outline of its canopy, which contributes to the softness of the scenery. The next most common tree is Wych Elm, while Elder, Hawthorn and Hazel are also plentiful on the lower ground, and Yew on the crags. On the steep cliffs there is a good deal of Rock Whitebeam, but this is mostly inaccessible.

Probably the most famous Dovedale plant is Alpine Currant, which is locally plentiful here and regarded as undoubtedly wild. When I came in May the bushes were very easy to find owing to the fresh green colour of their foliage, and they were laden with flowers. In August the foliage had gone dark, and it was less easy to spot the plants with their red fruits rather hidden under the leaves.

There is much Nottingham Catchfly and Spring Cinquefoil on the rocks and grassy slopes, and high up on the screes there is Rock Pepperwort and Germander Whitlow-grass. I am told that there is one patch of Angular Solomon's-seal, *Polygonatum odoratum* running down the cliff, and I saw Herb Paris. Greater Burnet-saxifrage, *Pimpinella major*, is plentiful—this has the purest white flowers of all the British Umbelliferae. On the lower ground there is also Long-stalked Cranesbill.

The western side of Dovedale is in Staffordshire, and it happened to be within this county that we found Lesser Teasel, *Dipsacus pilosus*, and Woolly-headed Thistle, *Cirsium eriophorum*. But the mystery plant of Dovedale is recorded as from the Derbyshire side. Madder, *Rubia peregrina*, is the largest of the British members of the Bedstraw Family (Rubiaceae). Its leaves and the angles of its perennial woody stem are rough with deflexed prickles. By means of these it scrambles over the bushes amongst which it grows. The leaves are dark green, arranged in fours, and some of them persist through the winter so that the plant is ready to renew its growth from fresh shoots immediately suitable weather returns in the spring. Formerly Madder was in great demand on account of the fast dye which was prepared from the root-stock.

The plant is most common on chalk and limestone cliffs on the south and west coasts, and it does not go north of Anglesey. Away from the sea it is very rare, though instances of its occurrence have already been given at Cheddar and the Wye Valley on Carboniferous Limestone and at Arundel in Sussex on the chalk. From this it will be clear that a record of Madder from thickets in Dovedale in the heart of England at an altitude of some 600 feet was a somewhat remarkable discovery. It was found by the Reverend R. Bindley of Mickleover about half a century ago and his specimens were checked by the Rev. W. R. Linton, so there can be no doubt about the identification. It is strange that no other botanist has ever seen it there, and it is to be hoped that now wider publicity has been given to the record the plant will be rediscovered.

The Rivers Dove and Manifold join between Ilam and Thorpe, and either of these villages would be a good centre for the exploration of both river valleys. Since it is in Staffordshire, the Derbyshire term " Dale " is not applied to the Manifold Valley, although in scenery and flora it forms an extension of the area just described. The trees —mostly Ash—cover many of the slopes but are restricted to the shelter of the valley, leaving the exposed tableland above devoid of woods and often leached. The flora of the Manifold is rather less rich than Dovedale, although the research undertaken by Mr. E. S. Edees and his friends in recent years has added considerably to the records.

The best part is the limestone about Wetton Mill, and here Rock Pepperwort, Spring Cinquefoil and Jacob's Ladder are to be found. Amongst other interesting plants are Soft-leaved Rose, *Rosa villosa*, and Melancholy Thistle. There is also at least one place in the Manifold Valley where the winter-flowering Mezereon, *Daphne mezereum*, occurs wild.

The Carboniferous Limestone of Derbyshire and Staffordshire is one of the richest parts of central England for wild flowers, famous both for the large number of species represented and for the luxuriance in which many of them occur. North of the dales from the Peak onwards there is one of the most deadly dull areas to the botanist in Britain. For 50 miles Millstone Grit (or "The Grit," as Yorkshire botanists disparagingly call it) is the rock of the Pennines. Here and there a few good plants are to be found, but in general the vegetation consists of a short list of calcifuges repeated with monotonous regularity. Going north, it is not until the upper valley of the Wharfe is reached that good limestone country is again to be found. Fortunately on the east side of the Pennines there is a narrow strip of limestone of another sort, and this will be considered before returning to the Carboniferous in Yorkshire.

CHAPTER 12

THE MAGNESIAN LIMESTONE

MAGNESIAN Limestone is exposed in a narrow outcrop on the east side of the Pennines. Its southern limit is near Nottingham. From here it extends northwards in a belt some five miles wide by way of Doncaster, Tadcaster, Knaresborough and Ripon. From Darlington it widens and curves eastwards to the Durham coast. The length of the outcrop is about 150 miles and the rocks vary considerably.

The most important geological subdivision consists normally of a thick-bedded yellow limestone containing a higher proportion of carbonate of magnesium than is usual in other limestones. It is to this that the Magnesian Limestone owes its name. When the proportion of that chemical is more than 20 per cent, the rock is known as dolomitic limestone. On the Durham coast as much as 44 per cent of magnesium carbonate may be present, but generally it is very much less.

Dolomitic limestones tend to be slightly heavier and harder than corresponding limestones without carbonate of magnesium. When tested in the usual way with cold hydrochloric acid effervescence is much less brisk than when the calcium carbonate is almost pure. With hot dilute acid they effervesce freely. No ecological comparison between dolomitic and other limestones has yet been made, but it is possible that the differences in chemical constitution may have an interesting influence on the vegetation. Some of the Carboniferous Limestones are also dolomitic.

The Magnesian Limestone is of Permian age. It is older than the Oolites and the Chalk, but more recent than the Carboniferous. It is a relatively soft rock, weathering easily to form rounded hills. Rugged cliffs like those of the Carboniferous Limestone are exceptional but occur in a few places. Because of its softness it gives rise to a good light dry soil suitable for cultivation. For this reason most of the Magnesian Limestone country has been under the plough for centuries and very little of the original vegetation is left. The botanist must search round old quarries for aboriginal turf with its treasures. For other plants the few natural scarps provide the best habitats.

The contrast between the lowland agricultural scenery of the Magnesian Limestone and the upland, or even mountainous, rough crags and uncultivated slopes of the Carboniferous Limestone is very great. The latter provides wild unspoiled country visited chiefly by shepherds and people in search of natural beauty. The former is relatively thickly populated. These differences are evident if a comparison is made between the Derbyshire Dales and the Magnesian Limestone between Mansfield and Worksop in the same latitude. There is an even greater contrast between the

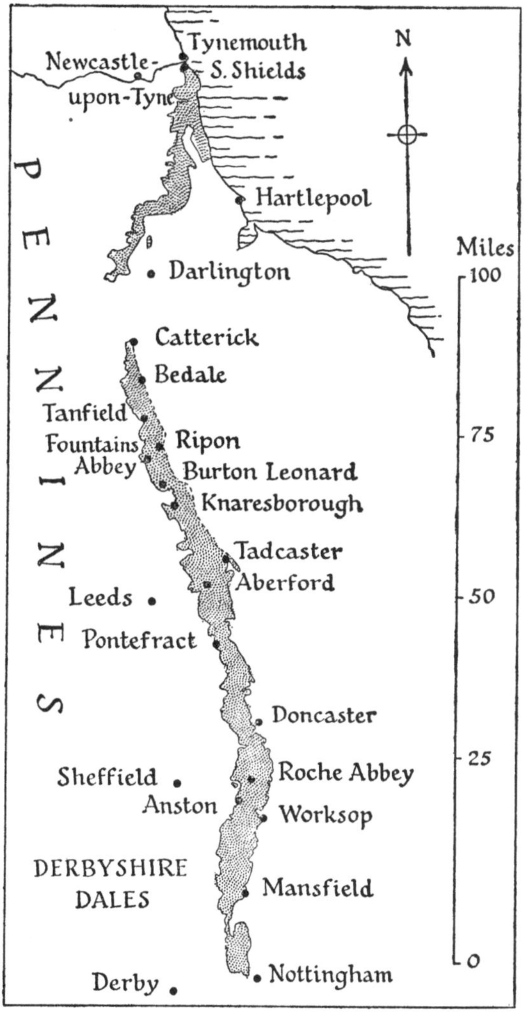

FIG. 13
The Magnesian Limestone

Carboniferous Limestone area of Craven in Yorkshire (see Chapter 13) and the corresponding Magnesian Limestone to the east.

The contrast in wild flowers is equally great. It is due less to differences in the character of the limestones than to variation in altitude. Height above sea-level influences the habitat factors under which plants grow—particularly temperature, precipitation, light and wind. On the high Pennine limestones species of northern distribution extend southwards. The Magnesian Limestone running parallel is all lowland. It is only in Durham that it attains an altitude of 600 feet and most of it is less than half that height. Flowers like Hoary Whitlow-grass, *Draba incana*, which are characteristic of mountain districts, are not to be found.

It is on the soil over this rock that a number of calcicoles reach their farthest north on the east side of England. Traveller's Joy, which is such a good and conspicuous indicator of calcareous ground, is thought to be native on Magnesian Limestone in south-west Yorkshire, but the reader is very unlikely to see it north of this except perhaps as an escape from gardens. Pasque Flower, *Pulsatilla vulgaris*, has been recorded as far north as Piercebridge on the Tees, but here, as in several Yorkshire stations farther south, it is now extinct. Nottingham Catchfly, *Silene nutans*, is still plentiful at Knaresborough but in England does not go beyond.

These are three particularly good examples, but the botanist travelling north along the Magnesian Limestone will be struck again and again with the ever-decreasing quantity of many of the common plants of the southern chalk. Such species as Stemless Thistle, *Cirsium acaulon*, and Black Mullein, *Verbascum nigrum*, just peter out. On the other hand, sufficient of the downland flowers extend north on this rock to make it extremely interesting to northern botanists. The flora of parts of the Permian Limestone in Yorkshire reminds me much more of the North Downs than any part of the Carboniferous.

One reason for this resemblance is the greater frequency of orchids. The Bee and the Fly Orchids, *Ophrys apifera* and *insectifera*, the Pyramidal, *Anacamptis pyramidalis*, and the Burnt Orchid, *Orchis ustulata*, so characteristic of our southern chalk, are still to be found on this formation as far north as County Durham. Spurge Laurel, *Daphne laureola*, is frequent in the woods. Purple Milk-vetch and Wild Liquorice, *Astragalus danicus* and *A. glycyphyllos*, which have been mentioned so often farther south, are widespread.

The southern aspect of the flora is emphasised by the prevalence of Tor-grass, *Brachypodium pinnatum*. In Derbyshire this is abundant on the Permian. In Yorkshire it is abundant locally on the same formation, and in fact Professor Sedgwick has pointed out how exactly it indicates the line of demarcation where it joins the lower sandstone. But it does not extend into Durham. The interesting fact is that this coarse downland grass is hardly known on the Derbyshire and Yorkshire Carboniferous Limestone, where its place is taken by the related *Brachypodium sylvaticum*. Similarly Upright Brome, *Bromus erectus*, is characteristic of the Chalk and the Permian.

There are two rare plants which are associated particularly with the Magnesian Limestone. One is the Thistle Broomrape, *Orobanche reticulata* (Plate XVII, p. 94), which is found in Britain only on the Magnesian Limestone from just east of Leeds to Ripon. It is a handsome species some 12 to 20 inches in height, with pinky-grey to amber-yellow flower-spikes to be seen in July. In its first discovered station it was parasitic on the Woolly-headed Thistle, *Cirsium eriophorum*, but in the place where I have seen it several times in quantity the host-plant is Creeping Thistle, *C. arvense*. At this spot it grows on a rough common by a busy road, and when the common was ploughed up during the war it was just pure luck that a little corner where the Broomrape grew best was left undisturbed. In all its localities this very rare plant varies a great deal in quantity from year to year. Since it depends for survival on the chance of its seeds falling by a suitable host-plant, picking specimens can endanger its existence.

The second special plant of the Permian is a very inconspicuous little sedge, *Carex ericetorum*. Most of the other places where this occurs in Britain are in East Anglia, where it grows on chalk and on calcareous sand over chalk (see p. 100), and its occurrence farther north was quite unsuspected until 1943.[1] In that year Mr. E. C. Wallace was serving with the R.A.F. at Harrogate and devoting his off-duty periods to botanizing. Early in May he discovered a small patch of aboriginal turf near some old quarries in the Burton Leonard district, and here the rare sedge was growing with a number of other chalk plants. This locality is 150 miles from the nearest place where it was previously known to grow. After it had been shown by this very unexpected discovery that it occurred on the Magnesian Limestone, other botanists started a search to try and fill in the gap in the dis-

[1] *The Naturalist* for 1943, p. 97 (1944).

tibution. A Sheffield naturalist, Mr. John Brown, soon found it at Markland Grips in Derbyshire and on Lindrick Common in the extreme south of Yorkshire. Since then *Carex ericetorum* has been found in more than one place on the Permian between Wallace's and Brown's stations. More recently it has been found on Carboniferous Limestone in Westmorland.

Space will only permit of notes on a few selected habitats on the Magnesian Limestone, and these will be given in sequence from south to north. In Derbyshire and Nottinghamshire the best places are in valleys where wall-like lines of rock have preserved the characteristic flora from destruction, as at Markland Grips, Cresswell Crags and Pleasley Park, and about quarries, as at Shireoaks. At the first-mentioned place Mountain Sedge, *Carex montana*, grows with *C. ericetorum.*

A short distance over the county boundary into Yorkshire the wooded crags of Anston have long been famous for their flora. A mile away the main road from Anston to Worksop runs across Lindrick Common on the limestone plateau, and here Stemless Thistle is abundant. Surrey botanists would regard this as one of the commonest of plants, but in the north it is a great rarity. When the Yorkshire Naturalists' Union went to Lindrick in 1947 they recorded with delight that there was so much of this Thistle that they had to pick their way between its prickly leaves. This place is probably the farthest north that it is plentiful, though it is to be found off the Permian at Rievaulx.

The Magnesian Limestone passes very close to Doncaster on the west side of the town, and some eight miles farther north it forms a most beautiful valley through which runs the River Went. In one place there is a good deal of Spring Cinquefoil, *Potentilla tabernaemontani*, with other attractive limestone flowers, and I have sometimes turned off the Great North Road at Wentbridge to see these. The main road (A.1) from here runs right along the middle of the Permian to just beyond Wetherby, and some of the best localities can be reached by making only slight diversions.

It is interesting to read the views of a Yorkshire naturalist on the characteristic plants of the Magnesian Limestone about Aberford. The following is taken from the preliminary notice[1] of an excursion to this district:

[1] Yorkshire Naturalists' Union, Circular 397 (1936).

"In the hedgerows Dogwood[1], *Cornus sanguinea*, and White Bryony, *Bryonia dioica*, with Black Horehound, *Ballota nigra*, and Tor-grass, *Brachypodium pinnatum*, may be taken to show quite clearly that we are on Magnesian Limestone, and in a less distinct way we might put Small Scabious, *Scabiosa columbaria*, Clustered Bellflower, *Campanula glomerata*, Hoary Plantain, *Plantago media*, Pyramidal Orchis, *Anacamptis pyramidalis*, Hedge Bedstraw, *Galium mollugo*, and Upright Brome, *Bromus erectus*."

These, we note, are all common plants of the southern chalk!

Much the same list might be produced from other interesting localities in the same district—from quarries near Tadcaster, roadsides near Collingham, and from Linton Common.

The Permian cliffs above the River Wharfe at Boston Spa and Thorp Arch are wooded and produce chiefly woodland plants. Of the rarer species two of the most characteristic are Wild Liquorice and Purple Milk-vetch, *Astragalus glycyphyllos* and *A. danicus*. The former I have only seen near Linton Common on a hedgebank, but the latter has several localities. Fingered Sedge, *Carex digitata*, is near Boston Spa. There are at least two places in the district where Baneberry, *Actaea spicata*, may be still found. This will be described in the next chapter in connection with the Yorkshire Carboniferous Limestone (see p. 186), where it is more plentiful, but its occurrence on the Permian at an altitude of only about 200 feet is interesting. At one place it is still growing at or very near the spot where Ray recorded it in 1670. In a few wet spots Bird's-eye Primrose, *Primula farinosa*, is to be found, but this again is much more plentiful on the Carboniferous Limestone.

The town of Knaresborough, by the Nidd, with its Castle, is built on cliffs which are mainly Magnesian Limestone, though the acid Millstone Grit is also exposed. On the calcareous rocks there is an abundance of naturalised plants like Wallflower, *Cheiranthus cheiri*, Parsley, *Petroselinum crispum*, and Ivy-leaved Toadflax, *Cymbalaria muralis*, which are doubtless escapes from ancient gardens. Nottingham Catchfly is still here in its most northern English station, although it has from time to time been reported as extinct. Bloody Cranesbill is also on the cliff with Pellitory-of-the-wall, *Parietaria diffusa*, and Field Garlic, *Allium oleraceum*.

Four miles north at Burton Leonard I made a long list of plants

[1] *Thelycrania sanguinea*.

from the aboriginal turf which would differ very little from a list made on similar ground at Box Hill in Surrey! Here, and in fact all the way to Fountains Abbey, I was surprised at the abundance of Greater Burnet-saxifrage, *Pimpinella major*.

The ruins of the Abbey are most beautifully sited in a lovely valley on the Permian limestone. The surrounding woods which are composed mainly of Ash and Wych Elm with a good deal of Yew and Sycamore, *Acer pseudo-platanus*, extend for over two miles through Mackershaw Wood by the River Skell. Most of the stone used for the construction of this richest of all Cistercian abbeys was obtained from quarries in the valley in which it was built, and the flowers which now grow on the ruins are therefore properly those of the Magnesian Limestone.

Fountains Abbey should be visited by everyone interested in lovely old buildings and their history. To a botanist there are added attractions. For four centuries the flowers have been struggling to establish themselves on the broken walls and, in spite of efforts to keep the place neat and tidy in recent years, they still add charm to the ruin. The most beautiful of all the blooms there are those of the Pink, *Dianthus plumarius* (Plate 43, p. 186). The full popular name is " Common " Pink, the prefix being necessary to distinguish it from its allies, but really satisfactory localities for the plant are few and far between. The usual colour of the flower, as its name suggests, is pink, but at Fountains white blooms are not uncommon and there are also some of a much deeper red colour. How long it has been there we do not know for certain, but there is at least a possibility that the Pink has been at the Abbey since the days of the monks. This old-fashioned garden flower has long been a favourite. It is particularly interesting to see the way the plant has climbed the ruins—it certainly ascends to at least 100 feet above ground level and probably higher.

The Permian is a yellow limestone, and the colour of the Abbey walls makes a perfect setting for the flowers which grow on them. Wallflower, *Cheiranthus cheiri*, and Welsh Poppy, *Meconopsis cambrica*, are old garden plants which, like the Pink, have found a home here. Ivy-leaved Toadflax, *Cymbalaria muralis*, is an alien which is thoroughly established. Other flowers I noticed include Pellitory-of-the-wall, Hoary Plantain, Small Scabious, Hairy Rock Cress and Common Lady's Mantle. Fingered Sedge, *Carex digitata*, grows in an open space in the woods a mile and a half away and Bird's-nest Orchid, *Neottia nidus-avis*, is plentiful under Beeches.

John Markham

BLOODY CRANESBILL *Geranium sanguineum;* a rather widespread species of chalk and limestone which is most frequent in the north and west. Yorkshire; July

PLATE 40

John Markham

MELANCHOLY THISTLE, *Cirsium heterophyllum;* a northern plant sometimes found on limestone. Yorkshire; July

I have never botanized seriously on the Magnesian Limestone north of Fountains Abbey, but it continues past Ripon, Tanfield and Catterick to the Tees at Manfield. In Durham it broadens out to form a triangle with the coast from Hartlepool to South Shields as its eastern edge. It includes Castle Eden Dene, where Lady's Slipper Orchid, *Cypripedium calceolus*, was once plentiful. Unfortunately the only recent papers dealing with this area are scattered notes in periodicals and a new full county flora is very much needed. In spite of industrialisation there can be no doubt that interesting plants are still to be found on the Permian in Durham, but it is not a district which appeals to botanists on holiday.

This chapter has covered country from central England to the north. From Nottingham and Derbyshire the journey has led far past the main mass of the Yorkshire Carboniferous Limestone with which the early part of the next chapter is concerned. But this is the usual approach of visitors from southern or central England who travel by road. They follow the Great North Road to Doncaster and along the stretch of Magnesian Limestone described, through Aberford and Bramham, and then turn west along the valley of the Wharfe. It is with Upper Wharfedale that the next chapter is first concerned.

CHAPTER 13

CRAVEN IN YORKSHIRE

NORTH OF the Derbyshire Dales there is a gap of some 50 miles before the next big exposure of Carboniferous Limestone in the Craven district of West Yorkshire. On the intervening stretches of the Pennines, Coal Measures and Millstone Grit give rise to acid soils with large areas of some of the most dreary vegetation in the whole of Britain. To this the varied flora of the limestone is a welcome contrast.

Craven is near the southern end of a large area marked as Carboniferous Limestone on small-scale geological maps. Stretching from coast to coast at the Solway Firth, and some 135 miles from south to north, this area includes much of Yorkshire and Northumberland and parts of Lancashire, Westmorland, Durham and Cumberland, and it extends into Scotland. In the south there are extensive exposures of massive limestone, the best of which are considered in this chapter. Going north along the Pennines, the limestone becomes increasingly replaced by beds of shale and sandstone. In Northumberland the latter predominate and beds of limestone are only exposed on a relatively small scale.

It is not easy to generalise about the flora of the limestone of the north of England, but I think its characteristic feature is its "upland" nature. Carboniferous Limestone descends to sea-level at Humphrey Head. It ascends so high on Ingleborough (2,373 ft.), Penyghent (2,273 ft.) and Mickle Fell (2,591 ft.) that it becomes the habitat of mountain flowers outside the scope of this book. Excluding these two extremes, most of the country favoured by botanists is upland rather than mountainous and the flowers are mostly northern species. The

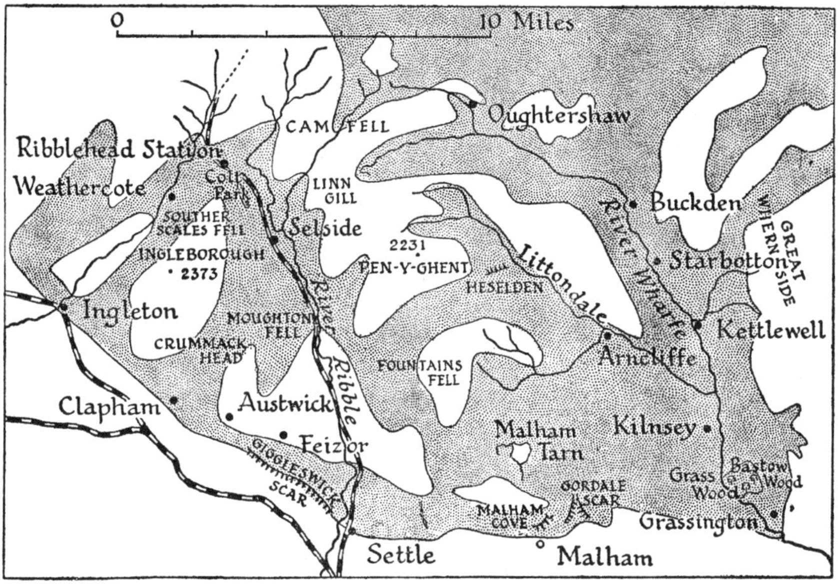

FIG. 14
Carboniferous Limestone of the Craven District of Yorkshire

Derbyshire Dales served as an introduction to this type of flora—in Yorkshire the northern plants are more numerous.

In this region magnificent cliffs are the homes of rare plants. The Yorkshire and Westmorland Scars, such as Gordale, Malham Cove, Dib Scar, Scout Scar, Whitbarrow Scar, and the sea-washed cliffs of Humphrey Head, are famous for the richness of their flora. Where the limestone comes down to low levels, as in the Silverdale district of Lancashire, it is often well wooded, but on higher ground only scattered trees and open scrub are to be seen except in sheltered places.

On the west side of the Pennines the Carboniferous Limestone shares the heavy rainfall for which the Lake District is famous, and here the interesting feature known as " limestone pavement " is locally extremely well developed. This is due to the same cause as leaching (see p. 13). Rain-water containing carbon dioxide in solution is capable of dissolving calcium carbonate to the extent of about 1 in 16,000 parts, and its action continued over many centuries has an important effect on limestone rock. Joints in the rock yield first; the jointing of the Carboniferous Limestone here, being rectangular, leads to a characteristic product of weathering. Yielding along the horizontal bedding-planes, it gives rise to a bare, jointed, flattish surface known as "clints." The vertical joints are widened into crevices (Plate 36, p. 155) called "grikes," which commonly extend down to a depth of 5 to 15 feet. These are the home of many interesting and rare plants which find shelter both from the desiccating action of the wind and from attacks of grazing animals, which are unable to reach them. The "Pot-holes," which are particularly well developed on Ingleborough, are also due to the solubility of the limestone and offer shelter to a luxuriant vegetation.

Maritime cliffs, upland crags, pavement and pot-holes, old mine workings, gorges through which run rivers and streams, and flat hill-tops are amongst the places where the botanist has to search in this vast and often wild stretch of country. Some of the localities have been the subject of pilgrimage throughout the history of British botany; others are inadequately explored even now.

Only the Craven district of west Yorkshire will be considered in the present chapter. This is a tract of wild hilly country extending east from Ingleborough. Here the rivers Wharfe and Aire, which drain to the North Sea, and the Ribble, which runs south-west to the Irish Sea, have their sources. All the important roads follow their valleys, which provide a convenient way of arranging the limestone habitats of Craven.

Wharfedale

The Wharfe runs through an interesting bit of wooded limestone at Bolton Abbey; but it is at Grassington, some nine miles farther up the valley, that the really exciting limestone country commences. Here there are good plants found on calcareous rocks by the river at Ghaistrills, and Grass and Bastow Woods and Dib Scar are famous for their flowers. Near Kilnsey Crag the valley forks. One branch leads through Kettlewell, Starbotton and Buckden; the other by Arncliffe and Littondale to Heseltine (Hesleden) Gill and the slopes of Penyghent. There are few more exciting places for the botanist in Britain.

John Markham

DARK-FLOWERED HELLEBORINE, *Epipactis atrorubens;* an orchid of northern distribution which is specially characteristic of the Carboniferous Limestone. Yorkshire; July

PLATE 42

Brian Perkins

Rigid Buckler Fern, *Dryopteris villarii*; locally plentiful over a small area where Westmorland and Yorkshire meet, and found in a few other places. The fronds of this fern are usually of the bluish-green colour shown in the photograph. Yorkshire; June

The sides of these two valleys are fairly steep and there is much bare limestone, but in many places there are also narrow strips of open scrub woodland—so open that much of it we should hardly regard as worthy of the name of wood in the south of England. Below the scrub on the open ground the limestone is often damp—at least locally—and here the most characteristic plant is the Bird's-eye Primrose, *Primula farinosa*. This little gem has numerous small lilac-purple flowers arranged on a common stalk like a Cowslip, and the lower surface of the leaves is mealy. Its distribution in Britain is limited to approximately the area considered in this and the next chapter, though it strays across the border into the south of Scotland. Near Kilnsey it grows with a plant which is usually found only on the coast—the Sea Plantain, *Plantago maritima*.

In several places the Bird's-eye Primrose is associated with one of the special rarities of this valley—the Bitter Milkwort, *Polygala amara*. They both thrive over wet limestone where there is no undue competition with coarser plants. Bitter Milkwort, like the Kentish Milkwort, *P. austriaca* (see p. 54), has very small flowers and a rosette at the base of the stem. Apart from the adjoining upper Aire valley, its only other British station is in Teesdale (Distribution Map 4, p. 217). The flowers are usually of a pale slaty-blue and not easy to find, and it was probably for this reason that it remained undetected in Wharfedale until the comparatively recent date of 1883.

Another very special rarity for which the valley is famous is the Lady's Slipper Orchid. The old botanists knew this farther west round Ingleborough, but there it has not been seen for many years. The days when ten Lady's Slippers could be bought at Settle market from a man who had brought about forty to sell, as Thomas Frankland informed Curtis in 1781,[1] are long over. We may deplore the destruction of the flowers which resulted from such transactions, but they indicate that the plant must have been tolerably plentiful. Formerly this orchid ranged over a fairly wide area : it extended into Westmorland on the Carboniferous, and grew on the Oolite in eastern Yorkshire and on the Magnesian Limestone in Durham (Distribution Map 15, p. 223). To-day it is one of the rarest and most elusive of British plants and one of the few I have not seen wild myself. The nearest I have come to getting practical knowledge of the Lady's

[1] Letter dated 30 November, 1781, quoted in Curtis, W. Hugh (1941), *William Curtis, 1746-1799*, p. 55.

Slipper is to be shown places where it has been found in previous years.

There is little doubt that, apart from its rarity, the chief reason why this orchid is so seldom seen is its shyness of flowering. Growing among Lily-of-the-Valley, or on limestone scree under scattered trees, its yellow sabot-shaped flowers are conspicuous enough not to be easily missed. Many of those which do occur are found by children from the villages. In the past they have often been transplanted into cottage and inn gardens. The fact remains that some plants rarely produce flowers, although there is a case on record where twenty blooms were cut from one clump in the space of seven years. Many botanists go to look for it too late in the year, being misled by the dates given in the text-books; the last week in May or early June would seem to be the best times.

It is not entirely easy to account for the decrease of the Lady's Slipper. The depredations of botanists and villagers are obviously to some extent responsible, but these may not be the only causes. From the records over three centuries it would seem that it has always been rare, but that there have been periodical " assurgences " when for a few years it has been found in increased quantity. It is likely that the occasional notes of a number of flowers being found in one or several places have coincided with these periods. There have been no " assurgences " during the present century and it is possible that one is almost due. But against this theory there is the undoubted fact that there have been important general changes in the vegetation of some of its old haunts. Thus Helks Wood, Ingleton, where botanists used to find it in the seventeenth century, is now a rather unlikely place for it to grow.

Calceolus Mariae, or Mary's Shoe, as it was once called, has shallow roots and an underground stem which creeps in leaf mould just below the surface of the soil. it can thus live for a number of years without flowering, while putting up pairs of leaves in shape and colour very similar to those of the Lily-of-the-Valley. The blooms have an elaborate mechanism for ensuring cross-pollination but, as Lees remarks that he never saw them visited by insects and that he doubted if they commonly ripened seed, it seems probable that in this country the mechanism is a failure. Nevertheless I very much hope that any reader finding a flower will follow the example of Yorkshire naturalists and leave it lightly covered with brushwood so that it stands a chance of fulfilling its mission.

There are three places on the high limestone west of Littondale where Mountain Avens, *Dryas octopetala*, is to be found. This is a most attractive little plant commonly obtainable from nurserymen. In cultivation many people find it a shy flowerer and have to rest content with the leaves, which are shaped rather like those of the oak (though very much smaller) and are downy white on their lower surface. In the wind-swept places where it grows wild there are usually plenty of blooms, and these with their commonly eight snowy white petals are a glorious sight in early summer. The fruits which follow are feathery and not unlike those of the Pasque Flower, *Pulsatilla vulgaris*, though this belongs to the Ranunculaceae and Mountain Avens to the Rosaceae.

These are some of the special rarities of Upper Wharfedale and Littondale, but a better idea of the interesting vegetation can be obtained from a brief description of a rough limestone valley near Grassington which I visited in July, 1946, for the second time. The valley ended in an amphitheatre of cliffs some 150 feet high, and these continued along its south side for about a quarter of a mile. A track ran along the bottom where there was a lot of Ash and Hazel and some Downy Birch, *Betula pubescens*, Mountain Ash, *Sorbus aucuparia*, and Aspen, *Populus tremula*. On the cliffs were a number of plants of Rock Whitebeam, *Sorbus rupicola*, and a great deal of Ivy.

Below the cliffs a scree ran down to the track, and on this we found common southern calcicoles, such as Fairy Flax, Small Scabious and Common Rock-rose, growing with Mountain Bedstraw, *Galium pumilum*, and northern plants like Grass-of-Parnassus, *Parnassia palustris*, Bird's-eye Primrose and Bitter Milkwort. Towards the top of the scree there was one place which even from a distance appeared blue—almost like that blue haze one associates with Bluebell woods. As we climbed up it became evident that this was caused by a glorious patch of Jacob's Ladder, *Polemonium caeruleum*, which has already been described in connection with the Derbyshire Dales (see p. 159).

The sheer limestone cliffs had a wonderful flora in their cracks and narrow ledges. There were ferns like Hart's-tongue, *Phyllitis scolopendrium*, Common Polypody, *Polypodium vulgare*, and Brittle Bladder Fern, *Cystopteris fragilis*, and the much rarer Limestone Polypody, *Thelypteris robertiana*, and Green Spleenwort, *Asplenium viride*. Then there were interesting flowers similar to those of the Derbyshire limestone such as Germander Whitlow-grass, *Draba muralis*, Hoary Whitlow-grass, *D. incana*, with its twisted pods, Bloody Cranesbill, *Geranium sanguineum*, Field Garlic, *Allium oleraceum*, and Mossy Saxifrage, *Saxifraga hypnoides*. With these were Hairy Rock-cress, *Arabis hirsuta*, Crosswort, *Cruciata chersonensis*, Horseshoe Vetch, Dropwort, Marjoram and Salad Burnet. The presence of these common plants of the southern chalk on this northern limestone cliff at an altitude of some 750 feet above sea-level serves to stress the " common factor " which exists between all the calcareous soils in Britain.

Grass Wood is a well-known place both for plants and picnics. Angular Solomon's-seal, *Polygonatum odoratum*, and Dark-flowered Helleborine, *Epipactis atrorubens*, are in the district. Much of the lower part of the woodland is planted and its character has been artificially changed. On the other hand, Bastow Wood, which adjoins it at a higher level (900-950 ft.), is more natural. The dominant trees are Ash and Downy Birch, widely spaced and dwarfed owing to the shallowness of the soil and exposure to winds. Many of them seem to be dying, and the dead stumps and branches scattered about give an eerie appearance which is enhanced by the dense webs of caterpillars which cover the Bird Cherries, *Prunus padus*.

Gordale Scar and Malham Cove

Six miles west of Grassington, across the watershed into the region drained by the head-waters of the Aire, there is another limestone district which every botanist should visit. The longest tributary of the river is Gordale Beck, which drains down from Malham Moor through a mile-long rocky gorge and then runs over a waterfall at Gordale Scar. This is one of the finest sights in Britain. The visitor is awed by the towering cliffs around him and the knowledge that to reach the ledges and the valley above he must climb up the difficult track by the waterfall.

The flowers of Gordale Scar are very much the same as those described for the valley at Grassington, but Small Meadow-rue, *Thalictrum minus*, is very much more abundant.

People who know Gordale Scar will readily appreciate how inaccessible are some of the ledges on the cliffs, and that a botanist, scrambling about, may, by chance, find his way on to one of them by a route not easily retraced. This is the simple explanation of how a locality for a rare little sedge was lost for sixty years although the locality was recorded so precisely that one would have supposed its rediscovery presented no difficulty. In June, 1878, William West found *Carex capillaris* growing on the terraced limestone rocks of Gordale " on the left-hand as the ascent is made, above the large mass of debris." It was previously unknown south of Teesdale and so the find was an important one. In the years which followed many botanists searched carefully for the little sedge without success, but it was ever in the minds of local naturalists. When I visited Gordale in 1935 with Mr. C. A. Cheetham, the Secretary of the Yorkshire Naturalists' Union, he expressed the view that it would one day be refound. His optimism was justified and in 1939 Mr. G. A. Shaw found *Carex capillaris* in a place which agreed with West's description. Since then several botanists have seen it.

From Gordale it is a short walk to Malham Cove, a magnificent amphitheatre of grand and precipitous cliffs (Plate 34, p. 147). On each side of the scar big screes lead down to the stream which issues from the bottom of the cliff. At the bottom and on the screes there is open woodland made up chiefly of Ash, Hazel and Hawthorn.

The glory of Malham Cove is a magnificent display of Jacob's Ladder (see pp. 159 and 181), which is all the more interesting on account of the fact that John Ray found it here over 270 years ago. The words in which he recorded it[1] are worth quoting :

" Greek Valerian, called by the vulgar Ladder to heaven or Jacob's Ladder. Found . . . about Malham Cove, a place so remarkable that it is esteemed one of the wonders of Craven. It grows there in a wood on the left hand of the water as you go to the Cove from Malham plentifully ; and also at Cordill or the Whern [Gordale Scar], a remarkable Cove where comes out a great stream of water, near the said Malham."

It is not to be found now at the *exact* spot indicated by Ray, and it seems to have disappeared completely from Gordale, where it was plentiful as late as 1805. As the eye follows the blue flowers up the scree at Malham Cove on a day when the sky is cloudless, one is tempted to follow the example of the " vulgar " and call it " Ladder to heaven."

The precipice at the Cove holds a botanical mystery which has not been blessed with a satisfactory solution like the one at Gordale

[1] Ray, John (1677) ; *Catalogus plantarum Angliae*, Ed. 2 : 299.

Scar. In 1862 L. C. Miall published a record on his own authority of Hoary Rock-rose, *Helianthemum canum*, as growing at " Malham, near the Cove." Later, F. Arnold Lees claimed to have confirmed the record (there is a specimen in his collection) and said that the plant grew " on the step-like ledges of rock near the top of the face of the Cove, with a S.W. aspect." He hastened to add that reaching it was risky for all but the cool-headed! Like *Carex capillaris*, this has acted as a challenge to a generation of Yorkshire botanists to break their necks, but the plant still eludes them.

The cliffs here are also adorned with Rock Whitebeam, and there is a good deal of Germander Whitlow-grass, Hoary Whitlow-grass, Bloody Cranesbill, Mountain Bedstraw and various Hawk-weeds. Just above the top is a small but famous bit of limestone pavement, but the plants that grow in it are so heavily grazed whenever they appear above the level of the clints that their description will be reserved for better examples.

Leaving the bottom of the Cove, visitors are very likely to find Spring Sandwort, *Minuartia verna*, and more locally they may see Alpine Penny-cress, *Thlaspi alpestre*. These occur in a good many places in Craven and particularly, as between Malham and Settle and at Grassington, about the workings from old lead-mines (compare p. 157). At Malham the Penny-cress, like Jacob's Ladder, suffers severely from the nibbling of grazing animals.

Ribblesdale

On the other side of the road west of Malham Cove and almost opposite to it (though half a mile farther up the steep hill from where the public track comes out), there is a gate labelled " To Settle via Stockdale Farm." This is the route to follow across the watershed into Ribblesdale. It is the way the old botanists used to reach Malham from Settle. The market town is just as good a centre to-day for exploring the limestone country as it was three centuries ago.

The period of greatest activity in the exploitation of the mineral mines of Craven seems to have started soon after A.D. 1600 and continued throughout that century. It is therefore almost certain that the workings at Pikedaw, Grizedales, Stockdale and Attermire Scar were either still being dug or had only recently been abandoned when

John Ray came along the track. The " lead-plants," Spring Sandwort and Alpine Penny-cress, were probably very much more plentiful than they are to-day.

A mile and a half north-west of Settle the wooded Giggleswick Scar borders the main road to Kirkby Lonsdale. From Settle to Clapham this road is almost the precise boundary between the Carboniferous limestone to the north and Millstone Grit to the south, and it therefore provides a useful opportunity of comparing their respective floras. Giggleswick Scar figures prominently in the old botanical records, many of which were given as " above the Ebbing and Flowing Well." This may still be seen by the side of the main road, and provided it is not choked up with fallen leaves and you have the time to spare to wait while it empties and fills, it will intrigue you. Several rare plants are still to be seen on the screes and cliffs of the Scar, but I fancy that the growth of the trees (Beeches have been planted on the lower part) and the digging of the quarry at the east end have made great changes.

From Settle there is a big area running south-west almost to Preston marked on the map as Carboniferous Limestone, but little calcareous rock is exposed on the surface. It is north of Settle up the Ribble valley beyond Horton that the best country is to be found. The road runs between the mighty hills of Ingleborough on the west and Penyghent on the east, rising all the time until it is over 1000 feet above sea-level, near Ribblehead station. The railway, the " Midland " route to Carlisle, runs near the road all the way, and Horton and Ribblesdale stations are convenient for exploring the dale. It is interesting to see from the train how the cuttings through rocks which are not limestone are immediately picked out by the presence of Foxglove, *Digitalis purpurea*, and Broom, *Sarothamnus scoparius*.

There is one plant which has been found in a number of places in Ribblesdale and on tracks leading up on to Ingleborough which is not known anywhere else in the British Isles. Yorkshire Sandwort, *Arenaria gothica*, was first found in 1889 at Ribblehead station, and there was considerable argument about its identity before it was named. A little tufted plant with small leaves and white flowers resembling those of the commoner Spring Sandwort, it is very closely allied to *Arenaria ciliata*, which only grows with us on the Ben Bulben range, Co. Sligo, and *A. norvegica*, which is restricted in Britain to north-west Scotland, the Hebrides, Shetland and Ireland. (Distribution

Map 5, p. 213). These three are regarded by some botanists as subspecies of one collective species, and it is remarkable that they are restricted to such very limited and widely scattered localities. Abroad the Yorkshire Sandwort has its main home in Sweden, but in spite of the fact that it was first noticed by a road near a railway station it is generally regarded as a native plant in Ribblesdale.

Between Selside and Ribblehead there is one of the most remarkable and uncanny woods in Britain. Colt Park is the best example in Britain of an aboriginal scar limestone ashwood, and the variety and interest of its flora is astonishing, having regard to the small area concerned. I was there last on 16 July, 1946, and my notes ran to four closely written pages, but as the general flora has been described fully in a fairly recent book,[1] only a brief account will be given here.

Colt Park Wood consists mainly of Ash, with some Bird Cherry (covered with caterpillar webs as at Grassington), Mountain Ash, various Sallows, Guelder Rose, *Viburnum opulus*, Soft-leaved Rose, *Rosa villosa*, Hawthorn and Elder. These grow on a limestone pavement with some of the widest and deepest cracks (grikes) that I have ever seen. In places it is difficult to jump across from one slab to the next, and the intervening crack may go down for some eight feet—in others the grikes are much less wide and shallower. Every footstep has to be carefully chosen if bruised shins and possibly even broken bones are to be avoided. On account of the danger to their limbs, grazing animals are kept out. Down in the cracks there is plenty of moisture and plants are sheltered from the wind. Here vegetable remains accumulate and plants which favour woodland humus thrive. Bracken is sometimes eight feet tall with its fronds expanding above the surface of the rock. Dog's Mercury, *Mercurialis perennis*, can be found a yard in height. The general ground vegetation is much as one would expect in an Ashwood but modified by the extraordinary conditions under which it grows.

Lily-of-the-Valley is abundant and so is Ramsons, *Allium ursinum*, which is easily distinguished by the pungent smell of onions which arises every time you tread on the lily-like leaves. Angular Solomon's-seal is there and so is Baneberry, *Actaea spicata* (see Plate 38, p. 159). This is a curious plant belonging to the Ranunculaceae, with divided leaves having their leaflets arranged in threes each side of the midrib, spikes of small white flowers, and purplish-black berries. Herb

[1] Tansley, A. G. (1939), *The British Islands and their Vegetation*, p. 434.

Brian Perkins

COMMON PINK, *Dianthus plumarius*, on the ruins of Fountains Abbey. Anciently introduced here on walls built of local Magnesian Limestone. Yorkshire; June

G. H. McLean

IRISH LIMESTONE PAVEMENT NEAR BLACK HEAD, CO. CLARE
The home of a unique association of plants of northern and southern distribution. July

Christopher, the old botanists called it ; but even Gerard and Johnson were unable to find a use for it. " I finde little or nothing extant in the antient or later writers, of any one good propertie wherewith any part of this plant is possessed : therefore I wish those that love new medicines to take heed that this be none of them, because it is thought to be of a venomous and deadly qualitie."[1] Perhaps this warning has played its part in preserving this rare species from destruction ! The area over which it is found in Britain is restricted to a narrow band across northern England (Distribution Map 7, p. 219). In Craven there are a fair number of localities and it extends westwards on the Carboniferous Limestone to near the shore of Morecambe Bay at Arnside. As already stated, it is also found east of Craven on the Magnesian Limestone and on Oolite near Scarborough. In addition there is one very puzzling locality in Yorkshire for Baneberry. Although elsewhere restricted to calcareous soils, it grows in a wood near Mirfield on the Coal Measures —but here it has been suggested that it has been introduced.

One of the glories of Colt Park Wood is sheets of a lovely large-flowered Pansy, *Viola lepida*, with very pretty variegated blooms. In one place there is Alpine Cinquefoil, *Potentilla crantzii*. Yellow Star-of-Bethlehem, *Gagea lutea*, grows here in its highest British locality. I have only seen leaves and believe it seldom flowers. Herb Paris is also to be found in the wood.

In the damper spots there is plenty of Melancholy Thistle, Meadow Sweet, *Filipendula ulmaria*, Water Avens, Wood Cranesbill, *Geranium sylvaticum*, and Giant Bellflower, *Campanula latifolia*. I also noticed Marsh and Soft Hawksbeards, *Crepis paludosa* and C. *mollis*, which are plants with a northern distribution. The former is fairly common in hilly or mountainous districts, but Soft Hawksbeard is a rare plant which I have only seen a few times. They are both rather like Hawkweeds and not too easy to tell apart before the fruits are ripe. This, however, did not present the slightest difficulty when I was last at Colt Park, for on 16 July the Marsh Hawksbeard was in full bloom while the later-flowering *Crepis mollis* was only just opening.

A mile and a half away, and on the other side of the road, there is a most beautiful gorge known as Ling Gill. The sides are clothed with a luxuriant vegetation thriving under the constantly moist atmosphere and protected from the wind and from grazing animals by the steepness of the slopes. There is only one way to see Ling Ghyll and

[1] Gerard, J., *The Herball*, Ed. 2, by Thomas Johnson (1636), p. 980.

that is by walking in the bed of the stream, and this presents considerable difficulty after heavy rain when it may be impossible to negotiate the waterfall half-way through.

The flowers here include Marsh Hawksbeard, Melancholy Thistle, Wood Cranesbill, Herb Paris, Giant Bellflower, Globe Flower and Mountain Everlasting, *Antennaria dioica*. There is also a record of London Pride, *Saxifraga umbrosa*, which I have seen under very similar conditions in Hesleden Gill on the other side of Penyghent. This is a little different from the larger-flowered London Pride commonly grown now in town gardens, but it seems to be the same as a form which was once cultivated in this country, now rejected by gardeners in favour of a more showy plant. It is possible that some scrap of it got into these remote Yorkshire Gills from cottage gardens, but this is not supported by the situations of the few human habitations in the district and it seems just as likely that it is a true native.

The district from Ling Ghyll and Cam Fell to Oughtershaw, to the east at the head of Wharfedale, may hold the key to another mystery of British field botany. The Eyebrights are quite a difficult critical group, but one of the most distinct of them is the Narrow-leaved Eyebright, *Euphrasia salisburgensis*, which occurs in some plenty on the limestones of the west of Ireland. As Praeger remarks, it "is easily recognised in the field by its dwarf bushy growth, characteristic colour, and jagged upper leaves." He adds that the latter assume a beautiful coppery brown colour when the plant grows in exposed places. In Britain it has only been found in Yorkshire (the Devon record is an error) and the finder was F. Arnold Lees.

As I write I have before me Lees' own annotated copy of Dr. G. C. Druce's *British Plant List*, edition 1, which was given to him by the author and eventually found its way into my library. Against *E. salisburgensis*, Lees has written : "Cam, Outershaw and on exposed table limestone to Conistone Cold !" but he never published the record. In his herbarium at the British Museum (Natural History) there are specimens from Outershaw and Buckden (farther down the Wharfe Valley) collected in 1885 and 1886 which H. W. Pugsley said exactly match the Irish plants. It will be seen that these place-names extend over a large area of country and it is perhaps not to be expected that the plant will be found again easily. The rediscovery of Narrow-leaved Eyebright in Yorkshire would be a find of first-class botanical importance.

Ingleborough

The fissured massive limestone of the Craven area reaches its finest development on the slopes of Ingleborough; a mighty hill which is most conveniently explored from Austwick, Clapham or Ingleton. The alpine plants which grow near the summit, like those of Penyghent, belong to a book on mountain flowers rather than to this volume, but there is plenty of interest on the scars and limestone pavements on the flanks of the hill. These are beautifully illustrated by the photographers in Plate 36 to 42, pp. 155-179.

One of the finest areas of limestone pavement is on Souther Scales Fell. This is less wooded than at Colt Park, a couple of miles to the north-east, but the main features are very similar. The fissures afford protection to the plants from grazing animals, and, if allowed, trees such as the Ash, Sycamore and Downy Birch grow up to form open woodland (Plate 37, p. 158). In places there are sheets of Lily-of-the-Valley (Plate 36, p. 155), while on account of the heavy rainfall and accumulation of humus in the cracks there is local development of plants which will grow under acid conditions, like Melancholy Thistle (Plate 40, p. 175), Bracken and Devil's-bit Scabious, *Succisa pratensis*. Baneberry (Plate 38, p. 159) is found in the district, and so are many other plants already mentioned. Just below, at Weathercote Cave, Chapel-le-dale, the Kidney-leaved Saxifrage, *Saxifraga hirsuta*, has been naturalised for over a century. It is rather like London Pride but has much rounder leaves with blunt teeth.

The south-west side of the hill is equally interesting, and especially about Crummack Head, Sulber and Moughton Scars. This is the area where a rare fern, the Rigid Buckler Fern, *Dryopteris villarii*, has its headquarters in Britain. It is particularly a plant of the tabular Carboniferous Limestone, growing in the cracks of the pavement or on the screes. To the east it is found in small quantity above Settle and at Malham, and to the west it is scattered through the south of Westmorland to Whitbarrow and Arnside Knott and into Lancashire at Warton Crag. There is a slight extension of its range north into the Eden drainage area and it has been found very rarely in North Wales (see p. 153). Apart from this it is a very local plant (Distribution Map, p. 223). Rigid Buckler Fern has fronds of a curious bluish-green colour and usually grows stiffly erect (Plate 42, p. 179). The Holly Fern, *Polystichum lonchitis*, has also been found near here and elsewhere in Craven, but it is intensely rare and it is to be hoped that anyone finding it will leave it undisturbed.

On Moughton Fell the Ecological Committee of the Yorkshire Naturalists' Union have been making a most interesting study of Juniper, *Juniperus communis.* It was noticed that this shrub was showing signs of decadence—that many of the old plants were sickly and that seedlings to take their place were rare. Several explanations have been offered, such as the attacks of rabbits and fungi, but in spite of the careful work of Mr. A. Malins Smith and his colleagues the reasons for the decrease of the Juniper here and in other places are not yet known.

The inconspicuous little Field Lady's Mantle or Parsley Piert, *Aphanes arvensis*, is common throughout the British Isles and grows on various soils. It is, for example, frequent on mole-heaps on the chalk downs. So-called " Common " Lady's Mantle, *Alchemilla vulgaris*, a much larger plant with rather inconspicuous green flowers, is rare in the south of England though plentiful enough in hilly districts in the north. It has now been divided into a number of segregates most of which are fairly easy to distinguish by the careful use of the keys in standard floras. The characters by which they are separated are derived mainly from the distribution of the hairs, and whether they are spreading or not, and the shape of the leaves and their toothing. *A. glaucescens* (*A. hybrida* auctt.) with spreading silky hairs, and *A. minima*, with rather few hairs, are small plants especially associated with the Ingleborough district.

The seeds of Lady's Mantles are known to remain capable of germinating after they have passed through the intestines of sheep, cows, horses and other grazing animals. In Derbyshire and Yorkshire I have noticed that the distribution of these plants often seems to be associated with the droppings of such beasts.

Grasses are not particularly the subject of this book, but it is hardly possible to leave Craven without mention of the Blue Moor Grass, *Sesleria caerulea.* Most visitors see it in the summer when the flower-heads are dry and look like chaff, and the leaves are coarse and yellow. In this state it is far from handsome. But as I first saw it one May, when snow still rested on the hills, with the spikes fresh and suffused with a bluish tint, the Blue Moor Grass looked very different. It is abundant on the limestone of the whole of this area and over many stretches by far the most common grass.

R. H. Hall

Limestone Polypody, *Thelypteris robertiana*; near Buxton

Judges Ltd.

Scout Scar, Kendal (Carboniferous Limestone)

Mention of the Mezereon, *Daphne mezereum*, has been intentionally left until last. This is partly because the little winter-blooming shrub is so persecuted by people who dig it up for their gardens that I dare give no clue to its precise localities. The other reason is that it is out of flower when most visitors go to Craven and therefore unlikely to attract their attention. Mezereon grows about two to three feet tall, and in February and March bears red flowers towards the end of its stem. The leaves are leathery and resemble those of its ally, the Spurge Laurel, *Daphne laureola*, but unlike those of that evergreen species they are shed in autumn. I have seen the two growing together in one scrub-wood in Craven and it is believed that they may hybridise. The Mezereon has been found in a number of wild and remote woods in the district, and to my mind it is more certainly wild here than in most of the other parts of England where it occurs. There is always the question whether birds have carried the seeds from gardens or if man transplanted the roots into cultivation at nearby cottages, but in Craven it seems likely that transport has been mainly in the latter direction.

Craven, with its fissured massive tabular limestone, is one of the most important calcareous areas in Britain. It has a characteristic flora with a number of rare species and a long botanical history. Grassington, Gordale Scar, Malham Cove and Ingleborough are places which every nature-lover should visit, and if it is necessary to omit any of them from an itinerary no time should be lost in making good the omission.

CHAPTER 14

OTHER LIMESTONE DISTRICTS OF NORTH ENGLAND

THERE IS no other large limestone region in the north of England to equal Craven. Elsewhere calcareous soils are more restricted, and although relatively small areas rival, or sometimes even exceed, limited stretches of Craven in the interest and variety of their flora, they are not of the same importance. Such places as Hutton Roof Crag, Scout Scar, Humphrey Head, and Upper Teesdale are wonderful hunting grounds for botanists. But enthusiasm over their treasures must not obscure the fact that as *limestone* areas they are dwarfed by the region described in the last chapter.

Geographically Craven is the headquarters of calcicole plants in the north of England. From this upland region it is only a few miles west to the limestones round the head of Morecambe Bay. Another tongue of the Carboniferous Limestone runs north-west through north Westmorland and Cumberland. There is a third extension through north Yorkshire, Durham and Northumberland, across the border into south Scotland. These will be discussed in that sequence, but it must be stressed that north of Craven the limestone is broken up by sandy and shaly sediments. In Northumberland and south Scotland calcareous rocks are subordinate to those of other types in the Carboniferous Limestone formation.

LIMESTONES ROUND MORECAMBE BAY

West of Kirkby Lonsdale there are three hills with an exceedingly good flora of an upland type similar to parts of Craven. The tops of

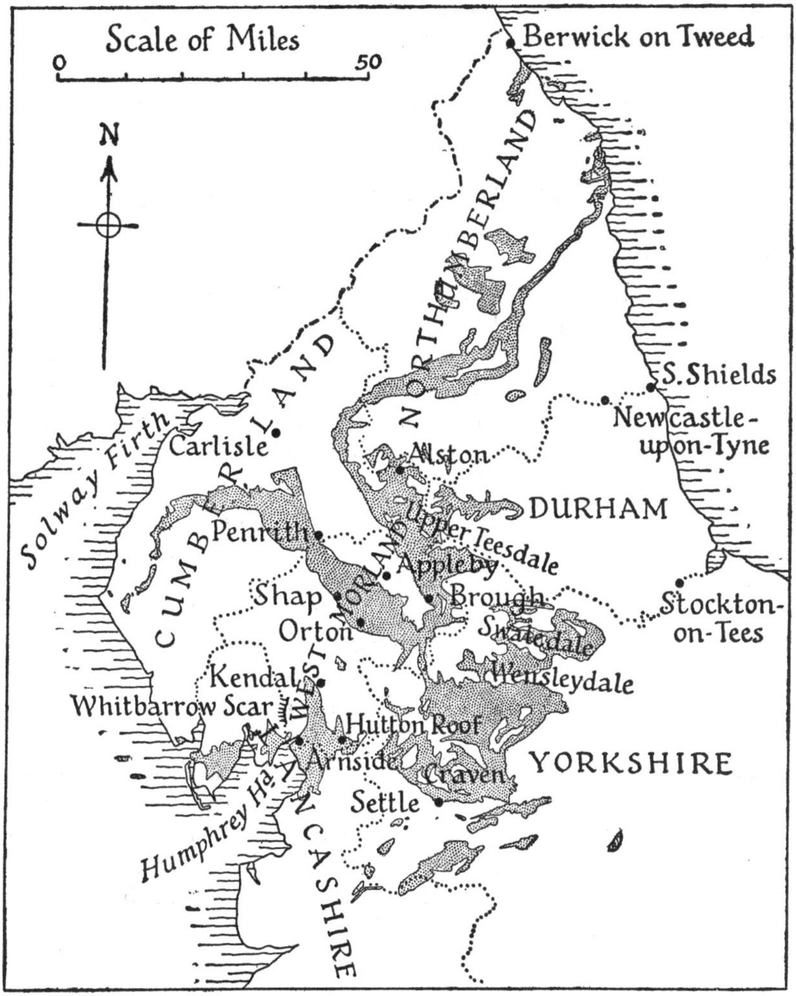

FIG. 15
Carboniferous Limestone areas of Northern England

Farleton, Hutton Roof and Dalton Crags have considerable exposures of limestone. The best known of these is Hutton Roof Crag, a rough and rocky hill rising to nearly 900 feet, and surmounted with a big area of limestone pavement. A luxuriant flora thrives in the grikes protected from grazing. The great variety of species present is indicated by the fact that on my third visit I failed to find several plants which I remembered seeing on the two previous occasions.

The flowers of this limestone pavement are in general very similar to those of comparable places in Craven. Ferns are abundant and include the rare Rigid Buckler Fern, *Dryopteris villarii*, and Limestone Polypody, *Thelypteris robertiana*, which are both plentiful. Blue Moor Grass and Mountain Melic abound. Small Meadow-rue, Dark-flowered Helleborine and Angular Solomon's Seal are among the choicer flowers. But the plant which most botanists visit Hutton Roof to see is the little Bird's-foot Sedge, *Carex ornithopoda*. This is more plentiful in Westmorland than in any other British county, and is found in a number of places near Kendal and also towards the north of the county. Elsewhere it is only to be seen in Derbyshire (see p. 160), although there is an old record from near Ripon in Yorkshire and one from Cumberland of which I have no details.

A little farther west the limestone hills of Silverdale flank Morecambe Bay and the estuary of the Kent. The highest of these is Arnside Knott, 522 feet, in Westmorland, but the Lancastrian Warton Crag, some four miles to the south, is nearly as high. The villages of Silverdale and Arnside are convenient centres for exploring this district.

The scenery of Silverdale is heavily wooded and of lowland type, and a complete contrast to the upland Fell limestone of Craven and Hutton Roof Crag. The wooded pavements of Middlebarrow, Gait Barrows, and Cringlebarrow have crowded well-grown trees which often form a continuous canopy. Nevertheless many of the rare plants are the same. Lady's Slipper Orchid (which has not been seen for many years), Dark-flowered Helleborine, and Stone Bramble are examples of woodland plants which also grow in open scrub at higher altitudes. Spring Cinquefoil, Bird's-eye Primrose and Spring Sandwort are amongst the Craven species which occur in the more open parts of Silverdale.

But the feature of the flora of this district which makes it so attractive to northern botanists is the presence of a number of plants which are

G. H. McLean

SPRING SANDWORT, *Minuartia verna;* a plant of widespread distribution on limestone. Co. Clare, Ireland; July

G. H. McLean

A Rare Saxifrage, *Saxifraga rosacea*. Allied Mossy Saxifrages are frequent on limestones of the wetter parts of Britain, but this species is known only from Ireland. Co. Clare; June

much more common in southern England. A Lancashire friend who had explored the Surrey chalk under my guidance described Silverdale as a " second-rate Box Hill." While the statement is perhaps unnecessarily disparaging, his meaning was clear. A number of species like Dropwort and Fly Orchid, which are frequent in Surrey, are regarded by northern botanists as rarities. They go to Silverdale to see them.

The limestone here comes right down to the coast. A walk along the top of the cliffs from Far Arnside, round the Park to the village of Arnside, is to be strongly recommended both for scenery and for flowers. Except for the abundance of Blue Moor Grass, the general flora recalls that of limestone areas in the south of England.

The limestone of Silverdale is continued on the opposite side of the Kent estuary in the cliffs near Grange-over-sands and at Humphrey Head. Western Spiked Speedwell, *Veronica hybrida*, grows on both sides of the water. In the place where I have seen it the plant is often 15 inches tall; equal to the finest the Great Orme and Avon Gorge usually produce. A colony of Maidenhair Fern, *Adiantum capillus-veneris*, is an indication of the mildness of the climate at sea-level.

Humphrey Head is a steep-sided hog's back of a hill jutting out into the sea at its highest end. It is the home of a number of flowers so beautiful and rare that I was at first inclined not to mention the promontory by name. But the steepness and inaccessibility of the limestone rocks affords such adequate protection that they are unlikely to come to any harm. Here Bloody Cranesbill, *Geranium sanguineum*, Hoary Rock-rose, *Helianthemum canum*, Spotted Catsear, *Hypochoeris maculata*, Goldilocks, *Crinitaria linosyris*, and Western Spiked Speedwell, *Veronica hybrida*, can be seen growing within a few feet of one another. The only other place where all these plants grow together in Britain is on the Great Orme. Most of them are also associated in the Avon Gorge and on one spot on the Gower coast. Collectively they form a group of rare plants characteristic of the coastal Carboniferous Limestone from Somerset to Humphrey Head.

Inland and to the north, two other ranges of limestone hills rise above the Silurian rocks which predominate in the south of Westmorland. The more westerly of these is Whitbarrow with its adjacent hills. Here Rigid Buckler Fern and Bird's-foot Sedge are again found, while Traveller's Joy, at the southern end of the hill, is an unexpected plant so far north.

The eastern range is a ridge running from north to south at an altitude of 600 to 700 feet. Its west-facing escarpment forms a series of scars—Cunswick, Underbarrow and Scout Scars. Below the cliffs there are screes and rocky woods. Scout Scar (Plate XXII, p. 191) is the one best known to botanists. The top is almost flat, littered with thin slabs of rock, and in a few places the limestone is shallowly fissured into an incipient " pavement." At first sight it would seem a most unpromising place to look for flowers and ferns. Yet here I was able to find six species of ferns, including Rigid Buckler Fern, Limestone Polypody, and Green Spleenwort, *Asplenium viride*, within an area of less than three square yards. Blue Moor Grass is abundant, and Squinancywort, Bird's-foot Sedge, Spring Sandwort, and Small Meadow-rue, *Thalictrum minus*, are other plants of the bare wind-swept top.

The limestone cliffs are a complete contrast. On these, brightly-coloured flowers abound, and there are few places in the whole of Britain which I have enjoyed so much. In June the prevailing colour of the flowers is yellow. Sheets of Hoary Rock-rose, Common Rock-rose, Horseshoe Vetch and Hawkweeds on the rock ledges form patches of yellow which tone admirably with the greyish-white colour of the limestone and the dark green foliage of the Yews. Flowers of other colours include Bloody Cranesbill and Dark-flowered Helleborine.

There is an interesting series of woods at the base of the escarpment below the scars. Their higher parts run up on to the rocky screes; their western and lower sides are on sticky calcareous clay. Cunswick, Barrowfield and Brigsteer Woods are the best known. In these Herb Paris, Lily-of-the-Valley, and Greater Butterfly Orchid, *Platanthera chlorantha*, occur in abundance. Lady's Slipper Orchid, Mezereon, Angular Solomon's seal, and Narrow-leaved Helleborine, *Cephalanthera longifolia*, are also recorded. In Barrowfield Wood I found Large-leaved Lime, *Tilia platyphyllos*, in a situation where it is likely to be native though previously unrecorded.

North Westmorland and Cumberland

The tongue of Carboniferous Limestone which runs north-west from Craven, curves round north of the Lake District to run south parallel to the Cumberland coast. The area of greatest interest is just north of the River Lune about Orton, Great Ashby and Shap, and is conveniently explored from the railway junction at Tebay.

Perennial Flax, *Linum anglicum*, is found at several places on calcareous soils in this district. The main distribution of this species in Britain is near the east coast, where it extends from Cambridgeshire to Durham (Distribution Map 6, p. 218). That it should also occur in an isolated and limited upland area in Westmorland is a surprising and somewhat incongruous fact. Alpine Bartsia, *Bartsia alpina*, is another rare flower in Britain known from the Orton area since the time of John Ray (1670). Like Bird's-eye Primrose, *Primula farinosa*, with which it grows here, it belongs to a group of plants which are not strictly calcicole. They favour wet ground which is rather peaty, but only where this is in limestone districts. Bird's-foot Sedge is also found in the vicinity. The flora of the Carboniferous Limestone in Cumberland is apparently of no special interest.

The meadows of limestone districts in the north of England in summer have as fine a display of flowers as any to be seen in the Alps. For beauty of combinations of colours, and delightful scent of the blossoms, they owe much of their charm to plants such as Common Milkwort, Lady's Bedstraw, Ox-eye Daisy, and Salad Burnet, which are common throughout Britain. But here they grow in a more colourful mass accompanied by Globe Flower, Melancholy Thistle, Mountain Pansy, and Wood Crane's-bill, and other northern plants. Every meadow differs in detail from its fellows and their charm never gets monotonous.

North Yorkshire, Durham and Northumberland

The Yorkshire Dales north of the Craven district have no massive fissured limestone. Calcareous rocks tend to be restricted to the scars along the sides of the valleys and to gorges where streams have cut themselves deep beds. Some of these have a very interesting flora, but it is of secondary importance by comparison with areas already described.

Wensleydale is drained by the Yore, which gives its name to the Yoredale Limestone. It is a wide valley with calcareous scars at intervals along its sides. In places, as from Askrigg to Carperby, these are almost continuous. The recorded plants include Hoary Whitlow-grass, Rock Pepperwort, Baneberry, Spring Cinquefoil, Mezereon and Limestone Polypody. Red Broomrape, *Orobanche alba* (which sometimes has whitish flowers in the Alps), has been found on the scars in several places, and towards the eastern end, at Leyburn Shaw, Perennial Flax has been observed.

Swaledale is the next valley. It has a similar series of limestone scars but the flora includes fewer rarities. Small Meadow-rue and Dark-flowered Helleborine are of interest. Near Richmond, where the castle stands on a limestone hill, Lesser Teasel, *Dipsacus pilosus*, reaches its farthest north in Britain.

Upper Teesdale is much better known to botanists. The exposures of limestone rock are restricted to the higher ground with one important exception. At High Force the Tees, which forms the boundary between Yorkshire and Durham, has cut right through the basalt to the limestone beneath. Below this magnificent waterfall, down to beyond Winch Bridge, a number of interesting calcicoles are to be found. These include Rock Whitebeam, *Sorbus rupicola*, Alpine Penny-cress, *Thlaspi alpestre*, Alpine Cinquefoil, *Potentilla crantzii*, and the Blue Moor Grass. Here (and higher up the river) Shrubby Cinquefoil, *Potentilla fruticosa*, is abundant. This is a shrub about a yard in height with yellow flowers. Although this very local species sometimes grows on soils which are not obviously basic, it seems to occur only where there are limestone rocks in the vicinity.

The finest areas of calcareous soils in Teesdale are on high ground, and their floras belong rather to a book on mountain flowers. Brief mention must be made, however, of the higher limestones, as some of the rare calcicoles occur at lower altitudes elsewhere. On the tops of two hills there are patches of a loosely granular crystalline limestone, which resembles an extremely coarse granulated sugar, and is known as "Sugar Limestone." Growing on this, in one place, there are masses of Hoary and Common Rock-roses in company with Mountain Avens, *Dryas octopetala*. The latter flowers here rather shyly and its tough little leaves hardly rise above the level of the soil in this windswept situation. Hoary Whitlow-grass is also in some quantity.

In wetter places there are four other rare plants which in Britain are found only in limestone districts though not necessarily on calcareous soils. Bird's-eye Primrose and Alpine Bartsia have already been referred to in this chapter. Bitter Milkwort, *Polygala amara*, is only to be seen elsewhere in Craven (see p. 179). In Teesdale it has been known since 1852 but it is very difficult to find and it is often reported as extinct. Nevertheless it was still there as recently as 1947

—a shorter, dumpier little plant than those from Grassington, where it is more plentiful. Spring Gentian, *Gentiana verna*, is one of the most charming plants in the British flora. It is only about two inches high but the flowers are large and a most glorious blue. In this country the colour is very uniform, but in Switzerland I have seen it in a remarkable range of variations, including white. Spring Gentian is so lovely that it is in demand as a rockery plant, and some years ago Teesdale was regularly raided by men armed with sacks and trowels, so that its numbers were sadly reduced. Fortunately the owners of one large estate took public-spirited measures to stop this shameful trade, and the Gentian is now flourishing again.

Another good hill is across the Tees. It is the only British station for Teesdale Sandwort, *Minuartia stricta*, which grows in wet open places over the limestone. This slender little plant, with very narrow leaves and an upright stem about three inches tall, has little to commend it besides its rarity. There is also a compact little violet, *Viola rupestris*, which grows on the Sugar Limestone. This has blue flowers in May, which seem disproportionately large in comparison with the small rounded leaves. Both these plants are very local, but a little sedge, *Carex capillaris*, is amongst the more abundant species. Indeed it is so plentiful that one cannot help feeling surprise that only about forty miles away in Craven it occurs only as a few individuals on a limestone ledge (see p. 183).

Widdy Bank Fell and the limestone on the north bank of the Tees at Winch Bridge are in Durham. The remainder of that county and Northumberland are not specially noted for their limestone floras. Exposures of calcareous rocks are small and few, and over large areas drift deposits cover the Carboniferous Limestone formation. Calcicoles are to be found at intervals but are not particularly important. The extreme north of England has many interesting botanical features but they do not include a good calcicolous flora.

CHAPTER 15

LIMESTONES OF SCOTLAND AND IRELAND

IN SCOTLAND and Ireland maps showing "solid" geology are of very little value as guides to the distribution of calcareous soils. In both countries limestone outcrops influence plants over only relatively small parts of the large areas marked as Carboniferous Limestone. Scotland also has calcareous rocks in other formations, but these are only of local importance. A greater number of calcicoles are to be found off the limestone. Some of these are on coastal dunes where accumulations of comminuted shells provide calcium carbonate. More of them are on basic soils formed from igneous rocks.

Many calcicoles appear to be indifferent whether the basic nature of soils is due to calcium or other salts. Species generally associated with limestone are also to be found on basic soils formed from igneous rocks. The latter are mostly at high altitudes and their mountain flowers are clearly outside the scope of this book. On lower ground in Scotland basic soils, whether derived from limestone or not, are often marked by the occurrences of such rarities as Sticky Catchfly, *Lychnis viscaria*, Wood Fescue, *Festuca altissima*, and Pyramidal Bugle, *Ajuga pyramidalis*. Only the more important stretches of limestones can be referred to here.

The most important of these is the exposure of Carboniferous Limestone on the north shore of the Firth of Forth. Early botanists crossing over from Edinburgh by ferry soon found that the Ferry Hills, North Queensferry, had a rich flora. One of the plants they recorded was a rare purple vetch, *Oxytropis halleri*, which was eventually destroyed by the construction of the Forth Bridge to carry the railway.

Another rarity of the Ferry Hills can still be seen. Great Meadow-rue, *Thalictrum majus*, may be distinguished from its allies by the more numerous fruits and large, but narrow, leaves. Most of the other plants of this Fife limestone are widely distributed. Spring Cinquefoil, Bloody Cranesbill, Wild Liquorice, Purple Milk-vetch, and Sea Cabbage have all been mentioned many times in previous chapters. Some of the flowers such as Hairy Violet, Common Rock-rose and Dropwort, are those which abound on the southern chalk.

The outcrops of Cambrian Limestone in the north-west of Scotland are thrilling places to a southern botanist, for here mountain flowers come down to low levels—even to sea-level. At Durness, about Inchnadamph, and at the Cnochan rocks on the Ross-Sutherland boundary, plants can be seen which usually necessitate a strenuous climb elsewhere. Mountain Avens, Hoary Whitlow-grass and Dark-flowered Helleborine are among the interesting species referred to earlier on the Carboniferous Limestone which are also found on the Cambrian. On one stretch of the rock in the Inchnadamph district I have seen Norwegian Sandwort, *Arenaria norvegica*. It also comes down off the hills on to the river shingle, but otherwise is found elsewhere in Britain only in a few other places (page 185). This charming little white flower is closely allied to the Yorkshire and Irish Sandworts, *A. gothica* and *A. ciliata*, which are also restricted to very small areas. The greenness of the vegetation of the Cambrian Limestone country is a remarkable contrast to the bareness of the dark peat on adjoining acid soils.

This Durness Limestone outcrops again in Skye, and there is oolitic limestone pavement at Applecross. The flora, like that of the Dalradian Limestone of Lismore, is not of outstanding general interest. It is on the small patches of basic soils scattered over the country that Scottish botanists find most of their calcicoles.

The flowers of these small outcrops cannot be described adequately in a short space and it is to be feared that the reader may obtain a false impression of the delights of the Scotch limestone.

Ireland

The central part of Ireland is occupied by the largest continuous area of Carboniferous Limestone in Europe. With its outliers scattered round the coast it is by far the most important geological formation in the country. Nevertheless its influence on the flora is less widespread than might be supposed. On the eastern side the limestone is obscured by drift, and in the centre much of it is covered by marshes and bogs, so that it is chiefly on the western side of Eire that the rock is exposed on the surface. The best exposures are in Galway and Clare, from Lough Corrib to the Shannon, and include the fascinating Burren district and the Aran Islands of Galway Bay. To the south of this area limestone forms important botanical ground by the Killarney Lakes; to the north, near Sligo. In addition good calcicole floras are to be found on the limy gravels in the Central Plain, in places on the Antrim basalt, on dunes and elsewhere. These are thoroughly described in Dr. R. Lloyd Praeger's brilliant survey of the Irish flora.[1]

There are important differences between the wild flowers of Ireland and those of England. In the first place, there are fewer species and, the evidence suggests that this is because England was separated from Ireland earlier than from the Continent. It was shown in Chapter 4 that some of the rarer plants of the Kentish chalk had failed to extend their ground very far westwards, and this is taken as an indication that they entered England from across the English Channel. Other European flowers which may have come in by the same route have spread more widely and are now to be found commonly over most parts of England, Wales and Scotland. Yet some of these have failed to cross the Irish Channel. A good example of an abundant limestone species of this kind is Small Scabious, *Scabiosa columbaria*. This occurs as far north as Angus and is often a conspicuous feature on calcareous soils; and yet it has never been found in Ireland. Wild Liquorice has been mentioned many times in this book on chalk and limestone. It extends well up into Scotland and yet has not crossed into Ireland. Two woodland species—Herb Paris and Lily-of-the-Valley—are similar.

In addition there are a number of flowers which are equally widespread on the mainland but extremely local and rare in the Emerald Isle. The best example is Common Rock-rose, *Helianthemum chamaecistus*. In Ireland it is intensely scarce. When it was found in Donegal in 1893, the record was discounted as a mere "casual escape or introduction," and it was not until its rediscovery on the same ground in 1933 that it was generally accepted as a native. Purple Milk-vetch, *Astragalus danicus*, which is particularly widespread on the

[1] Praeger, R. L. (1934): *The Botanist in Ireland*. Dublin.

PLATE 47

G. H. McLean

Mountain Avens, *Dryas octopetala*; a calcicole usually found on mountains, but which grows almost at sea-level in the north of Scotland and the west of Ireland. Co. Clare, Ireland; June

G. H. McLean

MAIDENHAIR FERN, *Adiantum capillus-veneris;* a fern found in calcareous places near the sea. Co. Clare, Ireland; July eastern side of England and Scotland, is rather paradoxically known only from the limestone of the Aran Islands on the west coast of Ireland. Dropwort, *Filipendula vulgaris*, is surprisingly local in view of its abundance in many English counties, while, to take an example from the ferns, Limestone Polypody, *Thelypteris robertiana*, is known as a native only on a limestone hill in Mayo.

Although they do not make up in numbers for the loss of so many plants with a " continental " type of distribution, the interest of the Irish limestone flora is maintained by the presence of a number of species with a " Mediterranean " or an " Arctic-alpine " distribution. Some of these are not known elsewhere in Britain. Thus the little Dense-spiked Orchid, *Neotinea intacta*, which is found on the Mediterranean and Atlantic coasts of southern Europe, with us grows only in Clare, Galway and Mayo. The Strawberry Tree, *Arbutus unedo*, of the west coast of Europe and the Mediterranean, is found only near Killarney and Sligo—and mostly on limestone. These are examples of plants with Mediterranean-Lusitanian distribution. An " Arctic-alpine " is Irish Sandwort, *Arenaria ciliata*, of which a special subspecies is found only on the Ben Bulben range in Sligo.

In addition to distributional differences, there are also changes in the behaviour of some species which occur both in England and Ireland. It is alleged that some plants which are restricted to calcareous soils in Ireland are less exacting in England. To some extent this is to be expected, as soil requirements partly are dependent on climatic conditions. It is not surprising if plants behave differently in the dry and more extreme temperatures of the Kentish chalk. But a careful comparison has yet to be made. That the converse may sometimes be true, and that English calcicoles may be less exacting in Ireland, is indicated by Praeger's statement about Madder, *Rubia peregrina*. This, he says, flourishes equally well on and off the limestone in Ireland. In England my experience suggests that it is a strict calcicole.

The most remarkable limestone flora in Ireland is that of the Burren district of Co. Clare, which is conveniently explored from the little village of Ballyvaughan or from Lisdoonvarna. The coast road round Black Head (Plate 44, p. 187) runs through some of the best areas. The Burren hills rise to a height of over 1100 feet, but their summits are of no special interest: most of the interesting plants are to be found on the lower slopes.

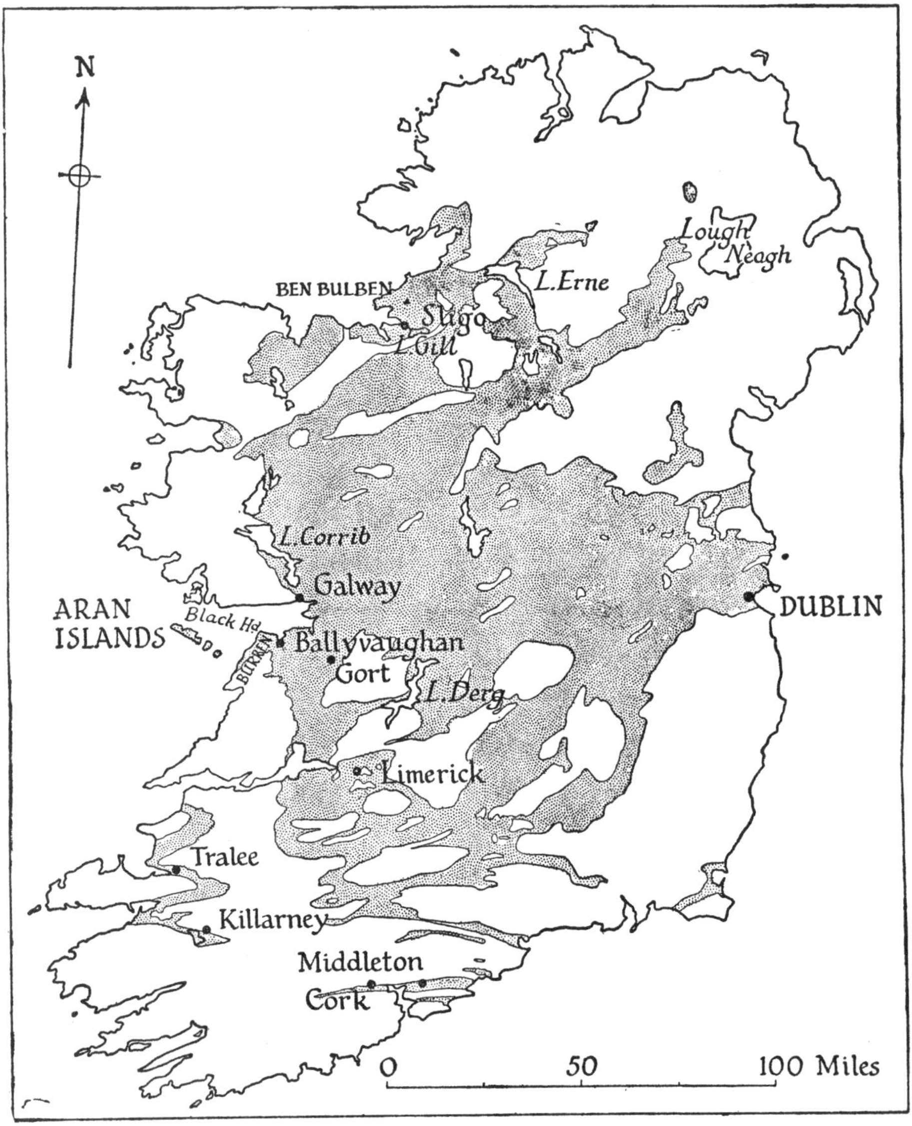

FIG. 16
Ireland. (Areas marked on geological maps as Carboniferous Limestone are stippled)

The feature which most impresses visitors is the vast extent of exposed limestone rock on which there is often very little vegetation to be seen. Streams are few and far between, and at first sight it would seem a bare, dry and most unpromising place to search for flowers. But in the deep crevices, where the atmosphere is always humid and the plants sheltered from the strong winds which are so prevalent, there is a luxuriant flora. Ferns are perhaps the best index of these conditions and they grow to an extraordinarily large size. Thus Maidenhair Fern, *Adiantum capillus-veneris* (Plate 48, p. 203), I found over a foot tall and very luxuriant. No doubt the complete absence of frosts (they are unknown here) partially accounts for the abundance of this and other tender species. It is also an important factor explaining the remarkably early appearance of the spring flowers. My own visit was made in mid-June and many blooms were past their best—even a month earlier there would have been a grand display of colour.

The showy flowers are found where a thin layer of soil has accumulated over the rock. A depth of only a couple of inches can lead to the formation of a peat-like soil in this humid district, and under such conditions calcifuges can thrive side by side with calcicoles. Of the former, Ling forms extensive sheets, while Tormentil, *Potentilla erecta*, is common. The flora includes a group of plants which seem particularly characteristic of peat over limestone and yet sometimes grow on the calcareous rock where the acid layer is absent. Good examples are the two Teesdale rarities (see pp. 198, 199), Spring Gentian, *Gentiana verna* (Distribution Map 9, p. 220), and Shrubby Cinquefoil, *Potentilla fruticosa*. The former is widespread and plentiful in the Burren and a glorious sight worth travelling many miles to see. Shrubby Cinquefoil is more local, and forms thickets about two feet high in hollows where more moisture is present. Near Ballyvaughan I found it with two kinds of flowers. The smaller were only three-eighths of an inch across, with deep chrome-orange petals much shorter than the sepals. The larger and commoner kind were an inch across and had much paler petals longer than the sepals. They grew on separate bushes and seemed to have no obvious connection with sex, though from the researches of a Swedish botanist it appears that in his country male and female blooms differ in size.

Two other plants which occur both on limestone and on thin peat over it are Mountain Avens, *Dryas octopetala*, and Narrow-leaved

Eyebright, *Euphrasia salisburgensis.* The former (Plate 47, p. 202) has been described in connection with its Yorkshire localities (see p. 181), and in the south it is generally regarded as a mountain flower, but in Scotland and here on the west coast of Ireland, as in Iceland and Scandinavia, it thrives very near sea-level. The Eyebright occurs over a considerable area in western Ireland, yet in Britain it is known only from Yorkshire (see p. 188). From other Eyebrights it is easily known by the narrow and jaggedly toothed leaves, bushy growth, and absence of stiff marginal hairs from its fruit capsules.

At the time of my visit the Dense-spiked Orchid, *Neotinea intacta,* was dried up and in fruit, but even then the short, dense heads of straw-coloured capsules were easily found. In mid-May, when it is in flower, I fancy that it must be more difficult to see. Two kinds of bloom occur. Commonly the flowers are greenish-white and the leaves unspotted (var. *straminea*), but sometimes the sepals have stripes and blotches of purplish-pink and the darker green leaves are faintly spotted with purple. In the British Isles this orchid is to be found only in the area around Galway Bay.

Pyramidal Bugle, *Ajuga pyramidalis,* is another plant which pleased me on the Burren, and my photograph (Plate XXIVb, p. 207) gives a good idea of the dense, shaggy bracts in which the flowers are half hidden. It is a northern and sub-alpine plant also found in Scotland. It flowers in May. Around Black Head and Ballyvaughan, and again in the Aran Islands a few miles to the west, there is a Saxifrage which grows in extremely beautiful patches on the limestone (Plate 46, p. 195). This was formerly known as *Saxifraga sternbergii* but, following a recent revision by Professor D. A. Webb of Dublin, it must now be included in *S. rosacea.* It belongs to a most puzzling group of species, and while the Burren plants on their own seem superficially distinct enough, he has shown that they must be grouped with others from elsewhere which look rather different.

The Burren flowers so far described are those of special rarity, but the greater part of the attraction of the flora is due to the immense profusion of commoner flowers which have already been mentioned in connection with other parts of Great Britain. Squinancywort, Dropwort and Yellow-wort recall the English chalk downs. Madder is associated with the Devon and Avon Gorge limestones. Dark-flowered Helleborine and Hoary Rock-rose, *Helianthemum canum,* remind one of the Great Orme. Mossy Saxifrage, *Saxifraga hypnoides,*

John Markham

a. Keys (fruits) of Ash, *Fraxinus excelsior*, a characteristic tree of limestone districts

A. T. Johnson

b. Mezereon, *Daphne mezereum*, in fruit

A. W. Graveson

a. Vernal Squill, *Scilla verna*; Pembrokeshire, April

J. E. Lousley

b. Pyramidal Bugle, *Ajuga pyramidalis*. The Burren, Co. Clare

and Stone Bramble, *Rubus saxatilis*, are plants of the Peak District; Small Meadow-rue, *Thalictrum minus*, Spring Sandwort and Bloody Cranesbill of the Peak District and Craven in Yorkshire. Red Broom-rape, *Orobanche alba*, to me recalls especially a patch of Scottish limestone, as does Pyramidal Bugle already mentioned. These examples serve to illustrate the wide distribution of many of the plants of calcareous soils.

The Burren is the meeting place of species of very varied types of distribution, and there is nowhere in Europe where Mediterranean and arctic-alpine plants grow together in a similar way. The warmth-loving southern Dense-spiked Orchid and Maidenhair Fern can be seen within a few yards of northern plants like Pyramidal Bugle and arctic-alpines such as Mountain Avens and Spring Gentian. The result is a unique flora full of interest for the plant-geographer.

The Aran Islands—sometimes called the South Islands of Aran to distinguish them from Arran in Donegal and Arran on the west coast of Scotland—are in Galway Bay just west of the Burren. There are three main islands, Inishmore, Inishmaan and Inisheer (Great, Middle and South Island respectively). The general surface of the land is a sloping flagged platform with crevices varying from a couple of inches to a foot or so in width, and it is in these fissures that most of the choicer plants are to be found. Here Maidenhair Fern has been seen over two feet in length, and Rustyback, *Ceterach officinarum*, is said often to have fronds a foot long. The general flora is very similar to that of the Burren, and Praeger suggests that the visitor will be most impressed by the abundance of Hoary Rock-rose, Narrow-leaved Eyebright, Spring Gentian, and the two ferns already mentioned. Rather surprisingly it seems that Mountain Avens and Dense-spiked Orchid have not been found in the Aran Islands, but as some compensation Purple Milk-vetch has here its only Irish station.

The characteristic flora of the Burren is at its best on the mainland in the area already described, but in decreasing richness it extends over many miles of country. To the south it is continued down to Ennis, to the east some of the species extend to the limestone shores of Lough Derg, to the north it spreads past Athenry and Galway to Lough Carra, where Spring Gentian reaches the northern limit of its Irish range.

North of this region there is an area near Sligo where the Carboniferous Limestone forms the magnificent hills of the Ben Bulben range and is also exposed on lower ground. The mountains here rise to over 2000 feet and the best of the calcareous rock is at about 1500 feet. Apart from the definitely Alpine plants found there, the flora is so interesting that it must receive brief mention. When I climbed King's Mountain from the Glencar valley, I observed the most remarkable and abrupt contrast between acid and basic soils, calcifuge and calcicole plants, that I have ever witnessed. The lower slopes are acid, with patches of arable land and bog, and as we plodded on past this towards the wall of limestone rock above we were surprised to meet donkeys loaded with paniers of peat coming down the track towards us. At first we were puzzled, but when we climbed above the limestone we found that the flattish top was covered with a thick layer of peat on which such extreme calcifuges as Ling, Whortleberry, Tormentil and Heath Bedstraw were flourishing. It was only where small patches of limestone broke through the peat that there was an abrupt change to calcicoles.

In certain places on the cliffs along this range we saw Irish Sandwort, *Arenaria ciliata*, which in Britain is only to be found here. The flowers are about three-eighths of an inch across but of a very clear white, and as each little plant produces them in large numbers the effect is extremely attractive. Irish Sandwort is closely related to Yorkshire Sandwort (see p. 185) and Norwegian Sandwort (see p. 201), but the reader need not be concerned about the slight differences by which they are separated. The fact that each is restricted to small areas in Ireland, Yorkshire and Scotland respectively is sufficient guide to identification.

The Sandwort grows with Hoary Whitlow-grass, *Draba incana*, and other plants like Mossy Saxifrage, *Saxifraga hypnoides*, Mountain Bedstraw, *Galium pumilum*, and Green Spleenwort, *Asplenium viride*, mentioned in the chapters on the limestones of northern England. On the same cliffs there is a very striking variety (*ballii*) of Common Milkwort, *Polygala vulgaris*, which has wiry stems and very large leaves and flowers. It is quite unlike the largest variations of the plant I have seen elsewhere and surely deserves further investigation.

The limestone on lower ground near Sligo is less interesting. There is quite a good flora on Knocknarea a few miles west of the town, and about Lough Gill. In chinks of limestone rock round this lake there are Strawberry Trees, *Arbutus unedo* (see below), growing with Yew and Rock Whitebeam, *Sorbus rupicola.* Praeger has shown that there are good reasons for regarding them as native here. On rocks near the coast and elsewhere the Maidenhair Fern has been found, and Narrow-leaved Eyebright also occurs in the district.

The third really important limestone area which I have visited in Ireland is about the Killarney Lakes. Here the rock is exposed in various places about Lough Leane, particularly round the promontory called Ross Island, and also by Muckross Lake. The dark evergreen leaves and reddish bark of the Strawberry Tree growing out of limestone (and other) rocks by the water are locally an important factor in the beauty for which the district is rightly famous. It is only in the Killarney woods, Waterville, and about Lough Gill (see above) that this tree, which belongs to the Lusitanian element in our flora, is to be found as a native in Britain to-day. It is believed that it once covered a much wider area in Ireland. The white, bell-shaped flowers appear in autumn and the fruit takes a full year to mature. When ripe it is crimson-scarlet with the surface roughened with little tubercles, and in size a little larger than a cherry. The resemblance to a strawberry is fairly close.

On Ross Island it grows with Rock Whitebeam and other Sorbi and many of the usual shrubs common on calcareous soils. A considerable number of widely distributed calcicoles occur in the district. Killarney is a lovely place and I was very fortunate in my botanizing there, and yet I returned with a vague feeling of disappointment. Efforts to extract the last penny from visitors have led to petty charges being made for entering the demesnes where the best plants grow. To have to pay to see a wild flower in its natural home always gives me the subconscious feeling that it is no longer wild and, however unjustified it may be, this destroys some of the enjoyment. If the Irish nationalised some of these estates and established them as Nature Reserves with no charge for admittance, Killarney would be an even more pleasant place.

There are many other limestone areas in Ireland in addition to the three important ones I have described. Some of these are excluded merely on account of their limited size and importance—like Carrickshane Hill, near Cork, where I saw a rare Stonecrop, *Sedum dasyphyllum*, apparently native. Others, like the district about Ballintra on Donegal

Bay, are more important but have not been visited by me. The reader will find plenty of scope for studying limestone flowers in Ireland, and if he happens to be English, he will find the differences in both the flora and the people he meets interesting and refreshing.

CHAPTER 16

SUMMARY AND CONCLUSION

Our travels in search of the flowers of chalk and limestone have taken us into almost every part of the British Isles. From the Isle of Wight to Sutherland, from Dover to the Burren, calcareous soils are scattered over our islands. They occur over rocks of various geological ages and range from sea-level to mountain-tops. They agree only in having a high proportion of calcium carbonate and certain physical characteristics. Apart from this their plants grow under a wide range of ecological conditions.

The presence or absence of lime in the soil determines more than any other chemical factor the nature of the flora to be found on it. Examples have been given in almost every chapter of striking differences between the vegetation of calcareous soils and adjoining acid areas. It has been demonstrated that locally chalk and limestone have characteristic flowers different from those of soils formed over rocks deficient in calcium carbonate. A few species like Hairy Violet are found on calcareous soils everywhere. Others, like Common Rock-rose and Dropwort, are to be seen over a very wide area. The great majority are limited in varying degrees to particular parts of the country. Climate as well as edaphic factors decide where they grow.

The limestones of the British Isles were laid down most extensively in Cretaceous, Jurassic, Permian, Carboniferous and Devonian times. Rocks of these ages differ considerably in hardness and purity, and one might expect that these differences would be reflected in the floras of the soils over them. It would seem that in general this is not the case. There are well-known contrasts in scenery between, for example, the massive limestones of the Carboniferous and the softer rocks of the Cretaceous and Permian ages. But the geographical separation of the outcrops of different geological formations entails important variations in climate which are of greater significance. Where outcrops of more than one age occur close together—as with the Cretaceous and Jurassic in Dorset, and the Permian and Carboniferous in north Yorkshire—there is scope for detailed work in comparing their floras. Any differences found to be due to soil variations between outcrops of different ages are likely to be slight. On the other hand, it has been shown in earlier chapters that widely separated calcareous soils, even of the same geological formation, each have their own characteristic selection of the less common plants.

The importance of geographical situation is well shown in the case of the Permian Limestone, on which the species of southern distribution are gradually replaced by northern plants along its range of some 300 miles. A similar south-to-north comparison can be made between the Carboniferous of the Derbyshire Dales and Craven. Along the Chalk there is a marked contrast between flowers of western and eastern distribution. The Jurassic combines south-to-north with west-to-east tendencies.

With such a wide range of climatic conditions over such a geographic spread it is not surprising that the flora of the chalk and limestone is extremely rich. A certain amount of alkalinity in the soil is favourable to plant life, and the great majority of British flowers will grow under such conditions. This applies even to some marked calcifuges provided they are not subject to competition from species which are better adapted to such places than themselves. Nevertheless I was astonished to find that I listed 585 species for inclusion in this book as having been seen by me on calcareous soils. All micro-species and most sedges and grasses were excluded. It is probably not an over-estimate to say that more than half of the 1550[1] British species of seed-plants and ferns are to be found on chalk and limestone.

This estimate of some 775 species includes not only a high proportion of attractive flowers but also an exceptionally high percentage of rare species. As Professor Good has shown, the term "rare" is used variously to cover sparsity in space, sparsity in number of individuals, and sparsity in time. Spur-lipped Coralroot, *Epipogium aphyllum* (see p. 89), is probably our rarest British plant. It has been found only in two small areas of Britain, and only a small number of

[1] This figure is based on 1513 given for seed-bearing plants only by W. B. Turrill, *British Plant Life*, 51, 1948.

individuals have been recorded at intervals since it was discovered in 1842. It is therefore rare on all three counts. Late Spider Orchid, *Ophrys fuciflora* (see p. 51), is found only over a few square miles in south-east Kent; the number of plants each year is small, but it never misses a season. It is rare on two counts. Lady Orchid, *Orchis purpurea* (see p. 51), is almost restricted to Kent, where it is in scattered colonies averaging perhaps 50 individuals which come up every year. It can only be said to be rare on two scores, and even then it is less so than the other two orchids. Every chapter contains examples of rarities. Some are found only very locally, some in small numbers, a few only occur in certain years.

Many of these rare plants might easily become extinct from a number of causes. Their life often hangs on a thread and this thread may be extremely thin. It can break under the slightest change in the conditions under which they exist. The most obvious threat comes from the unscrupulous collector. Such people are not botanists (or very rarely so) but rather persons with an adolescent mentality who derive pleasure from the possession of a specimen of a rare plant and will go to any lengths to secure it. Because such people exist I have been compelled to exercise discretion in describing places where scarce plants grow. For the same reason I must refuse to give any additional information to correspondents.

Secrecy is a purely negative method of protecting flowers. Positive action requires much more careful study, and a study of the associated vegetation as well as of the rarity concerned. Since we seldom know enough about any species to assess the ecological factors which are important to its existence, it is preferable to try to conserve whole communities in their present condition rather than particular plants. If the habitat is stabilised and saved from destruction the rarities it contains are likely to persist. Often the best way to protect communities is as parts of larger areas on which agricultural, pastoral or other uses are carried on as before.

Fortunately this approach to plant conservation has received official recognition. The Nature Conservancy was founded by Royal Charter in 1949 and it ranked as one of the four official Research Councils under the supervision of the Privy Council[1]. It was created " to provide scientific advice on the conservation and control of the natural flora and fauna of Great Britain; to establish, maintain and manage Nature Reserves in Great Britain, including the maintain-

[1]In May 1965 the Nature Conservancy became a committee of the National Environment Research Council.

ance of physical features of scientific interest; and to organize and develop the research and scientific services related thereto." By 1962, the total acreage of National Nature Reserves was over 190,000 acres, of Forest Nature Reserves over 4,100 acres, and of Local Nature Reserves 6,650 acres. These include some of the best chalk and limestone habitats such as Colt Park Wood, the Gower Coast, Kingley Vale, Knocking Hoe, and Wye and Crundale Downs, and permits are needed to visit some of these. Many more of the areas mentioned in this book have been scheduled as "Sites of Special Scientific Interest" (S.S.S.I.'s), which is recognition of their importance but in practice offers only very limited and inadequate protection.

Conservation, important though it is, is only one aspect of the work of the Nature Conservancy. Reserves require management, and scientific management must be based on research. In the long run the investigation of the complex interrelationships between plants, and between plants and animals, is likely to prove just as important as the initial step of saving downland from destruction. One example of this is the study of the changes in chalk grassland which followed the destruction of nearly the whole rabbit population in some areas by the 1954-55 epidemic of myxomatosis. It is essential to find ways of replacing the work of rabbits and other grazing animals if short downland turf with a varied flora is to be maintained.

The Conservation Corps of the Council for Nature is doing valuable work in clearing scrub on some of our chalk grassland. Naturalists' Trusts are also taking an active part in conserving important chalk and limestone areas, both by acquiring land and by advising on its management. There are now twenty-seven of these Trusts, some concerned with more than one county, and it is likely that the whole of England and Wales will soon be covered by their activities. The Botanical Society of the British Isles is amongst the other bodies taking an active part in conservation work, and helped to oppose recent threats to Teesdale and Berry Head. Work on the wider problems is being co-ordinated by the Society for the Promotion of Nature Reserves, which advises and assists the County Trusts, and by the Council for Nature, which represents natural history societies.

Chalk and limestone country takes a high priority in the programme for conservation. Our heritage of calcicoles—often beautiful and sometimes rare—deserves priority. There is no more interesting group in the British flora.

MAPS SHOWING THE RANGE OF SOME OF THE LESS WIDESPREAD PLANTS OF CHALK AND LIMESTONE

THE MAPS which follow show the distribution of some of the rarer and more interesting chalk and limestone flowers and ferns. They have been chosen to illustrate the restricted distribution of certain species in spite of the widespread occurrence of calcareous soils. The opportunity has been taken of including more than one flower on nine of the maps in order to show striking contrasts in types of distribution. On Maps 3, 4, 5, 9 and 11 these contrasts are between species belonging to the same genera.

The markings indicate localities from which the plants have been recorded and are based on published records, herbarium specimens and the writer's own field-work. In this way the true distribution is shown very much more accurately than by the more usual method of shading in whole divisions of counties (Watsonian Vice-counties) irrespective of whether the species has been found in a single locality or many. Nevertheless, it must be remembered that some parts of the British Isles have been investigated more thoroughly than others, and that some are covered by excellent modern local floras while others have only old floras or even none. For these reasons it is difficult to compile detailed distribution maps with absolute accuracy. The small scale employed has made it necessary in some cases to show groups of adjacent localities by single marks.

Localities are marked with the signs ●, ■ and ▲. These signs are placed in a circle for places where the species is believed to be extinct. In the case of the Military Orchid, the new locality mentioned on page 89 is not shown. A few records regarded as doubtful (either for determination or locality) are shown as a "?."

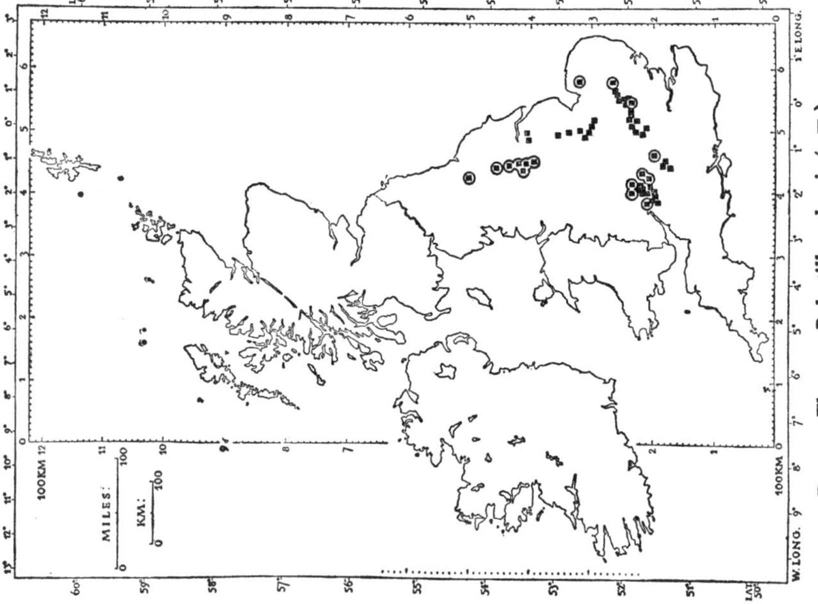

1. Pasque Flower, *Pulsatilla vulgaris* (■)

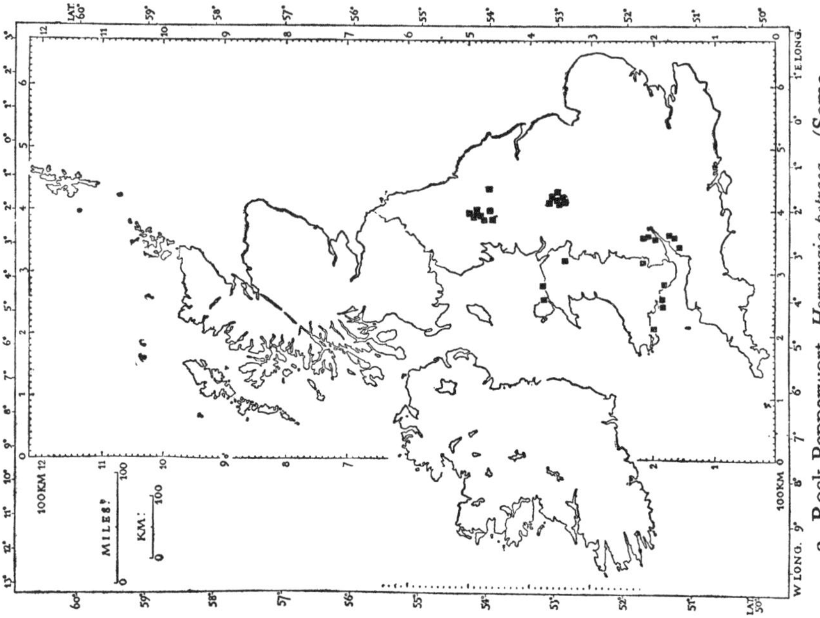

2. Rock Pepperwort, *Hornungia petraea*. (Some doubtful or alien records are excluded) (■)

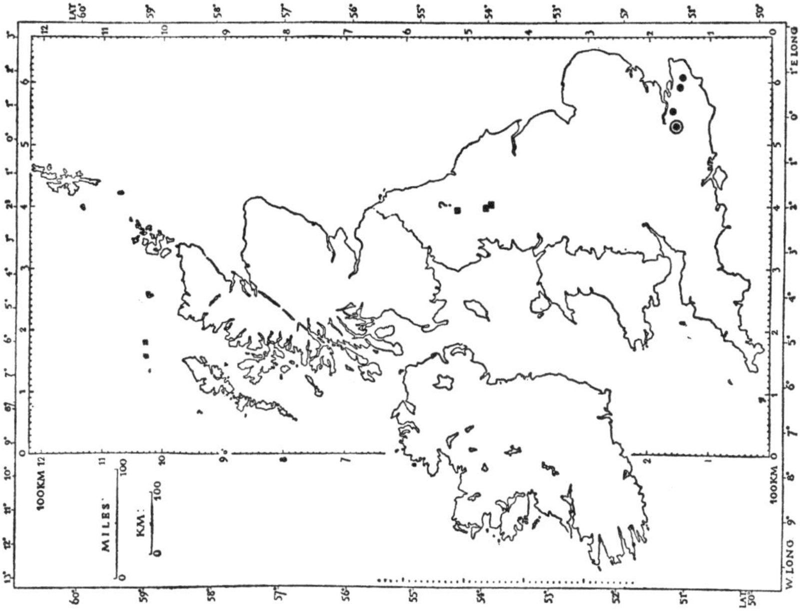

4. a. Bitter Milkwort, *Polygala amara* (■)
b. Kentish Milkwort, *P. austriaca* (●)

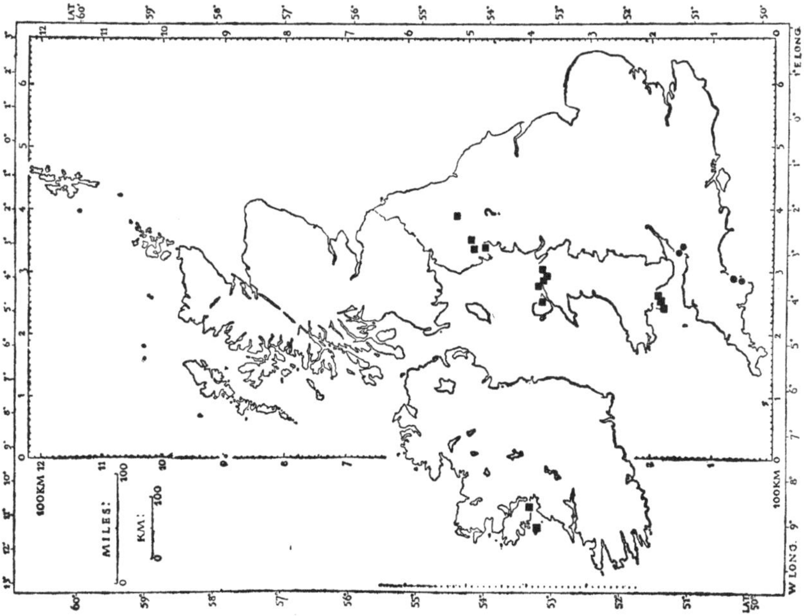

3. a. Hoary Rock-rose, *Helianthemum canum* (■)
b. White Rock-rose, *H. apenninum* (●)

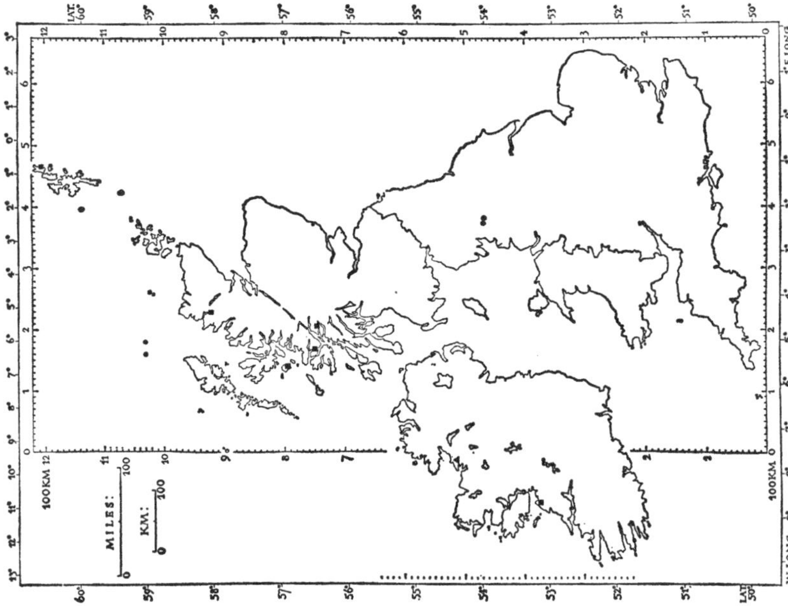

5. a. Yorkshire Sandwort, *Arenaria gothica* (●)
b. Norwegian Sandwort, *A. norvegica* (■)
c. Irish Sandwort, *A. ciliata* subsp. *hibernica* (▲)

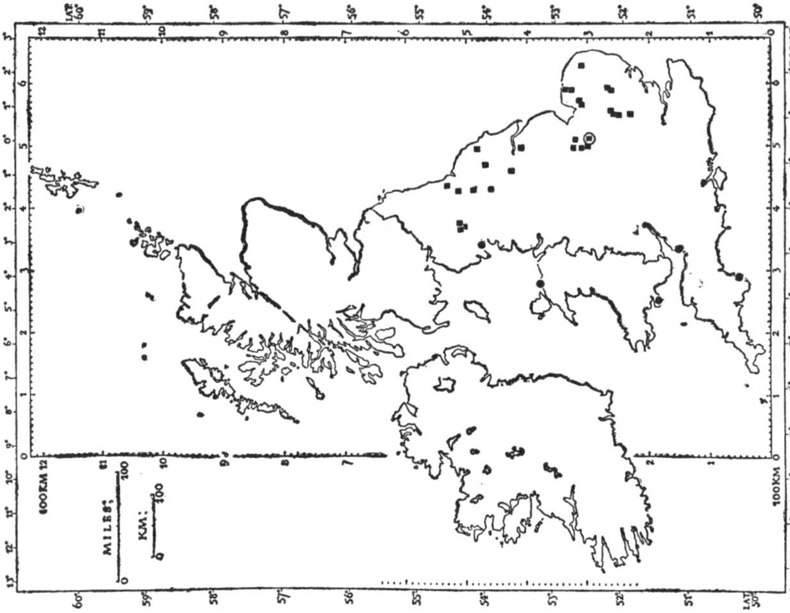

6. a. Perennial Flax, *Linum anglicum* (some doubtful records not shown) (■)
b. Hair-leaved Goldilocks, *Crinitaria linosyris* (●)

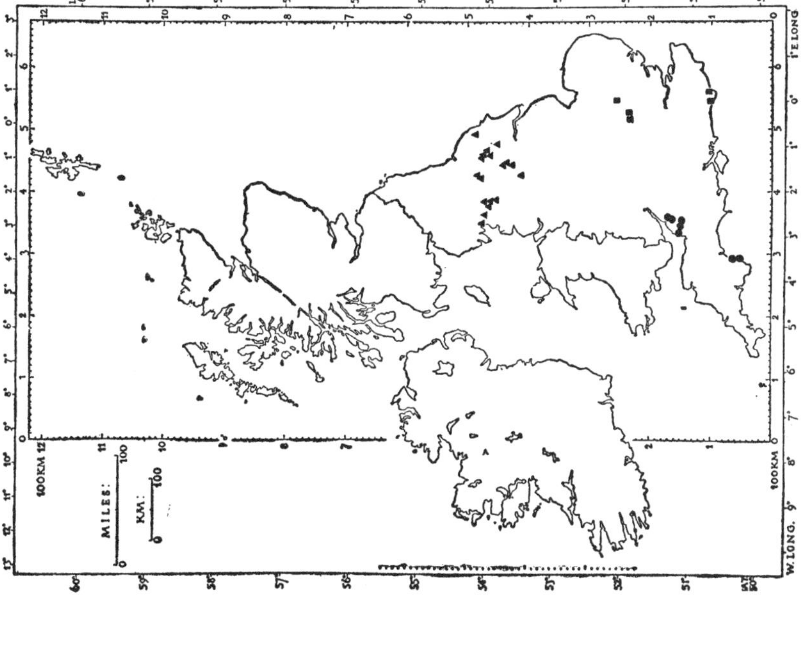

7. a. Honewort, *Trinia glauca* (●)
b. Mountain Stone-parsley, *Seseli libanotis* (■)
c. Baneberry, *Actaea spicata* (▲)

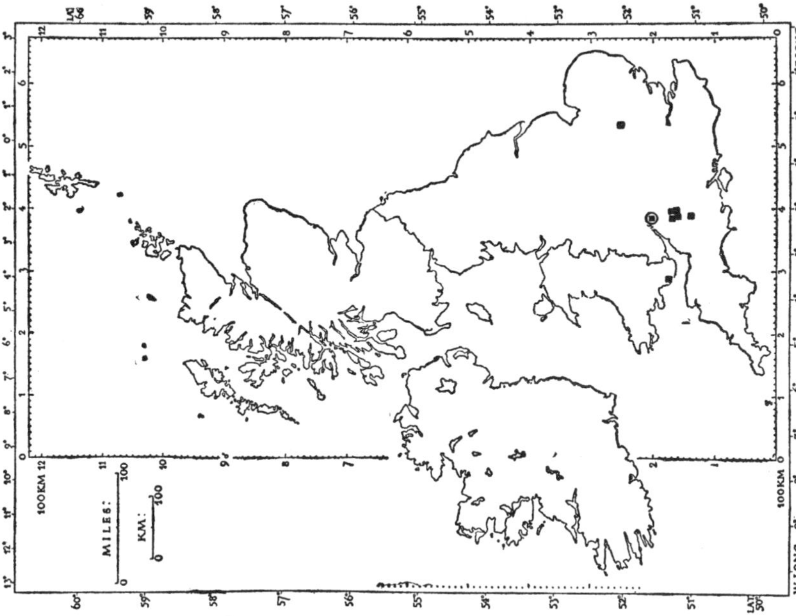

8. Tuberous Thistle, *Cirsium tuberosum* (■)

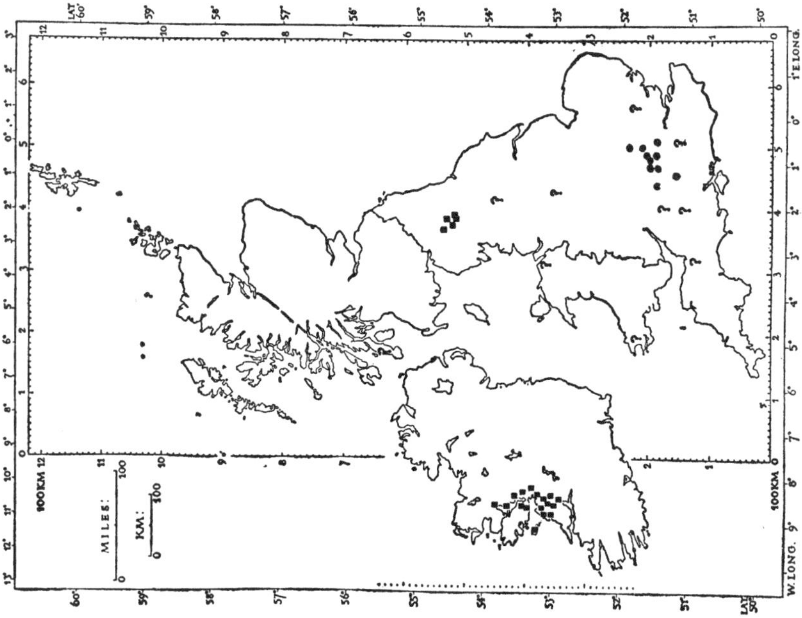

9. a. Spring Gentian, *Gentiana verna* (■)
b. Large Autumn Gentian, *Gentianella germanica* (● and ?—all queries refer to this species and most are due to errors of identification)

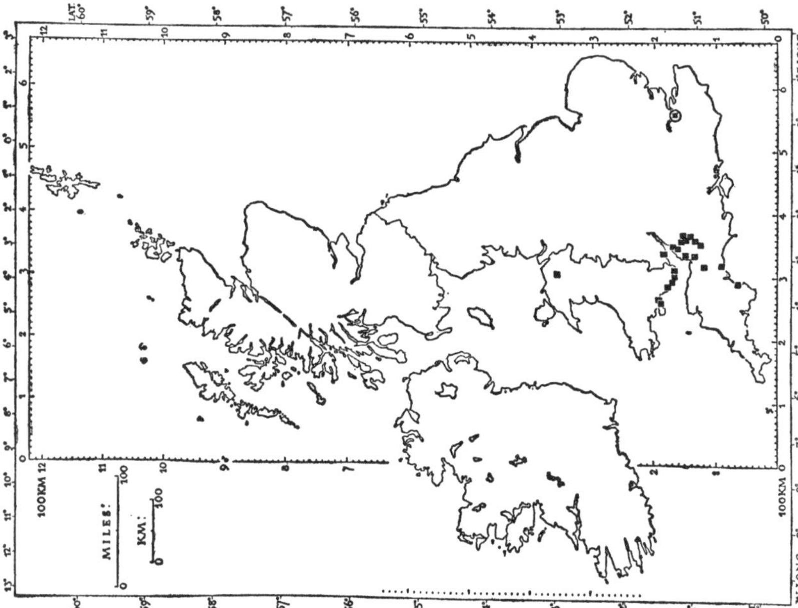

10. Blue Gromwell, ***Lithospermum purpurocaeruleum*** (■)

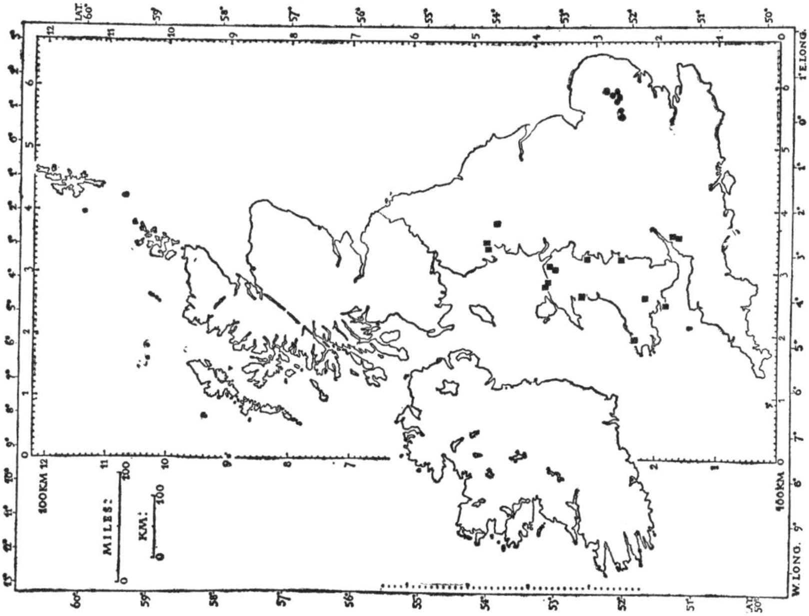

11. a. Western Spiked Speedwell, *Veronica spicata* subsp. *hybrida* (■)
b. Spiked Speedwell, *V. spicata* subsp. *spicata* (●)

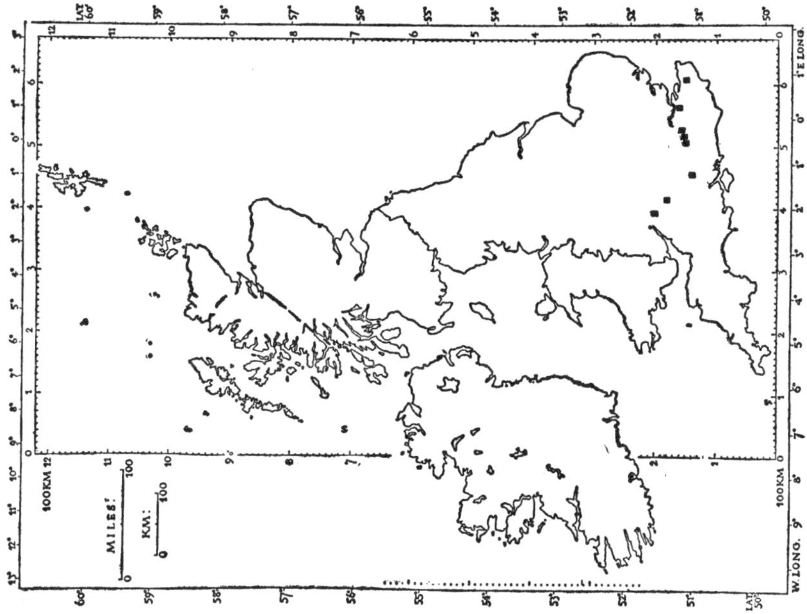

12. Cut-leaved Germander, *Teucrium botrys* (■)

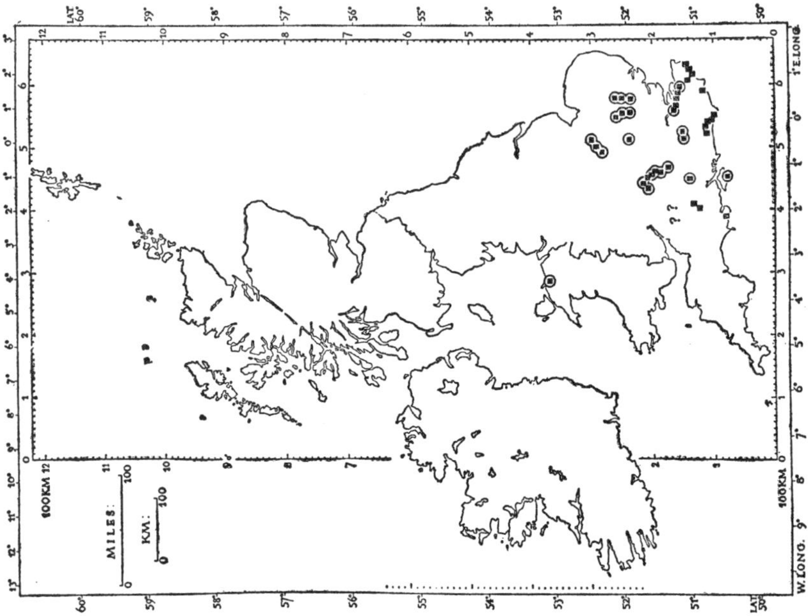

14. Early Spider Orchid, *Ophrys sphegodes* (■)

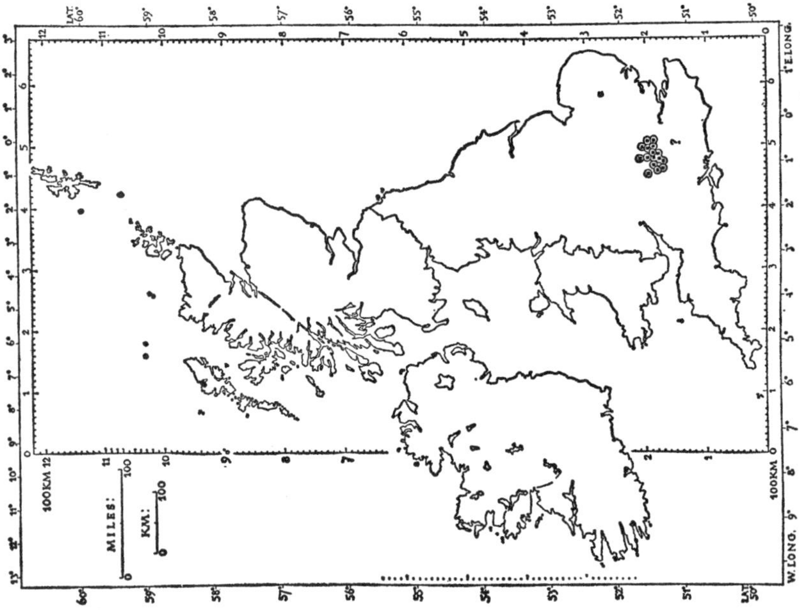

13. Military Orchid, *Orchis militaris* (■)

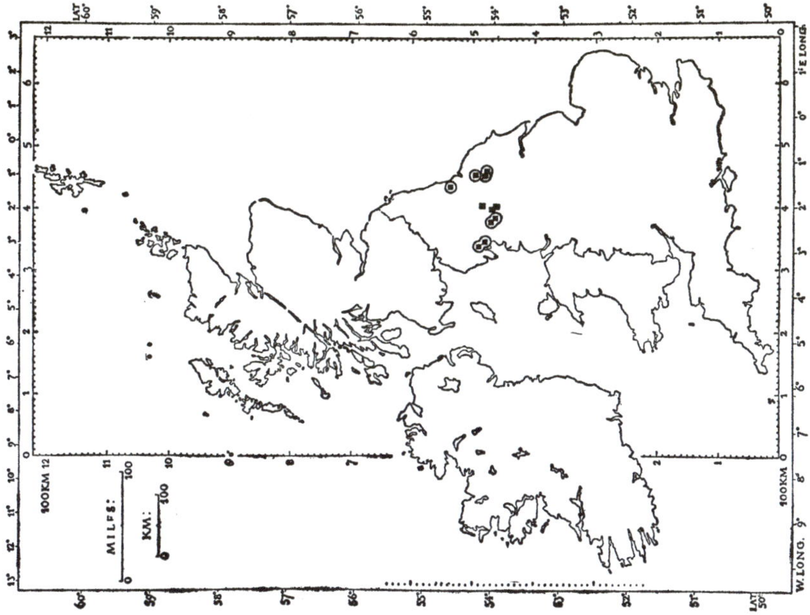

15. Lady's Slipper Orchid, *Cypripedium calceolus* (■)

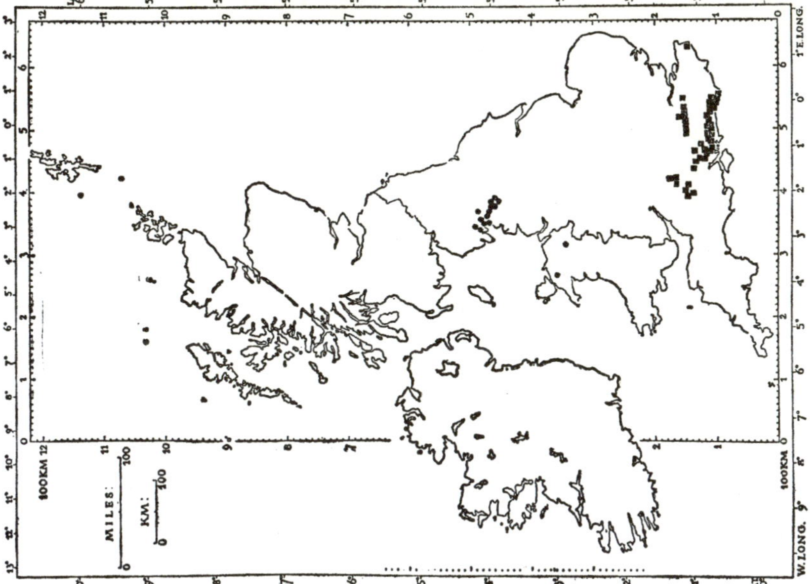

16. a. Roundheaded Rampion, *Phyteuma tenerum* (■)
b. Rigid Buckler Fern, *Dryopteris villarii* (●)

LIST OF VICE-COUNTIES

ENGLAND AND WALES

PENINSULA

1 West Cornwall with Scilly
2 East Cornwall
3 South Devon
4 North Devon
5 South Somerset
6 North Somerset

CHANNEL

7 North Wilts.
8 South Wilts.
9 Dorset
10 Isle of Wight
11 Hants, South
12 Hants, North
13 West Sussex
14 East Sussex

THAMES

15 East Kent
16 West Kent
17 Surrey
18 South Essex
19 North Essex
20 Herts.
21 Middlesex
22 Berks.
23 Oxford
24 Bucks.

ANGLIA

25 East Suffolk
26 West Suffolk
27 East Norfolk
28 West Norfolk
29 Cambridge
30 Bedford and detached part of Hunts.
31 Hunts.
32 Northampton

SEVERN

33 East Gloucester
34 West Gloucester
35 Monmouth
36 Hereford
37 Worcester
38 Warwick
39 Stafford and Dudley
40 Shropshire

SOUTH WALES

41 Glamorgan
42 Brecon
43 Radnor
44 Carmarthen
45 Pembroke
46 Cardigan

NORTH WALES

47 Montomery
48 Merioneth
49 Caernarvon
50 Denbigh and parts of Flint
51 Flint
52 Anglesey

TRENT

53 South Lincoln
54 North Lincoln
55 Leicester with Rutland
56 Nottingham
57 Derby

MERSEY

58 Cheshire
59 South Lancashire
60 Mid Lancashire

HUMBER

61 South-east York
62 North-east York
63 South-west York
64 Mid-west York
65 North-west York

TYNE

66 Durham
67 Northumberland, South
68 Cheviotland, or Northumberland, North

LAKES

69 Westmorland with North Lancashire
70 Cumberland
71 Isle of Man

SCOTLAND

W. LOWLANDS

72 Dumfries
73 Kirkcudbright
74 Wigtown
75 Ayr
76 Renfrew
77 Lanark and E. Dumbarton

E. LOWLANDS

78 Peebles
79 Selkirk
80 Roxburgh
81 Berwick
82 East Lothian
83 Midlothian
84 West Lothian

E. HIGHLANDS

85 Fife with Kinross
86 Stirling
87 South Perth with Clackmannan, and parts of Stirling
88 Mid Perth
89 North Perth
90 Angus or Forfar
91 Kincardine
92 South Aberdeen
93 North Aberdeen
94 Banff
95 Moray or Elgin
96 Easterness (East Inverness with Nairn)

W. HIGHLANDS

97 Westerness (West Inverness with North Argyll)
98 Argyll (Main)
99 Dumbarton (West)
100 Clyde Isles
101 Cantire
102 South Ebudes (Islay, etc.) and Scarba
103 Mid Ebudes (Mull, etc.)
104 North Ebudes (Skye, etc.)

N. HIGHLANDS

105 West Ross
106 East Ross
107 East Sutherland
108 West Sutherland
109 Caithness

NORTH ISLES

110 Outer Hebrides
111 Orkney
112 Shetland

IRELAND

113 (1) South Kerry
114 (2) North Kerry
115 (3) West Cork
116 (4) Mid Cork
117 (5) East Cork
118 (6) Waterford
119 (7) South Tipperary
120 (8) Limerick
121 (9) Clare with Aran Isles
122 (10) North Tipperary
123 (11) Kilmenny
124 (12) Wexford
125 (13) Carlow
126 (14) Leix
127 (15) South-east Galway
128 (16) West Galway
129 (17) North-east Galway
130 (18) Offaly
131 (19) Kildare
132 (20) Wicklow
133 (21) Dublin
134 (22) Meath
135 (23) Westmeath
136 (24) Longford
137 (25) Roscommon
138 (26) East Mayo
139 (27) West Mayo
140 (28) Sligo
141 (29) Leitrim
142 (30) Cavan
143 (31) Louth
144 (32) Monaghan
145 (33) Fermanagh
146 (34) East Donegal
147 (35) West Donegal
148 (36) Tyrone
149 (37) Armagh
150 (38) Down
151 (39) Antrim
152 (40) Derry

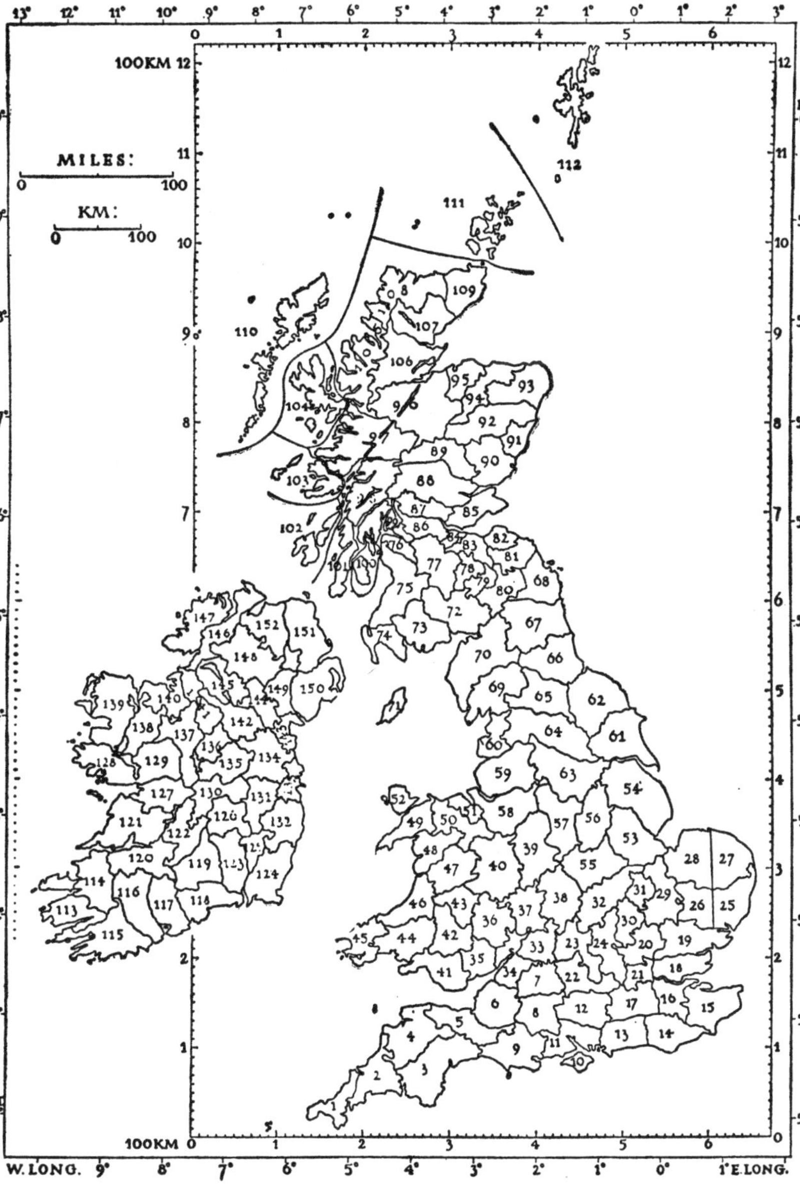

THE NEW NATURALIST VICE-COUNTY MAP OF THE BRITISH ISLES

REFERENCES

THE CLASSIFIED list of references given below is provided to enable the reader to check information given in the text (where this is not based on the writer's own observations) and to suggest further reading. Full details of the works are given in the bibliography.

GENERAL

Names of Plants : *Popular* : Pryor (1870) Rayner (undated). *Scientific* : Dandy, J. E. (1958). List of British Vascular Plants. London, Natural History Museum. *Identification* : Clapham, A. R., Tutin, T. G., & Warburg, E. F. (1962). Flora of the British Isles, Edition 2. Cambridge, University Press ; Clapham, A. R., Tutin, T. G., & Warburg, E. F. (1957—). Flora of the British Isles—Illustrations. Cambridge, University Press ; McClintock D., & Fitter, R. S. R. (1956). The Pocket Guide to Wild Flowers., London, Collins ; Butcher, R. W. (1961). A New Illustrated British Flora. London, Leonard Hill ; Ross-Craig, Stella (1948→). Drawings of British Plants. London, Bell.

CHAPTER I

General Ecology : Leach (1933), Tansley (1911, 1939, 1946), Turrill (1948). *Calcifuges and Calcicoles* : Contejean (1881), Salisbury (1921, 1925), Silva (1934), Tabor (1935), Hope-Simpson (1938), Webb & Hart (1945). *Geology* : Stamp (1946), North (1930), Holmes (1944). *Geographical Distribution of Plants* : Matthews (1937).

CHAPTER 2

Flora of Surrey : Salmon (1931). *Violets* : Walters (1946).

CHAPTER 3

General Ecology : Fagg (undated), Russell (1927), Tansley (1939), Turrill (1948). *Geology* : Dines & Edmunds (1933), Davies (1939). *Influence of slope* : Adamson (1922), Tansley & Adamson (1925). *Water-supply to chalk plants* : Anderson (1927, 1928), Locket (1946B). *Colonisation of bare chalk* : Hope-Simpson (1940A). *Chalk grassland* : Tansley (1922), Tansley & Adamson (1925, 1926), Hope-Simpson (1940A, 1941). *Beechwoods* : Adamson (1922), Watt (1934). *Aliens in bomb crater* : Lousley (1949).

CHAPTER 4

Kent : Hanbury & Marshall (1899), Smith (1829). *Lizard orchid* : Good (1936). *Continental southern element* : Matthews (1937). *Surrey* : Salmon (1931). *Selborne* : White (1788), Vaughan (1877).

CHAPTER 5

Sussex : Wolley-Dod (1937), Tansley & Adamson (1925), Hope-Simpson (1941). *Hampshire (including Isle of Wight)* : Townsend (1904), Rayner (1929). *Isle of Wight* : Bromfield (1856), Wulff (1896).

CHAPTER 6

Downland : Massingham (1936). *Hampshire* : Townsend (1904), Rayner (1929). *Wiltshire* : Grose (1957). *Dorset* : Linton (1900), Good (1948), Pugsley [*Calamintha boetica*] (1923). *Devon* : Martin & Fraser (1939), Harvey (1939). *Berkshire* : Druce (1897). *Thames meadows* : Druce (1926).

CHAPTER 7

Oxfordshire : Druce (1927). *Buckinghamshire* : Druce (1926). *Middlesex* : Trimen & Dyer (1869). *Hertfordshire* : Pryor (1887). *Bedfordshire* : Dony (1953). *Cambridgeshire* : Evans (1939). *Norfolk* : Nicholson (1914). *East Yorkshire* : Robinson (1902).

CHAPTER 8

Dorset : Linton (1900), Mansel-Pleydell (1895), Good (1948). *Devonshire* : Briggs (1880). Pugsley [*Silene angustifolia*] (1940), Phillips [*Carduus pycnocephalus*] (1939), Lousley (1935). *Ecology of Mendips* : Moss (1907). *Mendips and Avon Gorge* : White (1912).

CHAPTER 9

Bath and S. Cotswolds : White (1912). *Cotswolds* : Riddelsdell, Hedley & Price (1948). *Worcestershire* : Lees (1867). *Oxfordshire* : Druce (1927). *Buckinghamshire* : Druce (1926). *Northamptonshire* : Druce (1930), Hepburn (1942). *Rutland* : Horwood & Gainsborough (1933). *N. Yorkshire* : Baker (1906).

CHAPTER 10

Wye Valley : Shoolbred (1920), Purchas & Ley (1889), Riddelsdell, etc. (1948). *Glamorgan* : Riddelsdell (1907), Trow (1911), Vachell (1936). *Tenby* : Pugsley [*Limonium transwallianum*] (1924). *Anglesey and Caernarvonshire* : Griffith (1894). *Denbighshire* : Dallman (1911B, 1913). *Flint* : Dallman (1907, 1908, 1910, 1911). *Craig Breidden* : Lees (1851).

CHAPTER 11

Derbyshire : Linton (1903). *Ecology* : Moss (1913).

CHAPTER 12

Yorkshire : Davis & Lees (1878), Lees (1888), Lees, Cheetham & Sledge (1941). *Durham* : Baker & Tate (1868).

CHAPTER 13

W. Riding : Miall & Carrington (1862), Lees (1888), Lees, Cheetham & Sledge (1941). *Craven only* : Windsor (1873), Lees (1939).

CHAPTER 14

Lancashire : Wheldon & Wilson (1907). *Westmorland & Cumberland* : Baker (1885), Wilson (1938), Hodgson (1898). *N. Yorkshire* : Baker (1906). *Northumberland & Durham* : Baker & Tate (1868).

CHAPTER 15

Ireland : Praeger (1934). *Co. Kerry* : Scully (1916). *Aran Isles* : Hart (1875).

CONCLUSION

Conservation areas : Nature Reserves Investigation Committee Report (1945). Wild Life Conservation Special Committee Report (1947). The Nature Conservancy Annual Reports (1952→).

BIBLIOGRAPHY

ADAMSON, R. S. (1922). Studies of the Vegetation of the English Chalk—I. The Woodlands of Ditcham Park, Hampshire. *J. Ecol.*, *9*: 113–219.

ANDERSON, V. L. (1927). Studies of the Vegetation of the English Chalk —5. The Water Economy of the Chalk. *J. Ecol.*, *15*: 72–129.

ANDERSON, V. L. (1928). The Flora of the Chalk Downs. *Science Progress, London, No. 87, for January, 1928*: 444–60.

ARMITAGE, E. (1914). Vegetation of the Wye Gorge at Symonds Yat. *J. Ecol.*, *2*: 98–108.

BABINGTON, C. C. (1860). Flora of Cambridgeshire. London, Van Voorst.

BAKER, J. G. (1906). North Yorkshire: Studies of its Botany, Geology, Climate and Physical Geography. Edition 2. London, Brown.

BAKER, J. G., and TATE, G. R. (1868). A New Flora of Northumberland and Durham. Issued as Volume 2 of the Tyneside Naturalists' Field Club.

BRIGGS, T. R. A. (1880). Flora of Plymouth. London, Van Voorst.

BROMFIELD, W. A. (1856). [Edited by Sir W. J. Hooker and T. Bell Salter.] Flora Vectensis. London, Pamplin.

CLAPHAM, A. R. (1946). Check-List of British Vascular Plants. *J. Ecol.*, *33*: 308–47.

CONTEJEAN, C. (1881). Géographie botanique. Influence du terrain sur la végétation. Paris.

DALLMAN, A. A. (1907). Notes on the Flora of Flintshire. *J. Botany, London*, *45*: 138–53.

DALLMAN, A. A. (1908). Notes on the Flora of Flintshire, II. *J. Botany, London*, *46*: 187–96, 222–30.

DALLMAN, A. A. (1910). Notes on the Flora of Flintshire, III. *J. Botany, London* *48*: 40–53 and 90–98.

DALLMAN, A. A. (1911). Further Notes on the Flora of Flintshire. *J. Botany, London*, *49*: 8–14.

DALLMAN, A. A. (1911B). Notes on the Flora of Denbighshire. *J. Botany, London*, *49*: Supplement.

DALLMAN, A. A. (1913). Further Notes on the Flora of Denbighshire. *J. Botany, London*, *51*: Supplement.

DAVIES, G. M. (1939). Geology of London and South-East England. London, Murby.

DAVIS, J. M., and LEES, F. A. (1878). West Yorkshire, an account of its

Geology, Physical Geography, Climatology and Botany. London, Reeve.

DONY, JOHN G. (1953). Flora of Bedfordshire. Luton, Corporation of Luton Museum and Art Gallery.

DRUCE, G. C. (1897). The Flora of Berkshire. Oxford, Clarendon Press.

DRUCE, G. C. (1905). *Koeleria splendens* as a British Plant. *J. Botany, London, 43* : 313–17. Buncle.

DRUCE, G. C. (1926). The Flora of Buckinghamshire. Arbroath,

DRUCE, G. C. (1926B). Botany of the Upper Thames in The Natural History of the Oxford District (ed. J. J. Walker). London, Milford.

DRUCE, G. C. (1927). The Flora of Oxfordshire. Oxford, Clarendon Press.

DRUCE, G. C. (1930). The Flora of Northamptonshire. Arbroath, Buncle. Jackson.

EVANS, A. H. (1939). A Flora of Cambridgeshire. London, Gurney and

FAGG, C. C. (undated). The Vegetation of the Chalk. School Nature Study Union Publication, No. 51. London.

FAGG, C. C. (1941). Physiographical Evolution in the Croydon Survey Area and its effects upon Vegetation. *Proc. Croydon Nat. Hist. Sci. Soc., 11, for 1935–1941* : 29–60. Croydon.

GOOD, R. D'O. (1928). Notes on a Comparison of the Angiosperm Floras of Kent and Pas de Calais. *J. Botany, London, 66* : 253–64.

GOOD, R. D'O. (1936). On the Distribution of the Lizard Orchid (*Himantoglossum hircinum* Koch). *New Phytologist, 35* : 142–70.

GOOD, R. D'O. (1948). A Geographical Handbook of the Dorset Flora. Dorchester, County Museum.

GRIFFITH, J. E. (1894). The Flora of Anglesey and Carnarvonshire. Bangor, Nixon and Jarvis.

GROSE, DONALD (1957). The Flora of Wiltshire. Devizes, The Museum.

HANBURY, F. J., and MARSHALL, E. S. (1899). Flora of Kent. London, published privately.

HART, H. C. (1875). A list of Plants found in the Islands of Aran, Galway Bay. Dublin, Hodges, Foster & Co.

HARVEY, Mrs. C. (1939). Chalk Flora of Beer Head. In MARTIN, W. K., and FRASER, G. T. (1939), 33–35.

HEPBURN, IAN (1942). The Vegetation of Barnack Stone Quarries—A Study of the Vegetation of the Northamptonshire Jurassic Limestone. *J. Ecol., 30* : 57–64.

HIND, W. (1889). The Flora of Suffolk. London, Gurney & Jackson.

HODGSON, W. (1898). Flora of Cumberland. Carlisle, Meals.

HOLMES, A. (1944). Principles of Physical Geology. London and Edinburgh, Nelson.

HOPE-SIMPSON, J. F. (1938). A Chalk Flora on the Lower Greensand : Its use in Interpreting the Calcicole Habit. *J. Ecol.*, *26* : 218–35.

HOPE-SIMPSON, J. F. (1940A). Late Stages in Succession leading to Chalk Grassland. *J. Ecol.*, *28* : 386–402.

HOPE-SIMPSON, J. F. (1940B). The Utilisation and Improvement of Chalk Down Pastures. *J. Roy. Agric. Soc., England*, *100* : 1–6.

HOPE-SIMPSON, J. F. (1941). A Second Survey of the Chalk Grasslands of the South Downs. *J. Ecol.*, *29* : 217–67.

HORWOOD, A. R., and NOEL, C. W. F. (1933). The Flora of Leicestershire and Rutland. Oxford, University Press.

LEACH, W. (1933). Plant Ecology. London, Methuen.

LEES, EDWIN (1851A). Sketches of a Botanical Ramble in Wales. *Phytologist*, *4* : 116–24.

LEES, EDWIN (1851B). The Botanical Looker-Out. Edition 2. London, Hamilton, Adams.

LEES, EDWIN (1867). The Botany of Worcestershire. Worcester, Worcestershire Naturalists' Club.

LEES, F. ARNOLD (1888). The Flora of West Yorkshire. London, Reeve.

LEES, F. ARNOLD (1939). The Vegetation of Craven in Wharfedale. Arbroath, Buncle.

LEES, F. ARNOLD, CHEETHAM, C. A., and SLEDGE, W. A. (1941). A Supplement to the Yorkshire Floras. London, Brown.

LINTON, E. F. (1900). Flora of Bournemouth, including the Isle of Purbeck. Bournemouth, published privately.

LINTON, W. R. (1903). Flora of Derbyshire. London, Bemrose.

LITARDIÈRE, R. de (1928). Études sociologiques sur les pelouses xérophiles calcaires du domaine atlantique français. *Arch. Bot. Caen*, *2*, *Mem. No. 2* : 1–48.

LOCKET, G. H. (1946A). Observations on the Colonisation of Bare Chalk. *J. Ecol.*, *33* : 205–9.

LOCKET, G. H. (1946B). A Preliminary Investigation of the Availability to Plants of the Water in the Chalk. *J. Ecol.*, *33* : 222–29.

LOUSLEY, J. E. (1934). *Cirsium eriophorum* (L.) Scop. *x. C. lanceolatum* Scop. *J. Botany, London*, *72* : 171–73.

LOUSLEY, J. E. (1935). *Carduus pycnocephalus* L. (restr.). J. Botany, London, *73* : 257–58.

LOUSLEY, J. E. (1936). *Iberis amara* L. J. Botany, London, *74* : 197.

LOUSLEY, J. E. (1949). Botanical Records for 1948. *London Naturalist* for 1948 : 26–30.

MCLEAN, R. C., and COOK, W. R. I. (1946). Practical Field Ecology. London, Allen & Unwin.

MANSEL-PLEYDELL, J. C. (1895). The Flora of Dorsetshire. Edition 2. Dorchester, privately printed.

MARTIN, W. K., and FRASER, G. T. (1939). Flora of Devon. Arbroath, Buncle.
MASSINGHAM, H. J. (1936). English Downland. London, Batsford.
MATTHEWS, J. R. (1937). Geographical Relationships of the British Flora. *J. Ecol.*, *25* : 1–90.
MIALL, L. C., and CARRINGTON, B. (1862). The Flora of the West Riding. London, Pamplin.
MOSS, C. E. (1907). Geographical Distribution of Vegetation in Somerset : Bath and Bridgwater District. The Royal Geographical Society.
MOSS, C. E. (1913). Vegetation of the Peak District. Cambridge (publisher not stated).
NATURE RESERVES INVESTIGATION COMMITTEE (1945). Report on National Nature Reserves and Conservation Areas in England and Wales. London, The Society for the Promotion of Nature Reserves, British Museum (Natural History).
NICHOLSON, W. A. (1914). A Flora of Norfolk. London, West, Newman.
NORTH, F. J. (1930). Limestones, Their Origins, Distribution and Uses. London, Murby.
PHILLIPS, E. MASSON (1939). *Carduus pycnocephalus* on Plymouth Hoe. *Trans. Devonsh. Assoc.*, *71* : 243–47.
PRAEGER, R. L. (1934). The Botanist in Ireland. Dublin, Hodges, Figgis.
PRESTON, T. A. (1888). The Flowering Plants of Wilts. The Wiltshire Arch. and Natural History Society.
PRYOR, A. R. (1887). [Edited by B. J. Jackson.] A Flora of Hertfordshire. London, Gurney & Jackson.
PRYOR, R. C. A. (1870). On the Popular Names of British Plants. London, Williams & Norgate.
PUGSLEY, H. W. (1923). A new British *Calamintha*. *J. Botany, London*, *61* : 185–91.
PUGSLEY, H. W. (1924). A new *Statice* in Britain. *J. Botany, London*, *62* : 129–34.
PUGSLEY, H. W. (1940). An overlooked *Silene* in Devon. *J. Botany, London*, *78* : 94–9.
PURCHAS, W. H., and LEY, A. (1889). A Flora of Herefordshire. Hereford, Jakeman & Carver.
RAYNER, J. F. (undated). A Standard Catalogue of English Names of our Wild Flowers. Southampton, Gilbert.
RAYNER, J. F. (1929). A Supplement to Frederick Townsend's Flora of Hampshire. Southampton, published privately.
RIDDELSDELL, H. J. (1907). A Flora of Glamorganshire. *J. Botany, London*, *45* : Supplement.
RIDDELSDELL, H. J., HEDLEY, G. W., and PRICE, W. R. (1948). Flora of Gloucestershire. Cheltenham, Cotteswold Naturalists' Field Club.

ROBINSON, J. F. (1902). The Flora of the East Riding of Yorkshire. London, Brown.

RUSSELL, Sir. E. J. (1927). The Chalk Lands of England. London, School Nature Study Union Publication No. 65.

SALISBURY, E. J. (1921). The Significance of the Calcicolous Habit. *J. Ecol.*, *8* : 202–15.

SALISBURY, E. J. (1922). Stratification and Hydrogen-Ion Concentration of the Soil in Relation to Leaching and Plant Succession with Special Reference to Woodlands. *J. Ecol.*, *9* (*for 1921*) : 220–40.

SALISBURY, E. J. (1925). The Incidence of Species in relation to Soil Reaction. *J. Ecol.*, *13* : 149–60.

SALMON, C. E. (1931). [Completed by W. H. Pearsall.] Flora of Surrey. London, Bell.

SAUNDERS, J. (1911). The Field Flowers of Bedfordshire. London, Eyre & Spottiswoode.

SCULLY, R. W. (1916). Flora of County Kerry. Dublin, Hodges, Figgis.

SHOOLBRED, W. A. (1920). The Flora of Chepstow. London, Taylor & Francis.

SILVA, B. L. T. de (1934). The Distribution of " Calcicole " and " Calcifuge " species in relation to the content of the soil in Calcium carbonate and exchangeable Calcium and to Soil Reaction. *J. Ecol.*, *22* : 532–53.

SMITH, G. E. (1829). A Catalogue of Rare or Remarkable Phanerogamous Plants collected in South Kent. . . . London, Longman.

STAMP, L. D. (1946). Britain's Structure and Scenery. London, Collins.

TABOR, R. J. (1935). The Effect of Certain Physical Factors on the Determination of Plant Habitat. *South-Eastern Nat. Antiq.*, *40* : 32–39.

TANSLEY, A. G. (1911). Types of British Vegetation. Cambridge University Press.

TANSLEY, A. G. (1922). Early Stages of Redevelopment of Woody Vegetation on Chalk Grassland. *J. Ecol.*, *10* : 168–77.

TANSLEY, A. G. (1939). The British Islands and their Vegetation. Cambridge, University Press.

TANSLEY, A. G. (1946). Introduction to Plant Ecology. London, Allen & Unwin.

TANSLEY, A. G., and ADAMSON, R. S. (1925). The Chalk Grasslands of the Hampshire-Sussex Border. *J. Ecol.*, *13* : 177–223.

TANSLEY, A. G., and ADAMSON, R. S. (1926). A Preliminary Survey of the Chalk Grasslands of the Sussex Downs. *J. Ecol.*, *14* : 1–32.

THOMAS R. N. (1930). Flora of Paper-Mill Lime Waste Dumps near Glasgow. *J. Ecol.*, *23* : 333–51.

TOWNSEND, F. (1904). Flora of Hampshire, including the Isle of Wight. Edition 2. London, Lovell Reeve.

TRIMEN, H., and DYER, W. T. (1869). Flora of Middlesex. London, Hardwicke.

TROW, A. H. (1911). The Flora of Glamorgan. Vol. 1 (all published). Cardiff, Cardiff Naturalists' Society.

TURRILL, W. B. (1948). British Plant Life. London, Collins.

VACHELL, E. (1936). Glamorgan Flowering Plants and Ferns *ex* Glamorgan County History. Vol. 1, Natural History. Cardiff, Lewis.

VAUGHAN, J. (1877). Notes on the Botany of Selborne. *J. Botany, London, 25 :* 366–70.

WALTERS, S. M. (1946). Observations on Varieties of *Viola odorata. Bot. Soc. & Exch C., 1943–4 Report :* 834–39.

WATT, A. S. (1934). The Vegetation of the Chiltern Hills with special reference to the Beechwoods and their seral relationships. *J. Ecol., 22 :* 230–70, 445–507.

WEBB, D. A., and HART, A. V. (1945). Contributions towards an Understanding of the Calcicole and Calcifuge Habit in some Irish Plants. *Sci. Proc. Roy. Dublin Soc., n. ser., 24 :* 19–28.

WHELDON, J. A., and WILSON, A. (1907). The Flora of West Lancashire. Liverpool, Young.

WHITE, GILBERT (1788). The Natural History of Selborne, quoted from 1941 edition edited by James Fisher. London, Harmondsworth, Penguin.

WHITE, J. W. (1884). Life-History of *Lithospermum purpureo-coeruleum* Linn. *J. Botany, London, 22 :* 74–76.

WHITE, J. W. (1906). *Prunella laciniata* L. in Britain. *J. Botany, London, 44 :* 365–66.

WHITE, J. W. (1912). The Flora of Bristol. Bristol, Wright.

WILD LIFE CONSERVATION SPECIAL COMMITTEE (1947). Conservation of Nature in England and Wales. London, H.M. Stationery Office.

WILMOTT, A. J. (1939). Nomenclature of Two British Alchemillas. *J. Botany, London, 77 :* 249–50.

WILMOTT, A. J. (1934). Some interesting British *Sorbi. Proc. Linn. Soc., London,* Session *146* for *1933–34 :* 73–79.

WILSON, A. (1938). The Flora of Westmorland. Arbroath, Buncle.

WILSON, M. (1911). Plant Distribution in the Woods of North-East Kent, Part 1. *Ann. Bot., 25 :* 857–902.

WINDSOR, J. (1873). Flora Cravoniensis. Manchester, published privately.

WOLLEY-DOD, A. H. (1937). Flora of Sussex. Hastings, Saville.

WULFF, T. Jnr. (1896). Some Remarks on the Flora of the Isle of Wight, England. *Botaniska Notiser, Lund,* for *1896 :* 53–64.

[Most of the County and Local British Floras included in this bibliography are the most recent dealing with the areas to which they refer. A few older works have been included where of special interest in connection with the text. Many of these local floras were published privately or by subscription, and in some cases the " publishers " given on the title-page were really only printers of the works. Most have long been out of print and copies are scarce and often obtainable only through second-hand dealers who specialise in botanical books.]

INDEX

Figures in heavy type refer to pages opposite which illustrations appear. Figures followed by an asterisk refer to pages on which Distribution Maps appear. Place names are indexed only when of special importance or their flora is described in the text.

Acer campestre, 20
Acer pseudo-platanus, 20, 47, 174
Aceras anthropophorum, 24, **35**, 38, 53, 61, 71, 79, 91, 134
Acinos arvensis, 164
Actaea spicata, 136, **159**, 173, 186, 219*
Adiantum capillus-veneris, 8, 107, 144, 195, **203**, 205
Adonis annua, 79
Ajuga chamaepitys, 58, 61, 63, 77, **82**
Ajuga pyramidalis, 200, 206, **207**
Ajuga reptans, 43
Alchemilla glaucescens, 190
Alchemilla minima, 190
Alchemilla vulgaris aggr., 156, 190
Alexanders, 76, 83, 119
Allium oleraceum, 173, 182
Allium sphaerocephalon, 119
Allium ursinum, 186
Alpine Bartsia, 197, 198
Alpine Cinquefoil, 187, 198
Alpine Currant, 164, 165
Alpine Penny-cress, 113, 184, 185, 198
Alpine Woundwort, 128
Althaea hirsuta, 58, 61
Alum Bay, 74
Amberley Mount, 71
Anacamptis pyramidalis, **14**, 24, 54, 61, 74, 79, 128, 170, 173
Anderson, V. L., 38
Antennaria dioica, 97, 151, 188
Anglesey, 148
Angular Solomon's-seal, 126, 165, 182, 186, 194, 196
Anthyllis vulneraria, 16, 26, 77
Antirrhinum major, 59, 119
Antrim, 83
Aphanes arvensis, 190
Aquilegia vulgaris, 136
Arabis caucasica, 158
Arabis hirsuta, 74, 164, 182
Arabis stricta, 118
Aran Islands, 207
Arbutus unedo, 203, 209
Arctium spp., 47
Arenaria ciliata subsp. *hibernica*, 8, 185, 201, 203, 208, 218*
Arenaria gothica, 8, 185, 201, 218*
Arenaria norvegica, 8, 185, 201, 218*
Armeria maritima, 75, 76, 150
Arum maculatum, 44, 72, 76, 106, **106**
Arum neglectum, 72, 76, **107**
Arundel, 72
Ash, 19, 77, 106, 111, 156, 159, 165, 174, 181, 182, 183, 186, 189, **206**
Ash-wood, 186
Aspen, 181
Asperugo procumbens, 97
Asperula cynanchica, 27, 134
Asplenium ruta-muraria, 117
Asplenium viride, 156, 181, 196, 208
Astragalus danicus, 79, 93, 100, 102, 122, 131, 170, 173, 202

Astragalus glycyphyllos, 58, 65, 135, 170, 173
Atropa belladonna, 32, **47**, 102, 134, 136
Aubrey, John, 55, 128
Autumn Gentian, 31, 38, 65, 66, 68, 69, 86
Autumn Lady's Tresses, 25, **30**, 54, 61, 106, 136
Autumn Squill, 107
Avon Gorge, **74**, 116-120

B.D.H. Capillator Outfit, 15
B.D.H. Soil Testing Outfit, 14
Babington, C. C., 95, 97
Ballota nigra, 173
Baneberry, 136, **159**, 173, 186, 189, 197, 219*
Bargate Beds, 65
Barmouth, 147-148
Bartsia alpina, 197
Basil Thyme, 164
Bastard Toadflax, 75, 135
Bath, 123-126
Bath Asparagus, 123
Beachy Head, 67 *seq.*
Beam, 19
Bedford Purlieus, 134
Bedfordshire, 94
Bee Orchid, **15**, 25, 38, 52, 61, 79, 102, 125, 127, 134, 136, 170
Beech, 5, **11**, 19, 37, 42, 43, 55, **62**, 88, 102, 140, 142, 156, 174, 185
Beech hangers, 43
Beechwood, climax forest, 45
Beechwood, escarpment type 44
Beechwood, plateau type, 44, 92
Beer Head, 82
Ben Bulben, 208
Bennett, W., 62
Berkshire, 85-87
Berry Head, **59**, 106-109
Beta maritima, 67, 76
Betchworth Hill, 62
Betonica officinalis, 68
Betula pendula, 20, 42, 117
Betula pubescens, 20, 181
Bindley, R., 166
Binstead, 77
Bird Cherry, 155, 182, 186
Bird's-eye Primrose, 8, 173, 179, 181, 194, 197, 198
Bird's-foot, 117
Bird's-foot Sedge, 155, 160, 194, 195, 196, 197
Bird's-nest Orchid, 44, 66, 89, 136, 174
Bitter Milkwort, 179, 181, 198, 217*
Black Horehound, 173
Black Knapweed, 68, 74
Black Mullein, *see* Dark Mullein
Blackstone, John, 27, 92
Blackstonia perfoliata, 16, 27, **27**, 61, 134
Bladder Campion, 110
Bloody Cranesbill, 16, 118, 141, 146, 148, 150, 154, 161-162, 173, **174**, 182, 184, 195, 196, 201, 207
Blue Fleabane, *see* Field Fleabane
Blue Gromwell, 82, 114, 143, 147, 152, 220*
Bluebell, 37
Blue Moor Grass, 190, 194, 195, 196, 198
Bomb-crater, alien plants in, 47
Borage, 83
Borago officinalis, 83
Boulder Clay, 14, 99, **121**
Bowles, Dr., 133
Box, 5, 18, **26**, 37, 43, 55, 61, 94, 128
Box grove, interior, **19**
Box Hill, 17-48, **18**
Box Hill, geology, 35
Box Hill, Yorkshire, 137
Box-woods, 43, 46
Boxley, 55

Boxwell, 128
Brachypodium pinnatum, 15, 47, 77, 171, 173
Brachypodium sylvaticum, 171
Bracken, 36, 107, **154**, 189
Brambles, 37, 68
Brassica oleracea, 50, 143, 150
Breckland, 100
Breidden Hill, 153
Brenan, J. P. M., 132
Bristol Rock Cress, 118
Brittle Bladder Fern, 181
Broad-leaved Cudweed, 58
Broad-leaved Helleborine, 44, 66, 92
Bromus arvensis, 99
Bromus erectus, 15, 87, 156, 171, 173
Broom, 3, 185
Brown, John, 172
Bryonia dioica, 173
Buckland Hill, 43, 62
Buckman, Prof., 81
Bucknall, Cedric, 128
Buddleja davidii, 3, 119
Bunium bulbocastanum, 93, 98
Bupleurum baldense, 69, 108
Bupleurum rotundifolium, 79
Burdocks, 47
Burford Downs, 131
Burges, R. C. L., 131
Burnet Rose, 148, 162
Burnt Orchid, 87, 100, 170
Burren, 203-207
Büsgen, M., 19
Buxus sempervirens, 5, 18, **26**, 61, 94, 128

Calamintha ascendens, 84
Calamintha baetica, 84
Calamintha sylvatica, 75, 84
Calcareous Rocks, table of, 6, 7
Calceolus Mariae, 180
Calcicoles, 2
Calcicoles, defined, 3
Calcicolous, 2
Calcifuges, defined, 3
Calcipete, 3
Calciphile, 3
Calciphobe, 3
Calcium carbonate, 3
Calluna vulgaris, 3, 15, 36, 85
Cambridge Ragwort, 97
Cambridgeshire, 94-99
Campanula glomerata, 2, **11**, 16, 31, 87, 173
Campanula latifolia, 158, 187
Canadian Fleabane, 56-57
Candytuft, **83**, 89
Caper Spurge, 55-56, 73, 134, 140, 147
Carboniferous Limestone, characteristics, 138-139
Carboniferous Limestone, distribution of outcrops, Fig. 1c, p. 12
Carboniferous system, 11
Cardamine bulbifera, 92
Cardamine impatiens, 65, 141
Cardaria draba, 57
Carduus nutans, **10**, 29
Carduus pycnocephalus, 109
Carduus tenuiflorus, 67, 68, 82, 109
Carex capillaris, 183, 184, 199
Carex depauperata, 65, 114
Carex digitata, 120, 139, 141, 160, 173, 174
Carex ericetorum, 98, 100, 171, 172
Carex filiformis, 130
Carex flacca, 41
Carex humilis, 80, 82, 119, 141
Carex montana, 139, 141, 143, 172
Carex ornithopoda, 155, 160, 194
Carisbrooke Castle, 75
Carlina vulgaris, 2, 29
Carline Thistle, 2, 29, 75, 77
Caucalis latifolia, 97
Caucalis platycarpos, 97
Cecidomyia taxi, 18

Cefn-yr-Ogof, **151**
Centaurea calcitrapa, 55, 61, **70**
Centaurea nemoralis, 68
Centaurea scabiosa, 80
Centaurium capitatum, 68, 75
Centranthus ruber, 59, **72**, 119
Cephalanthera damasonium, 44, 127
Cephalanthera longifolia, 44, 79, 137, 196
Cephalanthera rubra, 126
Cerastium arvense, 77, 101
Cerastium pumilum, 64, 120, 132
Ceterach officinarum, 109, 117, 159, 207
Chalk, a limestone, 1
Chalk, distribution of outcrops, Fig. 1a, p. 12
Chalk grassland, 40
Chalk Milkwort, 2, 23, 54, 77, 86, 131, 135
Chalk pit, Cambridgeshire, **123**
Chalk pit, disused, **72**
Chalk scrub, 42
Chalk Violet, 23, 143
Chalk woodland, 43
Chanctonbury Ring, 71
Cheddar Gorge, 111-114, **143**
Cheddar Pink, 112
Cheetham, C. A., 183
Cheiranthus cheiri, 111, 119, 173, 174
Chilterns, 88-93
Chipstead Valley, 45
Chrysanthemum leucanthemum, 113
Ciliate Pearlwort, 117
Cirsium acaulon, **3**, 28, 41, 125, 170
Cirsium arvense, 171
Cirsium eriophorum var. *britannicum*, **110**, 122, 123, 143, 165, 171
Cirsium heterophyllum, 155, 162, **175**
Cirsium tuberosum, 81, 98, 143, 219*
Clay-with-Flints, 11, 37
Clematis vitalba, **2**, 15, 22, 87
Clematis vitalba var. *timbali*, 77
Climax forest, 45
Clinopodium vulgare, 30
Clints, 178
Clipsham Quarries, 135
Clove-scented Broomrape, 54, 61
Clustered Bellflower, 2, 8, **11**, 16, 31, 47, 87, 102, 156, 173
Cochlearia danica, 105
Cochlearia glastifolia, 47
Cochlearia officinalis, 150
Coeloglossum viride, 79, 127
Colley Hill, 62
Colt Park Wood, 186-188
Common Birch, 20
Common Birdsfoot Trefoil, 2, 8, 26, 38, 41, 102, 125
Common Buckthorn, 42, 87, 150
Common Bugle, 43
Common Calamint, 84
Common Eyebright, 31
Common Gromwell, 156
Common Hawkbit, 41
Common Honeysuckle, 72
Common Houndstongue, 47
Common Lady's Mantle (aggr.), 156, 174, 190
Common Milkwort, 24, 54, 197, 208
Common Oak, 20, 37
Common Pink, 174, **186**
Common Polypody, 181
Common Rock-rose, 16, 26, 38, 42, 47, 74, 83, 102, 106, 115, 131, 146, 148, 181, 196, 198, 201, 202, 211
Common Scurvy-grass, 150
Common Self-heal, 106, 113
Common Star-of-Bethlehem, 98, 100
Common Teasel, **98**
Conservation areas, 214
Continental Southern Element, 61
Convallaria majalis, 134, 136, 158
Conyza canadensis, 56
Conyza canadensis x *Erigeron acer*, 56
Coralroot, 92
Corfe Castle, 83

Corn Salad, 106
Cotoneaster horizontalis, **151**
Cotoneaster integerrimus, 150
Cotoneaster microphyllus, 151
Cotoneaster simonsii, 151
Cotswolds, 126-130
Cowslip, 99
Cranborne Chase, 82
Crataegus monogyna, 21
Craven, 176-191
Creeping Thistle, 171
Crepis mollis, 187
Crepis paludosa, 187
Crested Cow-wheat, 14, 99, 133, 134, 135
Cretaceous system, 10
Crinitaria linosyris, 108, 115, 146, 151, 195, 218*
Crithmum maritimum, 50, 67, 76, 82, 105, 150
Crosswort, 182
Cruciata chersonensis, 182
Cuckoo Pint, 44, 73, 76, 106, **106**
Culver Cliff, 73-74
Curtis, W. Hugh, 179
Curtis, William, 179
Curtis's Mouse-ear Chickweed, 64, 120, 132
Cut-leaved Germander, 59, 62, 63, 79, 130, 221*
Cut-leaved Self-heal, 79, 92, 106, 113-114
Cymbalaria muralis, 173, 174
Cynoglossum germanicum, 64, 132
Cynoglossum montanum, *see C. germanicum*
Cynoglossum officinale, 47
Cypress Spurge, 63, **82**
Cypripedium calceolus, 136, 175, 223*
Cystopteris fragilis, 181

Dactylorhiza maculata, 79
Dactylorhiza praetermissa, 60, 79
Dallas, J. E. S., 149, 150
Dane's Blood, 129
Danish Scurvy-grass, 105
Daphne laureola, 44, 170, 191
Daphne mezereum, 71, 166, 191, **206**
Dark-flowered Helleborine, 2, 152, 153, 161, **178**, 182, 194, 196, 198, 201, 206
Dark Mullein, 16, **27**, 29, 135, 136, 159, 170
Darwin, Charles, 60
Daucus carota, 28, 69, 83
Daucus gummifer, 83
Deadly Nightshade, 32, 43, **47**, 102, 134, 136
Delphinium ambiguum, 97
Dense-spiked Orchid, 203, 206, 207
Derbyshire, 155-167
Devil's-bit Scabious, 189
Devon, 82-83
Dianthus deltoides, 101
Dianthus gratianopolitanus, 112
Dianthus plumarius, 174, **186**
Digitalis ambigua, 47
Digitalis ferruginea, 47
Digitalis lanata, 47
Digitalis lutea, 47
Digitalis purpurea, 3, 15, 185
Dillenius, J. J., 115, 116
Dillenius's Hair-grass, 114
Dipsacus fullonum, **98**
Dipsacus pilosus, 159, 165, 198
Dog Rose, 21, 162
Dog's Mercury, 37, 43, 44, 186
Dogwood, 16, 20, **31**, 42, 77, 82, 105, 111, 117, 140, 173
Dorset, 82-84, 104-106
Dovedale, 165-166
Dover, 49 *seq.*
Downy Birch, 20, 181, 182, 189
Downy Oat, 87
Downy Sedge, 130
Downy Woundwort, 122, 132, 134

Draba aizoides var. *montana*, 144, 146
Draba incana, 155, 161, 170, 182, 208
Draba muralis, 72, 123, 161, 182
Drake, Sir Francis, 110
Drift Deposits, 11
Dropwort, 16, 77, 87, 102, 107, 156, 162, 182, 195, 201, 203, 206, 211
Druce, G. C., 85, 115, 131, 134
Dryas octopetala, 181, 198, **202**, 206
Dryopteris villarii, 153, **179**, 189, 194, 223*
Durness, 201
Dutchman's Pipe, 44
Dwarf Centaury, 68, 69, 75
Dwarf Sedge, 80, 82, 119, **141**
Dwarf Spurge, 68, 69

Early Gentian, 62, 64, 82, **90**, 105
Early Purple Orchid, **63**
Early Spider Orchid, 52, 61, 69, 95, 105, 131, **142**, 222*
Earthworks, 85
Echium vulgare, 60
Ecology, definition, 34
Edees, E. S., 166
Elder, 165, 186
Elecampane, 47
Endymion non-scriptus, 37
Epipactis atrorubens, 2, 152, 161, **178**, 182
Epipactis helleborine, 44, 92
Epipactis leptochila, 91
Epipactis palustris, 60
Epipactis purpurata, 44
Epipogium aphyllum, 52, 89, 212
Epsom Downs, 63
Erica cinerea, 15, 107
Ericaceae, 3
Erigeron acer, 56
Eriophyes geranii, 162
Eryngium campestre, 59, 61, **73**, 79, 110
Euonymus europaeus, 22
Euphorbia amygdaloides, 44
Euphorbia cyparissias, 63, **82**
Euphorbia lathyrus, 55, 73, **134**, **140**
Euphorbia nalensis, 63
Euphorbia pilosa, 125
Euphorbia platyphyllos, 99
Euphorbia portlandica, 74, 82, 105
Euphorbia stricta, 140
Euphrasia officinalis (aggr.), 30
Euphrasia nemorosa, 31
Euphrasia nemorosa var. *calcarea*, 31
Euphrasia pseudokerneri, 31, 86, **91**
Euphrasia salisburgensis, 188, 206
Eyebrights, 30, 69

Fagus sylvatica, 5, 19, **62**, 88
Fairy Flax, 27, 38, 41, 102, 181
Falcaria vulgaris, 57
False Oxlip, 99
False Sweetbriar, 22
" Father of English Botany," 50, 116
Festuca altissima, 155, 158, **200**
Fiddle Dock, 83
Field Bugloss, 74
Field Cow-wheat, 99
Field Eryngo, 59, 61, **73**, 79, 110
Field Fleabane, 56-57, 156
Field Fleawort, 56, 65, 69, 86, 93, 94, 97, **127**, 129, 131
Field Garlic, 173, 182
Field Lady's Mantle, 190
Field Madder, 69
Field Maple, 20, 77, 140
Field Mouse-ear Chickweed, 77, 101
Field Rose, 21, 162
Field Scabious, 29
Filago spathulata, 58
Filipendula ulmaria, 162, 187
Filipendula vulgaris, 16, 77, 87, 162, 203
Fine-leaved Heath, 15, 107
Fine-leaved Sandwort, 64, 77, 101, 129, 159
Fingered Sedge, 120, 139, 141, 160, 173, 174

Fly Honeysuckle, 71
Fly Orchid, **30**, 43, 54, 136, **170**, 195
Forest Marble, 131
Fountains Abbey, 174
Foxglove, 3, 15, 185
Foxgloves, alien, 47
Fragaria vesca, 43
Fragrant Orchid, **14**, 24, 54, 60, 79, 134
Frankland, Thomas, 179
Fraxinus excelsior, 19, **206**
Freshwater Downs, 74
Friar's Crowns, 123
Frog Orchid, 79, 127
Fumaria micrantha, 97
Fumaria parviflora, 97
Fumaria vaillantii, 97
Fumitories, 97

Gagea lutea, 79, 122, **125**, **132**, 137, 187
Galeobdolon luteum, 44
Galium mollugo, 54, 173
Galium parisiense, 134
Galium pumilum, 16, 181, 208
Galium saxatile, 15
Gentiana collina, 31
Gentiana verna, 199, 205, 220*
Gentianella amarella, 31, 38, 68, 86
Gentianella anglica, 62, 64, 82, **90**, 105
Gentianella germanica, 86, 89, **114**, 220*
Geological Survey Maps, 14
Geranium columbinum, 164
Geranium lucidum, 65, 83
Geranium pratense, 85, 125, 127
Geranium robertianum var. *hispidum*, 109
Geranium sanguineum, 16, 118, 136, 141, 146, 148, 154, 161, **174**, 182, 195
Geranium sylvaticum, 187
Gerard, 27, 32, 59, 161, 187
Germander Whitlow-grass, 72, 117, 123, 161, 165, 181, 184
Giant Bellflower, 158, 187, 188
Gibson, G. C., 95
Giggleswick Scar, 185
Gilmour, John, 134
Glacial Drift, 13
Glaucous Rose, 155, 162
Gladdon, 72, 82, 147
Glaucium flavum, 50, 61, 74, 150
Glaucous Sedge, 41
Globe Flower, 8, 155, 164, 188, 197
Godalming, 65
Gog Magog Hills, 98, **123**
Goldilocks, *see* Hair-leaved Goldilocks
Good, R. D'O., 52, 212
Goodenough, Bishop, 81
Goodyer, John, 27
Gordale Scar, 182-183
Goring, Charles, 71
Gorse, 68, 83, 107
Gower Peninsula, 144-147
Graham, R., xvii
Grape Hyacinth, 98, 100
Grass-of-Parnassus, 181
Grass Woods, 182
Graveson, A. W., 132
Grazing, a biotic factor, 46
Great Doward, 140
Great Meadow-rue, 201
Great Mullein, 30
Great Orme's Head, **75**, 148-152
Great Pig-nut, 93, 98
Greater Burnet-saxifrage, 165, 174
Greater Bur-parsley, 97
Greater Butterfly Orchid, 196
Greater Calamint, 75
Greater Knapweed, 80
Greek Valerian, *see* Jacob's Ladder
Green-flowered Helleborine, 91
Green Hellebore, 141
Green-leaved Houndstongue, 64, 132

Green Spleenwort, 156, 181, 196, 208
Gregory, Mrs. E. S., 113, 114
Grikes, 178
Grime's Graves, 101
Grose, J. D., xvii, 81
Ground Pine, 58, 61, 63, **77, 82**
Guelder Rose, 186
Gunther, R. W. T., 65
Gymnadenia conopsea, **14,** 24, 54, 79, 134

Habitat Factors, 34
Hackhurst, Downs, 62
Haines, J. W., 126
Hair-leaved Goldilocks, 108, 115-116, 146, 151, 195, 218*
Hairy Mallow, 58, 61
Hairy Rock Cress, 74, 164, 174, 182
Hairy Spurge, 125
Hairy Violet, 16, 22, 38, 42, 60, 65, 73, 102, 131, 149, 201, 211
Hall, R. H., xvii, 159, 160, 161
Hampshire, 65-66, 73, 78-79
Harefield, 92
Hartstongue, 117, 181
Harvey, Mrs. Clare, 82
Hawthorn, 21, 42, 150, 165, 183, 186
Hazel, 117, 165, 181, 183
Heath Bedstraw, 15
Hedera helix, 77
Hedge Bedstraw, 54, 173
Hedge Woundwort, 128
Helianthemum apenninum, 2, 107, 115, 217*
Helianthemum apenninum x *chamaecistus*, 115
Helianthemum canum, 146, 184, 195, 207, 217*
Helianthemum chamaecistus, 16, 26, 38, 146, 202
Helictotrichon pubescens, 87
Helleborus foetidus, 56, 72, 141
Helleborus viridis, 141
Henbane, **68,** 83
Herb Christopher, *see* Baneberry
Herb Paris, 152, 159, 165, 187, 188, 196, 202
Herb Robert, 109
Herminium monorchis, 25, 77, 127
Hertfordshire, 93-94
Hieracium spp., 92, 150, 164
Hieracium cambricum, 150
Hieracium exotericum, 126
High Taper, 30
Himantoglossum hircinum, 52, 61, 71, 94, **122**
Hippocrepis comosa, 2, 26, 38, 86, 131
Hirschfeldia incana, 58, 71
Hoary Cress, 57
Hoary Mustard, 58, 71
Hoary Plantain, 16, 27, 46, 77, 102, 173, 174
Hoary Rock-rose, 146, 148, 149, 195, 196, 198, 207, 217*
Hoary Stock, 70, 75, 76, 82, 143
Hoary Whitlow-grass, 155, 161, 170, 182, 184, 197, 198, 201, 208
Hog's Back, 65
Holly, 117, 140, 158
Holly Fern, 189-190
Honewort, 108, 114, 115, 116, 117, 218*
Hope-Simpson, J. F., xvii
Hordelymus europaeus, 92, 126, 158
Hornungia petraea, 118, 141, 161, 216*
Horseshoe Vetch, 2, 8, 26, 38, 74, 86, 106, 131, 182, 196
How, William, 133
How, W. W., 153
Hudson, William, 27
Humphrey Head, 195
Hutton Roof Crag, 194
Hydrogen Ion Concentration, 15
Hyoscyamus niger, **68,** 83
Hypericum montanum, 16, 83
Hypericum perforatum, 4, 38

Hypochoeris maculata, 94, 100, 151, 195
Hythe Beds, 58

Iberis amara, **83**, 89
Inchnadamph, 201
Ingall, T., 62
Ingleborough, **155**, **158**, 189-190
Inula conyza, 32
Inula helenium, 47
Ireland, 201-210
Iris foetidissima, 72, 82
Irish Sandwort, 8, 201, 203, 208, 218*
Isatis tinctoria, 47
Isle of Wight, 73-77
Italian Catchfly, 60
Ivinghoe Beacon, 94
Ivy, 77, 105, 111, 117, 181
Ivy Broomrape, **66**, 76, 83, 105, 109, 113, 118, 147
Ivy-leaved Toadflax, 173, 174

Jacob, John, 53
Jacob's Ladder, 155, 159, 166, 181, 183
Johnson, Thomas, 27, 59, 116, 161, 187
Juniper, 21, 42, 150, 190
Juniper Hall Field Centre, 17
Juniperus communis, 21, 190
Jurassic, distribution of outcrop, Fig. 1b, p. 12
Jurassic Limestones, 120 *seq.*

Kent, 49-62
Kent, D. H., 87, 92
Kentish Milkwort, 54, 179, 217*
Kentish Rag, 58
Kidney-leaved Saxifrage, 189
Kidney Vetch, 16, 26, 65, 77, 148
Killarney, 209
King Lear, 50
Kingley Vale, 73
Knaresborough, 173
Knautia arvensis, 29
Koeleria vallesiana, 114

Lady Orchid, 51, 61, **69**, 91, 213
Lady's Bedstraw, 148, 197
Lady's Slipper Orchid, 136, 175, 179-180, 194, 196, 222*
Lake, Dr., 27
Lambert, A. B., 81
Larch, 47
Large Autumn Gentian, 86, 89, **114**, 220*
Large-flowered Chalk-eyebright, 30, 86, **91**
Large-leaved Lime, 140, 142, 196
Large White Helleborine, 44, 127
Larkspur, 97
Late Spider Orchid, **42**, 51, 61, 213
Lathkill Dale, 159
Lathyrus aphaca, 72
Lathyrus slyvestris, 132, 134
Leaching, 13, 156
Lecoq's Poppy, 97
Lees, F. A., 180, 184, 188
Leigh Woods, 119-120
Lenham Beds, 68
Leontodon hispidus, 41
Leonurus cardiaca, 47
Lepidium draba, see Cardaria draba
Lepidium graminifolium, 47
Lesser Burnet-saxifrage, 41, 68
Lesser Bur-parsley, 97
Lesser Butterfly Orchid, 79
Lesser Teasel, 159, 165, 198
Lesser Wintergreen, 92, 126
Lewes, 71
Lias, 121, 122
Lightfoot, John, 131
Ligustrum vulgare, 4, 20
Lilium martagon, 64, 139
Lily-of-the-Valley, 134, 136, 158, 180, 186, 189, 196, 202

Lime, 3
Limestone, defined, 3
Limestone, tests for, 4
Limestone pavement, Irish, **187**
Limestone pavement, Yorkshire, **155**, **158**, 177-178, 184
Limestone Polypody, 113, 142, 153, 181, **190**, 194, 196, 197, 203
Limestones, nature of, 9
Limestones, older compared with Chalk, 103
Limestone soils, characteristics, 4
Limonium binervosum, 82, 105, 147
Limonium recurvum, 105
Limonium transwallianum, 147
Linaria repens, 86
Lincolnshire, 101-102, 135
Lindley, John, 57
Ling, 3, 15, 36, 85, 101, 110
Ling Gill, 187-188
Linton, W. R., 166
Linum anglicum, 98, 102, 135, 197, 218*
Linum catharticum, 27, 38, 41
Lithospermum officinale, 156
Lithospermum purpurocaeruleum, 82, 114, 143, 147, 152, 220*
Little Doward, 140
Lizard Orchid, 52, 61, 71, 94, **122**
Llandudno, 148-152
Lobularia maritima, 75
London Pride, 164, 188
Longleaf, 57
Long-stalked Cranesbill, 164
Lonicera periclymenum, 72
Lonicera xylosteum, 71, 72
Lotus corniculatus, 2, 26, 38, 41, 125
Lousley, Job, v, 86
Lychnis viscaria, 154, 200
Lycopsis arvensis, 74
Lynchets, 46

McClintock, D., xvii, 146
Madder, 72, 77, 82, 105, 109, 113, 118, 143, 147, 166, 203, 206
Madwort, 97
Magnesian Limestone, 168-175
Maianthemum bifolium, 136
Maidenhair Fern, 8, 107, 110, **144**, 195, **203**, 205, 207, 209
Maiden Pink, 101
Malham Cove, **147**, 183-184
Man, a biotic factor, 46, 47
Man Orchid, 24, **35**, 38, 42, 53, **61**, 71, 79, 91, 134
Manning & Bray, 18
Marjoram, 30, 60, 74, 102, 182
Marlborough Downs, 84
Marsh Hawksbeard, 187, 188
Marsh Helleborine, 60
Marsh Orchid, 60, 79
Marshfield, 125-126
Martagon Lily, 64, 139-140
Mary's Shoe, 180
Matlock, 158-159
Matthews, J. R., 61
Matthiola incana, 70, 75, 82, 143
May Lily, 136
Meadow Clary, 56, 58, 61, 71, 131
Meadow Cranesbill, 85, 125, 127
Meadow Sage, 56
Meadow-sweet, 162, 187
Meconopsis cambrica, 113, 174
Melampyrum arvense, 76, 84, 99
Melampyrum cristatum, 14, 99, 133, 134
Melancholy Thistle, 155, 162, 166, **175**, 187, 188, 189, 197
Melica nutans, 134, 139, 155, 158
Melica uniflora, 158
Mendips, 110-116
Mercurialis perennis, 37, 43, 44, 186
Meum mutellina, 117
Mezereon, 66, 71, 166, 191, 197, **206**
Miall, L. C., 184

Middlesex, 92-93
Military Orchid, 2, 87, 89-91, 93, **115**, 215, 222*
Mill, John Stuart, 94
Miller Christy, 99
Miller's Dale, **95**
Mills, Dr. W. H., 98
Millstone Grit, 167
Mil-mountaine, 27
Minuartia hybrida, 64, 77, 101, 129, 159
Minuartia stricta, 199
Minuartia verna, 113, 149, 157, 184, **194**
Mistletoe, 21
Monkey Orchid, 2, **69**, 91
Monotropa hypopithys, 44, 89
Morecambe Bay, 192-196
Morvern, 83
Mossy Saxifrage, 113, 139, 164, 182, 207, 208
Motherwort, 47
Mountain Ash, 181, 186
Mountain Avens, 181, 198, 201, **202**, 206, 207
Mountain Bedstraw, 16, 181, 184, 208
Mountain Everlasting, 97, 151, 188
Mountain Melic, 134, 155, 158, 159, 194
Mountain Pansy, 155, 197
Mountain St. John's Wort, 16, 83
Mountain Sedge, 139, 141, 143, 172
Mountain Stone-parsley, 69, 94, 98, 219*
Mouse-ear Hawkweed, 148
Muscari atlanticum, 98, 100
Musk Orchid, 25, 60, 77, 127
Musk Thistle, **10**, 29, 77
Myrrhis odorata, 47

Narcissus obvallaris, 147
Narrow-leaved Bitter-cress, 65, 141
Narrow-leaved Everlasting Pea, 132, 134
Narrow-leaved Eyebright, 188, 206, 207
Narrow-leaved Helleborine, 44, 79, 137, 196
National Parks, 214
Nature Conservancy, 213
Nature Reserves Investigation Committee, 214
Navelwort, *see* Wall Pennywort
Neotinea intacta, 203, 206
Neotinea intacta var. *straminea*, 206
Neottia nidus-avis, 44, 89, 136
Norbury Park, 43
Norfolk, 100-101
North, F. J., 87
North Downs, 49-66
Northamptonshire, 133-134
Norwegian Sandwort, 201, 208, 218*
Nottingham Catchfly, 60, 73, 82, 87, **111**, 164, 165, 170, 173

Old Man's Beard, 22—*see* Traveller's Joy
Oligocene, 77
Ononis reclinata, 107, 146
Oolite, 121, 122
Ophrys apifera, **15**, 25, 38, 52, 61, 79, 102, 125, 127, 134, 136, 170
Ophrys fuciflora, **42**, 51, 61, 213
Ophrys insectifera, **30**, 54, 136, 170
Ophrys sphegodes, 52, 61, 69, 95, 105, 131, **142**, 222*
Ophrys trollii, 122, 127, **146**
Orchids of a Hampshire beechwood, **99**
Orchis mascula, **63**
Orchis militaris, 2, 51, 87, 89, **115**, 222*
Orchis purpurea, 51, 61, **69**, 91, 213
Orchis simia, 2, **69**, 91

Orchis ustulata, 87, 100, 170
Origanum vulgare, 30
Ornithogalum pyrenaicum, 123
Ornithogalum umbellatum, 98, 100
Ornithopus perpusillus, 117
Orobanche alba, 197, 207
Orobanche caryophyllacea, 54, 61
Orobanche elatior, 80, 83, 134, 135
Orobanche hederae, **66**, 76, 83, 105, 109, 147
Orobanche picridis, 54, 61
Orobanche reticulata, **94**, 171
Orthilia secunda, 139
Oxalis acetosella, 37
Ox-eye Daisy, 113, 197
Oxfordshire, 88 *seq.*, 130-132
Oxlip, 14, 99
Oxtongue Broomrape, 54, 61
Oxytropis halleri, 200

Paeonia mascula, 115
Pale Toadflax, 86
Papaver hybridum, 97
Papaver lecoqii, 97
Parietaria diffusa, 109, 173
Paris quadrifolia, 152, 159
Parkinson, John, 116, 117
Parnassia palustris, 181
Parsley, 173
Parsley Piert, 190
Pasque Flower, **51**, 86, 93, 94, 95, 97, 122, 129, 131, 133, 135, 170, 216*
Pastinaca sativa, 28, **98**
Pellitory-of-the-Wall, 109, 113, 173, 174
Perennial Flax, 98, 102, 135, 136, 197, 198, 218*
Perfoliate Penny-cress, 122, 129-130, 131, 132
Perfoliate Yellow-wort, *see* Yellow-wort
Perforate St. John's Wort, 4, 38
Permian Limestone, *see* Magnesian Limestone
Permian system, 11
Petroselinum crispum, 173
Pewley Hill, 62
*p*H values, 15
Pheasant's Eye, 79, 80, 106
Phleum phleoides, 101
Phyllitis scolopendrium, 117, 181
Phyteuma orbiculare, *see P. tenerum*
Phyteuma tenerum, **2**, 62, 68, 77, 85, 223*
Pigott, D., 98
Pilgrim's Way, 59
Pimpinella major, 165, 174
Pimpinella saxifraga, 41, 68
Pinus sylvestris, 20
Plant communities, Box Hill, 39
Plant soil indicators, 15, 16
Plantago lanceolata, 41
Plantago maritima, 179
Plantago media, 16, 27, 173
Plantago sabrinae, 115
Platanthera bifolia, 79
Platanthera chlorantha, 196
Ploughman's Spikenard, 32, 43
Plowmans-spikenard, 32
Plymouth, 109-110
Poa bulbosa, 132
Polemonium caeruleum, 155, 159, 181
Polygala amara, 179, 198, 217*
Polygala austriaca, 54, 179, 217*
Polygala calcarea, 2, 23, 54, 77, 131, 135
Polygala vulgaris, 24, 54
Polygala vulgaris var. *ballii*, 208
Polygonatum odoratum, 126, 165, 182
Polypodium vulgare, 181
Polystichum lonchitis, 189
Populus tremula, 181
Portland, Isle of, 105-106
Portland Sea-lavender, 105
Portland Spurge, 74, 82, 105, 109

Potentilla crantzii, 187, 198
Potentilla erecta, 118, 205
Potentilla fruticosa, 198, 205
Potentilla recta, 94
Potentilla rupestris, 154
Potentilla verna, 99, 100, 118, 141, 146, 149, 164, 172
Poterium sanguisorba, 2, 24, 38, 41
Poverty Weed, 76
Praeger, R. L., 188, 202, 203, 207, 209
Prentice, J. E., xvii
Primrose, 99
Primula elatior, 14, 99
Primula elatior x *veris*, 99
Primula elatior x *vulgaris*, 99
Primula farinosa, 8, 173, 179, **197**
Primula veris, 99
Primula veris x *vulgaris*, 99
Primula vulgaris, 99
Privet, 4, 20, 42, 65, 74, 77, 82, 105, 111, 140, 150
Prunella laciniata, 79, 92, 106, 113
Prunella laciniata x *vulgaris*, 106, 113
Prunella vulgaris, 106, 113
Prunus padus, 155, 182
Pteridium aquilinum, 13, 36, **154**
Pugsley, H. W., 31, 32, 84, 147, 188
Pulsatilla vulgaris, **51**, 86, 93, 94, 122, 129, 170, 216*
Purbeck, 83
Purchas, W. H., 141
Purging Flax, 27
Purple Cow-wheat, 76
Purple Helleborine, 44
Purple Milk-vetch, 79, 93, 94, 95, 97, 100, 102, 122, 131, 134, 170, 173, 201, 202, 207
Purple Star-thistle, 55, 61, 70
Pyramidal Bugle, 200, 206, 207, **207**
Pyramidal Orchid, **14**, 24, 54, 60, 61, 74, 79, 125, 170, 173
Pyrola minor, 92, 126
Pyrus cordata, 140

Quercus robur, 20, 37

Rabbits, 46, 47, 68-69
Ramsons, 186
Ranunculus auricomus, 108
Ranmore, 43
Raphanus maritimus, 76
Rare Cuckoo Pint, 72, 76, **107**
Rarity, 212
Raven, John, xvii
Ray, John, 98, 110, 116, 128, 152, 157, 173, 183, 185, 197
Red Broomrape, 197, 207
Red Helleborine, 126-127
Red Valerian, 59, **72**, 111, 119
Reigate Hill, 62
Relhan, R., 97
Rendzina, 35
Residual Deposits, 11
Rhaetic Beds, 143
Rhamnus catharticus, 42
Rhododendron, 3
Ribblesdale, 184-188
Ribes alpinum, 164
Ribwort Plantain, 41
Rigid Buckler Fern, 153, **179**, 189, 194, 195, 196, 223*
Rock Cinquefoil, 154
Rock Pepperwort, 118, 120, 141, 142, 146, 148, 149, 153, 161, 165, 166, 197, 216*
Rock Sea-lavender, 82, 105, 147
Rock Spurry, 82
Rock Stonecrop, 108, 113
Rock Whitebeam, 142-143, 156, 158, 165, 181, 184, 198, 209
Rosa agrestis, 71
Rosa arvensis, 22, 162
Rosa canina, 21
Rosa dumalis, 155
Rosa micrantha, 22

Rosa pimpinellifolia, 148, 162
Rosa rubiginosa, 22
Rosa villosa, 155, 166, 186
Rose, Francis, 51, 54, 56
Rough Round-headed Poppy, 97
Round-headed Garlic, 119
Round-headed Rampion, 2, 62, 65, 68, 70, 77, 85, 223*
Round-leaved Hare's-ear, 79
Rubia peregrina, 72, 77, 82, 105, 109, 147, 166, 203
Rubus fruticosus (aggr.), 37, 68, **117**
Rubus saxatilis, 136, 159, 207
Rumex acetosella, 15
Rumex pulcher, 83
Rustyback, 109, 117, 159, **207**
Rutland, 134-135

Sagina ciliata, 117
St. Vincent's Rocks, 116
Salad Burnet, 2, 24, 38, 41, 74, 83, 87, 102, 106, 182, 197
Salisbury Plain, 79-81
Salomon's Memorial, view from, 35
Salvia pratensis, 56, 58, 61, 71, 131
Samphire, 50, 60, 67, 76, 82, 105, 150
Sarothamnus scoparius, 3, 185
Saxifraga hirsuta, 189
Saxifraga hypnoides, 113, 139, 164, 182, 207, 208
Saxifraga rosacea, **195**, 206
Saxifraga umbrosa, 164, 188
Scabiosa columbaria, 4, 16, 28, 41, 68, 87, 173, 202
Scarce Sweetbriar, 71
Scilla autumnalis, 107
Scilla verna, 146, 148, 149, **207**
Scotland, 200-201
Scots Pine, 20
Scout Scar, **191**, 196
Sea Beet, 67, 76
Sea Cabbage, 50, 60, 71, 143, 150, 201
Sea Campion, 150
Sea Carrot, 83
Sea Radish, 76
Sedgwick, Prof., **171**
Sedum acre, 108
Sedum album, 108
Sedum dasyphyllum, 209
Sedum forsteranum, 108, 154
Selborne, 66
Selborne Hanger, **43**, 66
Senecio integrifolius, 56, 69, 86, 93, **127**, 129
Seseli libanotis, 69, 94, 98, 219*
Sesleria caerulea, 190
Seven Sisters, **50**, 68
Shakespeare's Cliff, Dover, **34**, 50
Shakespeare, Wm. (quoted), 50
Shaw, G. A., 183
Sheep, 78
Sheep's Sorrel, 15
Shepherd's Purse, 130
Sherardia arvensis, 69
Shining Cranesbill, 65, 83
Shoolbred, W. A., 139
Shrubby Cinquefoil, 198, **205**
Silbury Hill, 85
Silene italica, 60
Silene maritima, 150
Silene nutans, 60, 73, 82, **111**, 164
Silene otites, 100
Silene vulgaris, 110
Silene vulgaris subsp. *macrocarpa*, 110
Silverdale, 194-195
Sledge, W. A., xvii
Slender-headed Thistle, 67, 68, 82, 109
Slender Tare, 99, 106
Slope, influence on vegetation, **37**, 38
Small Hare's-ear, 69, 108
Small-leaved Lime, 119, 134, 136, 140, 142, 152
Small Meadow-rue (aggr.), 100, 101,

107, 113, 135, 147, 161, 182, 194, 196, 207
Small Rest-harrow, 107, 146
Small Scabious, 4, 16, 28, 41, 68, 74, 87, 173, 174, 181, 202
Smith, A. Malins, 190
Smith, Sir J. E., 81
Smyrnium olusatrum, 76, 83, 119
Snapdragon, 59, 119
Soft Hawksbeard, 187
Soft-leaved Rose, 154, 162, 166, 186
Soil, chemical tests, **14**
Soil, defined, 9
Soil indicators, 3
Soldier Orchid, 91
Somerset, 110-119
Sorbus aria, 5, 16, 18, 117, 120, 143, 156
Sorbus aucuparia, 181
Sorbus bristoliensis, 120
Sorbus leyana, 143
Sorbus minima, 142
Sorbus porrigentiformis, 107, **142**
Sorbus rupicola, 142, 156, 158, 181, 198, 209
Sorbus vagensis, 140
Spergularia rupicola, 82, 105
Spergularia marina, 105
South Downs, 67-73
South Hawke, 62
Spanish Catchfly, 100, **101**
Spiked Speedwell, **58**, 98, 101, 221*
Spiked Star-of-Bethlehem, 123
Spindle Tree, 22, 42, 87, 117
Spiranthes spiralis, 25, **30**, 54, 61, 106, 136
Spotted Catsear, 94, 100, 151, 195
Spotted Orchid, 79
Spreadbury, W. H., 25
Spring Cinquefoil, 99, 100, 118, 141, 146, 149, 164, 165, 166, 172, 194, 197, 201
Spring Gentian, 199, 205, 207, 208, 220*
Spring Sandwort, 113, 149, 157, 158, 184, 185, 194, **194**, 196, 207
Spurge Laurel, 44, 66, 170, 191
Spur-lipped Coralroot, 52, 89, 212
Squinancywort, 27, 60, 65, 74, 77, 83, 106, 134, 156, 196, 206
Stachys alpina, 128
Stachys germanica, 122, 132, 134
Stachys sylvatica, 128
Stamp, Sir L. Dudley, **xvii**
Steep Holm, 115
Stemless Thistle, **3**, 28, 41, 77, 125, 156, 170, 172
Sticky Catchfly, 154, 200
Stinking Hellebore, 56, 66, 72, 141, 147
Stone Bramble, 136, 159, 194, 207
Strawberry Tree, 203, 209
Succession, 45
Succisa pratensis, 189
Suffolk, 100-101
Sugar Limestone, 198-199
Sulphur Clover, 99, 135
Superficial Deposits, 11
Surrey, 62-65
Swaledale, 198
Sweet Alyssum, 75
Sweetbriar, 22
Sweet Cicely, 47
Sweet-scented Orchid, *see* Fragrant Orchid
Sweet-scented Violet, 23
Sycamore, 20, 47, 174, 189
Symond's Yat, 140-141

Tall Broomrape, 80, 83, 134, 135
Tansley, A. G., 186
Taxus baccata, 5, 18, **26**
Teesdale Sandwort, 199
Tenby Daffodil, 147
Tetragonolobus maritimus, 125

Teucrium botrys, 59, 62, 79, 130, 221*
Teucrium chamaedrys, 143
Thalictrum babingtonii, 100, 101
Thalictrum majus, 201
Thalictrum minus (aggr.), 107, 113, 135, 147, 161, 182, 196, 207
Thames water, 87
Thanet, 57
Thelycrania sanguinea, 16, 20, **31**, 173
Thelypteris robertiana, 113, 142, 153, 181, **190**, 194, 203
Thesium humifusum, 75, 135
Thetford, 100-101
Thistle Broomrape, **94**, 171
Thlaspi alpestre, 113, 157, 184, 198
Thlaspi calaminare, 157, 158
Thlaspi perfoliatum, 122, 129
Thrift, 75, 76, 150
Thymus drucei, 4, 30, 38, 41
Tilia cordata, 119, 134, 136, 140, 152
Tilia platyphyllos, 140, 196
Toadstone, 157
Toothed Wintergreen, 139
Tor-grass, 15, 47, 77, 127, 171, 173
Tormentil, 110, 118, 205
Torquay, 106-109
Traveller's Joy, **2**, 15, 22, 42, 65, 74, 77, 82, 87, 102, 105, 107, 111, 117, 135, 136, 156, 170, 195
Trifolium ochroleucon, 99, 135
Trinia glauca, 108, 114, 116, 129*
Trollius europaeus, 8, 155, 164
Tuberous Thistle, 81, 85, 98, 143-144, 219*
Turner, William, 50, 116
Turrill, W. B., 34, 212
Twiggy Spurge, 63

Ulex europaeus, 68, 83
Ulmus glabra, 19, 158
Umbilicus rupestris, **67**, 109, 141
Upper Teesdale, 198-199
Upright Brome, 15, 87, 156, 173
Upright Cinquefoil, 94

Vaccinium myrtillus, 15, 36
Vachell, E., 143, 146
Valerianella eriocarpa, 106
Vaughan, J., 66
Ventnor, 76
Verbascum lychnitis var. *album*, 60, 72
Verbascum nigrum, 16, **27**, 29, 135, 159, 170
Verbascum nigrum x *V. thapsus*, 30
Verbascum thapsus, 30
Verbena officinalis, 77
Vernal Squill, 146, 147, 148, 149, **207**
Veronica hybrida, 99, 118, 146, 148, 151, 154, 195, 221*
Veronica spicata, **58**, 98, 100, 221*
Vervain, 77
Via Gellia, 159
Viburnum lantana, 16, 20, **46**
Viburnum opulus, 186
Vicia sylvatica, 136
Vicia tenuissima, 99
Viola calcarea, 23, 143
Viola hirta, 16, 22, 38, 149
Viola lepida, 187
Viola lutea, 155
Viola odorata, 23
Viper's Bugloss, 60
Viscum album, 21

Walcheren Expedition, 56
Wales, 142-153
Wallace, E. C., xvii, 171
Wall Bedstraw, 134
Wallflower, 111, 119, 173, 174
Wall Germander, 143
Wall Pennywort, **67**, 109, 113, 141
Wall-rue, 117
Walters, S. M., 23
Walton Downs, 63
Warty Spurge, 99
Wasp Orchid, 122, 127-128, **146**

Water Avens, 187
Water-content of soil, 39, 40
Water supply, influence on vegetation, 38
Wayfaring Tree, 16, 20, 42, **46**, 65, 74, 77, 82, 87, 105, 117, 131, 156
Welsh Poppy, 113, 174
Welsh Stonecrop, 154
Wensleydale, 197
West, William, 183
Western Spiked Speedwell, 118, 146, 148, 151, 152, 154, 195, 221*
Wharfedale, 178-182
White Arabis, 158-159
Whitebeam, 5, 16, 18, 42, 65, 111, 117, 119, 120, 140, 156
White Birch, 20, 42, 117
White Bryony, 173
White Downs, 62
White, Gilbert, 43, 65, 66, 67
White, J. W., 113, 118, 119
White, Mullein, 60, 72
White Rock-rose, 2, 107, 115, 217*
White Stonecrop, 108
Whortleberry, 15, 36, 110
Wild Basil, 30
Wild Carrot, 28, 69, 74, 83
Wild Columbine, 136
Wild Cotoneaster, 150
Wild Liquorice, 58, 135, 170, 173, 201
Wild Mignonette, 87
Wild Paeony, 115
Wild Parsnip, 28, **98**
Wild Pear, 140
Wild Strawberry, 43
Wild Thyme, 4, 30, 38, 41
Wilks, H. M., 91
Willmott, A. T., 141
Wilmott, A. J., 120, 140
Wiltshire, 79-81, 84-85
Winchester, 79
Withering, Dr. W., 31
Woad, 47
Wood Barley, 92, 126, 158
Wood Betony, 68, 74
Wood Cranesbill, 187, 188, 197
Wood Fescue, 155, 200
Wood Melic, 158
Wood Sorrel, 37
Wood Spurge, 44
Wood Vetch, 136
Woolly-headed Thistle, **110**, 122, 123, 125, 129, 134, 136, 143, 165, 171
Wotton-under-Edge, 128
Wulff, T., 75
Wych Elm, 19, 158, 159, 165, 174
Wychwood, 131
Wye Valley, 139-142
Wyndcliff, 139

Yellow Archangel, 44
Yellow Bird's-nest, 44, 66, 89
Yellow Sea-Poppy, 50, 60, 61, 74, 150
Yellow Star-of-Bethlehem, 79, 122, 125, 132, 137, 187
Yellow Stonecrop, 108
Yellow Vetchling, 72
Yellow Whitlow-grass, 144
Yellow-wort, 16, 27, **27**, 60, **61**, 74, 83, 135, 156, 206
Yew, 18, **26**, 37, 42, 43, 55, 64, 65, 73, 111, 117, 119, 140, 158, 174, 209
Yew-wood, 43, 46, 72
Yorkshire, East Riding, 102, 135-136
Yorkshire, North Riding, 102, 136
Yorkshire, Sandwort, 185, 201, 208, 218*

Yellow Whitlow-grass, 144
Yellow-wort, 16, 27, **27**, 60, 61, 74, 83, 135, 156, 206
Yew, 18, **26**, 37, 42, 43, 55, 64, 65, 73, **90**, 111, 117, 119, 140, 158, 174, 209
Yew-wood, 43, 46, 72
Yorkshire, East Riding, 102, 135-136
Yorkshire, North Riding, 102, 136
Yorkshire Sandwort, 185, 201, 208, 218*